Sabine Baring-Gould

The Lives Of The Saints

Volume 14, November, Pt. 2

Sabine Baring-Gould

The Lives Of The Saints
Volume 14, November, Pt. 2

ISBN/EAN: 9783741199479

Manufactured in Europe, USA, Canada, Australia, Japa

Cover: Foto ©Andreas Hilbeck / pixelio.de

Manufactured and distributed by brebook publishing software (www.brebook.com)

Sabine Baring-Gould

The Lives Of The Saints

Nov., Part II.—Front.

S. JOSEPHVS. S. ANTONIVS. S. BENEDICTVS. S. CLODOALDVS. S. LEDNARDVS. S. HVBERTVS. S. PLACIDVS. S. CAROLVS MAGNVS. S. EGIDIVS. S. LAZARVS. S. STEPHANVS HVNGARI. S. HENRICVS.

THE
Lives of the Saints

BY THE

REV. S. BARING-GOULD, M.A.

New Edition in 16 Volumes

Revised with Introduction and Additional Lives of
English Martyrs, Cornish and Welsh Saints,
and a full Index to the Entire Work

ILLUSTRATED BY OVER 400 ENGRAVINGS

VOLUME THE FOURTEENTH

November—PART II

LONDON
JOHN C. NIMMO
NEW YORK: LONGMANS, GREEN, & CO.
MDCCCXCVIII

CONTENTS

A

	PAGE
S. Agapius	458
,, Aignan, B. of Orleans	378
,, Alexander Nevski	511
SS. Alphæus and Zacchæus	378
S. Amphilochius	509
,, Andrew, Apost. M.	593
SS. Appia & Philemon	501
,, Arethas and comp	514

B

SS. Barlaam & Josaphat	562
S. Barlaam of Antioch	413
,, Bellinus	548

	PAGE
S. Bernward, B. of Hildesheim	466
,, Bilhild	574

C

S. Cæcilia	502
,, Catherine	540
,, Chrysogonus	513
,, Clement	506
,, Columbanus	489
,, Conrad, B. of Constance	547

D

S. Dionysius, B. of Alexandria	371

v

Contents

E

	PAGE
S. Edmund, K.	462
„ Elizabeth of Hungary	415

F

SS. Facundus & Primitivus	562
S. Faustus	412
„ Felix of Valois	485
„ Fergus	395
SS. Flora and Mary	525
S. Francis Xavier	602

G

S. Gelasius, Pope	487
„ Gregory III., Pope	579
„ Gregory the Wonder-Worker	375
„ Gregory, B. of Tours	381

H

S. Hilda	390
„ Hugh, B. of Lincoln	395

J

B. James de la Marca	586
S. James Intercisus	566
„ John of the Cross	526
„ Justus	564
SS. Josaphat & Barlaam	562

L

S. Leonard of Porto-Maurizio	549

M

	PAGE
B.V. Mary, Presentation of	486
S. Maudez	402
„ Maxentia	461
„ Maximus of Rome	412
„ Maximus, B. of Riez	569
„ Mercurius	540
SS. Mary and Flora	525

N

SS. Narses and comp.	460

O

S. Odo	404

P

S. Paul, B. of Skalholt	413
„ Peter of Alexandria	544
SS. Philemon & Appia	501
S. Pontianus, Pope	411
Presentation of the B.V. Mary	486
SS. Primitivus and Facundus	564

R

S. Radbod, B. of Utrecht	597
„ Reolus	542
„ Romanus	401

S

S. Saturninus	589
„ Secundinus, B. in Meath	578

	PAGE
S. Simeon Metaphrastes	574
„ Sosthenes	577
„ Stephen the Younger	583

T

S. Trojanus	598
„ Trudo	511
„ Tugdual	599

V

	PAGE
S. Virgilius, B. of Salzburg	570

X

S. Xavier, Francis	602

Z

SS. Zacchæus and Alphæus	378

LIST OF ILLUSTRATIONS

PROCESSION OF SAINTS . . *Frontispiece*
    From a Fresco.

PROCESSION OF SAINTS . . *to face p.* 371
    From a Fresco.

S. HILDA . . ,, 392

S. JOHN OF BEVERLEY, ABP. OF YORK (*see May 7th*) . . . . ,, 394

S. HUGH OF LINCOLN . . ,, 396
    After CAHIER.

THE PRESENTATION IN THE TEMPLE . 400
    After a Fresco by GIOTTO, *at Padua.*

THE PRESENTATION IN THE TEMPLE . . ,, 410
    After the Picture by FRA BARTOLOMMEO, *in the Vienna Gallery.*

S. ELIZABETH OF HUNGARY . . . . ,, 422
    After the Painting by HANS HOLBEIN (*the elder*), *one of the wings of the altar-piece of S. Sebastian, in the Pinakothek, Munich.*

S. ELIZABETH — THE MIRACLE — "I SEE ONLY JESUS CHRIST" . . ,, 424

S. ELIZABETH DRIVEN FROM THE WARTBURG . *to face p.*	438
S. ELIZABETH WASHING BEGGARS ,,	448
MARBOURG — CHURCH OF S. ELIZABETH, TOMB AND RETABLE . ,,	456
HIGH ALTAR, CHURCH OF S. ELIZABETH ,,	456
S. EDMUND . . ,, *After* CAHIER.	462
PRESENTATION OF MARY IN THE TEMPLE . ,, *After a Picture by* ISRAEL VAN MECKEN, *in the Museum at Munich.*	486
S. CÆCILIA ,,	502
S. CÆCILIA — THE MARRIAGE FEAST — "I WILL TELL YOU A SECRET" ,,	504
S. CÆCILIA — THE ANGEL'S VISIT — THE BROTHER'S CONVERSION . . ,,	506
S. CÆCILIA — HER HUSBAND IS BAPTIZED — SHE CONVERTS FOUR HUNDRED . ,,	508
S. CÆCILIA — BROUGHT BEFORE THE ROMAN PREFECT — SUFFERS MARTYRDOM . ,,	510
S. CATHERINE . . . . ,, *From the Vienna Missal.*	540

List of Illustrations

S. Catherine Contending with the
Doctors . . . . *to face p.* 542
After a Fresco by Masaccio, *in the Church of
S. Clemente at Rome.*

Martyrdom of S. Catherine „ 544

S. Catherine (*see p.* 540) . *on p.* 576

Altar of Gold, in the Cluny Museum . *to face p.* 576
*Presented to the ancient Cathedral of Basle by
the Emperor Henry II.*

S. Andrew, Ap. (*see p.* 593) *on p.* 588

S. Andrew, Apostle and Martyr . *to face p.* 594
After Wilhelm Kandler.

S. Francis Xavier . . . . „ 602
After Cahier.

Lives of the Saints

November 17.

S. Dionysius, *B. of Alexandria*; A.D. 264.
S. Gregory the Wonder-worker, *B. of Neocæsarea*; *circ.* A.D. 270.
SS. Alphæus and Zacchæus, *MM. in Palestine*; A.D. 303.
SS. Arsiclas and Victoria, *MM. at Cordova*; *circ.* A.D. 304.
S. Aignan, *B. of Orleans*; A.D. 453.
S. Gregory, *B. of Tours*; A.D. 594.
S. Leontius, *B. of Saintes*; A.D. 626.
S. Hilda, *V. Abss. of Whitby*; *circ.* A.D. 679.
S. Fergus, *B. at Glamis in Scotland*; 8*th cent.*
S. Hugh, *B. of Lincoln*; A.D. 1200.

S. DIONYSIUS, B. OF ALEXANDRIA.

(A.D. 264.)

[Roman Martyrology. Usuardus, Ado, &c. By the Greeks on Oct. 3, 4, and 5. Authority :—Euseb. H. E. vi. c. 33; vii. 11, 15-22. S. Jerome, Catal. c. 69.]

IONYSIUS, whom his contemporaries surnamed "the Great," on account of the services he rendered to the Church, was born at Alexandria of a distinguished family. He was a pagan and a rhetorician, but he renounced in the school of Origen his religion and his profession, devoted himself to theology, and succeeded Heraclas as head of the Catechetical School in his native city. Like his master, he devoted himself to the work of converting heretics, and for that purpose he studied their writings and systems. After having exercised his functions as head of the school for sixteen years, in 247, on the death of Heraclas, the choice of the clergy of Alexandria called him to the episcopal dignity, and he remained in-

vested with it during seventeen years of vicissitude and peril. From the date of his election the hostility of the pagans against the Christians began to manifest itself openly, and reached its greatest violence on the promulgation of the edict of persecution by Decius. Dionysius awaited his fate with patience, and it was only with difficulty that he was persuaded to place himself in security by hiding. But on his way to the place of concealment he was surprised by soldiers who overran the country, and was conveyed by them to the little town of Taposiris. The Christians of the place, hearing who was arrested, rose and delivered him from the hands of the soldiers, and conveyed him with two priests to an asylum where they would be safe. From this place he continued to direct his afflicted Church, by letters, or by sending priests and deacons to it, who penetrated Alexandria at the risk of their lives.

The Church suffered greatly in this persecution; a large number of Christians apostatized, and the schism of the Novatians came to aggravate the evil. Dionysius showed great moderation and gentleness towards those who by weakness had fallen, but he was stern and peremptory in his dealings with Novatian. When Novatian sent him notice of his election, he wrote in response: "If thou hast been really forced to take the office, as thou sayest, prove it by retiring from it. Thou shouldst have suffered anything rather than rend the Church. It is not less glorious to die for the unity of the Church than for the faith against heathenism. According to my idea, the first is the most glorious of the two. For in the latter case one dies for the advantage of one's own soul only, in the former for the entire Church."

In the Council of Antioch, 252, Dionysius made every effort to re-establish unity. In the following year, when the storms which had risen during the reign of Gallus were dissipated, and the Church breathed again in peace, Dionysius directed his attention towards Millenarianism. Nepos, a priest of Arsinoe, had adopted the old Cerinthian doctrine that Christ would reign on earth for a thousand years, and he composed a book on the subject, which was widely circuculated, entitled "Confutatio Allegoristarum." Dionysius answered it in two books, "De Promissionibus," and he made a journey to Arsinoe to meet and argue with Nepos and those who followed his teaching. This conduct had its desired effect; his persuasive eloquence and calm logic satisfied the Chiliasts, and they all abandoned their fantastic theory.

He used his best endeavours in like manner to bring to amicable terms the bishops who strove about the validity of heretical baptism. Pope S. Stephen had conducted himself with great violence in this matter. He allowed such baptisms, and excommunicated those bishops who denied them to be valid. S. Cyprian maintained the necessity of the iteration of baptism in the case of the previous baptism having been administered by a heretic. He called a council of African bishops, which supported his view against that of the Pope. S. Dionysius gave in his adhesion to the practice of S. Cyprian, and wrote a forcible letter of indignant remonstrance to Stephen on his violent conduct. He urged S. Firmilian, and those who agreed with him, to cease from controversy, and he exhorted S. Xistus II., the successor of Stephen, not to meddle with the Churches, but leave each to follow its traditional practice.

During this interior fermentation, Sabellius appeared at Pentapolis. His heresy exacted all the care and energy of the great bishop to oppose it. On first hearing of it he wrote to Xistus of Rome and to the bishops of Africa to unite against the heresiarch. He wrote four books in refutation of Sabellianism, but in this dogmatic discussion he used expressions which the Arians afterwards fastened upon.

They were less guarded than they might have been, had he anticipated the rise of such a heresy as that of Arius.

In 257 the persecution of Valerian broke out, and Dionysius was arrested. He confessed his faith boldly, and was exiled to Kephro in the Libyan desert. There he enjoyed the consolation of being in the midst of a large Christian community, partly of native believers, and partly of refugees from Alexandria. But after a while he was transferred to a place in Mareotis, nearer Alexandria, but more lonely. There he remained till 261, when the fall of Valerian allowed his return home. The change was, however, from one peril to another. The capital became, under Gallienus, the theatre of a bloody civil war, and of a desolating plague. The pest made dreadful ravages, and among the pagans fear stifled their pity for the sick, whom they abandoned, even when relatives. The heroic bishop revived the courage of the faithful, and stirred them up to deeds of charity and self-devotion towards the plague-struck, which excited the wonder and admiration of the heathen. The physical powers of Dionysius were exhausted by his labours, but not so his pastoral solicitude and zeal for the good of the Church. And indeed a new heresiarch arose to call forth his energies in the defence of the true faith. This was Paul of Samosata, bishop of Antioch, who took the converse line to Sabellius, and exaggerated it into heresy. Dionysius was invited by the bishop of Palestine to visit Antioch. His advanced age did not permit him to undertake so laborious a journey, but he wrote to the Church of Antioch a dogmatic epistle on the matter in question. This was his last work. A few days after, in 264, he ended his agitated and useful life.

His indefatigable activity for the interests of the Church, his ardent zeal for the conversion of the heathen, for the welfare of the faithful, for the reunion of schismatics; the firmness with which he combated error, the moderation he showed towards those who had fallen, the charity which embraced the whole Catholic Church, the constancy which remained unshaken under persecution, and, lastly, the amiable modesty he exhibited in the midst of the admiration of his age; all these qualities united to obtain for him from his contemporaries the title of the Great, and from S. Athanasius the epithet of " Master of the Catholic Church."

Only fragments of his writings have been preserved to us by Eusebius.

S. GREGORY THE WONDER-WORKER, B.

(ABOUT A.D. 270.)

[Roman Martyrology. Ado, Usuardus, Notker, &c. By the Greeks also on Nov. 17. Usuardus inaccurately calls him a martyr. Authorities :—His Life written by Gregory Nyssen (d. 390), this is so full of legend and marvel as to be of little historical value. Socrates, lib. iv. 12; Eusebius, lib. vi. 30, vii. 14. Above all, Gregory's panegyric on Origen, which is the best source of authentic material for his life. Mention by Jerome, Rufinus, and Theodoret, &c.]

ATHENODORUS and Theodorus were two brothers, natives of Pontus, who were attracted to Cæsarea by the celebrity of Origen. They were of good family, and brought up in paganism. Theodore, afterwards called Gregory, lost his father when he was fourteen; he then became imperfectly acquainted with Christianity, and an accident having brought him and his brother to Cæsarea, they were so charmed with Origen's teaching, that they continued with him five years, and were instructed by him not only in the Gospel, but in the whole range of philosophy and literature.

In the reign of Gordian, Origen quitted his retreat in Cappadocia, whither he had escaped from persecution, and went into Greece. In 239 he returned to Cæsarea, and his pupil Theodore, or, as we may henceforth call him, Gregory, who had gone to Alexandria when Origen left Cæsarea, rejoined him. Soon after, Gregory revisited his native Pontus, received ordination, and was appointed bishop of Neocæsarea; but before he left Palestine he delivered a public oration in praise of Origen, which is still extant. The celebrity of his character appears to have pointed him out for his station as bishop; and, if we may believe the accounts which were circulated in the fourth century, he distinguished himself still further by working the most stupendous miracles. But Eusebius, who was a contemporary, makes no mention of this marvellous power.

He is said to have erected a handsome church at Neocæsarea, which remained uninjured, when many public buildings were shaken by earthquakes.

When the Decian persecution broke out, Gregory saved himself by concealment. On the cessation of the storm he returned to his flock, and, seeing that one cause why the heathen were attached to their religion was the observance of festivals in connection with their gods, Gregory ordered that the anniversaries of the martyrs should be observed with solemnity and assembly of the faithful.

The plague which raged in Carthage and Alexandria in 253, spread into Asia Minor. Gregory emulated the activity of Cyprian and Dionysius. His disregard of contagion, his indefatigable care of the dying, his liberality to the needy, created a lively emotion in the hearts of the pagans, and many joined the Church which could produce such devoted pastors.

A certain Ælian, a heathen, wrote a book against the Christians, accusing them of believing in a plurality of gods. The charge was founded on the fact that Divine worship was paid to each Person in the Trinity. Gregory is said to have published an answer to this attack; and in attempting to explain to the heathen that the Father and the Son were one hypostatically, *i.e.* in substance or essence, he appeared to say that they were not really two, but only metaphysically so. The Sabellians claimed this explanation as favouring their views, but Leontius of Byzantium says that the authenticity of this treatise, now unfortunately lost, was doubted by many.

The Eastern part of the empire had for some time been suffering from another scourge, which appears to have begun in the same year as the pestilence. This was the irruption of the Goths, and other barbarians, into the provinces of Asia Minor. They swept through the country like a torrent, carrying away many of the inhabitants as prisoners. These incursions produced much misery and fatal consequences to Christians as well as heathen. A letter of Gregory is extant, in which he laments that so many Christians had fallen away from the faith they had professed.

Gregory was present in 265 at the council held at Antioch against Paul of Samosata, but it is questionable whether he assisted at the second Antiochian council in 270. His name is not in the synodal letter addressed to Pope Dionysius. He died in 270, and—if we may trust Gregory Nyssen—had the happiness of leaving in Neocæsarea only seventeen heathens, which was just the number of Christians he had found in the city when he took possession of the diocese. His renown, says Rufinus, filled the North as well as the East; his actions were celebrated in every church, resounded from every mouth; and S. Basil assures us that the enemies of Christianity, amazed at the many miracles he wrought, called him a second Moses.[1]

---

[1] Basil. de Spirit. Sanc. c. 29.

SS. ALPHÆUS AND ZACCHÆUS, MM.

(A.D. 303.)

[Roman Martyrology. By the Greeks on Nov. 18 and Dec. 18. Authority :—Eusebius, Hist. Eccl. viii. ("Martyrs of Palestine," c. 1.)]

ALPHÆUS and Zacchæus suffered in the persecution of Diocletian at Cæsarea in Palestine, and they were the only martyrs there who on that occasion lost their lives. They were scourged and scraped with iron hooks, and racked, with their feet stretched for a night and a day to the fourth hole, which would dislocate all their joints, and then were decapitated on November 17.

S. AIGNAN, B. OF ORLEANS.

(A.D. 453.)

[Roman and Gallican Martyrologies. Usuardus, Ado, &c. Authorities :—Gregory of Tours, Hist. Franc. ii. 7, and a Letter of Sidonius Apollinaris.]

S. AIGNAN, in Latin Anianus, was born at Vienne in Gaul of refugee parents from Hungary, probably of Roman origin; they were Catholics, and the Arian Goths menaced both their faith and their substance. They saved both by a timely flight within the frontiers, where the failing arm of Rome was not altogether powerless. Aignan had a brother, Leonianus, who became an abbot, and is commemorated by Gallican Martyrologists on November 16.

At an early age Aignan retired to a hermitage near Vienne, and remained in it till he heard of the virtues of S. Evurtius of Orleans,[1] when he went to him for guidance in the religious life. S. Evurtius ordained him priest, and then made him abbot of S. Laurence outside the city walls. About 391, when he was far advanced in age and looking forward to

---

[1] Died 391; called Enurchus in Anglican Kalendar.

his death, Evurtius determined to resign the bishopric and appoint a successor. He assembled the electors and bade them write the names of those for whom they voted on slips of parchment and place them in a box. A little child was enjoined to draw the lot, and the name drawn was that of Aignan. S. Evurtius then consulted the Sortes Sacræ. The Psalter was opened, then the book of Epistles, and then the Gospels, at hap-hazard. The text at the head of the page in the Psalms where the book opened was, "Blessed is the man whom Thou choosest and receivest unto Thee: he shall dwell in Thy courts." That in the Epistle was, "Other foundation can no man lay than is laid." That in the Gospel, "On this rock will I build my church, and the gates of hell shall not prevail against it." This convinced every one that Aignan was chosen by Providence. S. Evurtius therefore consecrated and installed him in his room.

Aignan at once asked the governor of Orleans to release the prisoners in the town. Agrippinus, the governor, refused. But a stone having fallen on his head and bruised it whilst he was at church, he thought this was a warning not to disregard the request of the new bishop, and he opened the jails, and released all the criminals.

Aignan buried S. Evurtius in the field of a senator named Letradus, on his death, shortly after his own election. Gaul was at this time troubled with the invasion of the Huns under Attila. In 451 his swarm of ferocious barbarians swept to the gates of Orleans. Romans, Gauls, Visigoths, Burgundians, Franks, and Alans united under Aetius to resist the terrible invader, who had also in his ranks Goths, Burgundians, Gepidæ, Alans, and Franks, from beyond the Rhine. It was a wild chaos and conflict of barbarians, of every name and race, disputing one with another, pell-mell, the remnants of the Roman empire, torn asunder and in dissolution.

When Attila laid siege to Orleans, S. Aignan sustained the courage of the besieged by promising them aid from Aetius and his allies. The aid was slow to come; and the bishop sent to Aetius the message, "If thou be not here this very day, my son, it will be too late." Still Aetius came not. The people of Orleans determined to surrender; the gates flew open; the Huns entered; the plundering began without much disorder; "waggons were stationed to receive the booty as it was taken from the houses, and the captives, arranged in groups, were divided by lot between the victorious chieftains." Suddenly a shout rang through the streets: it was Aetius, Theodoric, and Thorismund, his son, who were coming with the eagles of the Roman legions and with the banners of the Visigoths. A fight took place between them and the Huns, at first on the banks of the Loire, and then in the streets of the city. The people of Orleans joined their liberators; the danger was great for the Huns, and Attila ordered a retreat. It was the 14th June, 451, and that day was for a long time celebrated in the church of Orleans as the date of a signal deliverance. The Huns retired towards Champagne, which they had already crossed at their coming into Gaul. Aetius and all his allies followed them, and Attila, perceiving that a battle was inevitable, halted in position at Châlons-sur-Marne, for giving it. "It was," says Jornandes, "a battle which for atrocity, multitude, horror, and stubbornness has not the like in the records of antiquity." Theodoric was killed, but the Huns were defeated and driven out of Gaul. This was the last victory in Gaul, gained still in the name of the Roman empire, but really for the advantage of the German nations which had already conquered it. Twenty-four years afterwards the Roman empire of the West disappeared with Augustulus.

Aignan died, at the age of ninety-five, in 453, and was buried in the church of S. Laurence, where he had been abbot. His relics were burned by the Huguenots in 1562, but some small fragments are preserved in the cathedral at Orleans.

S. GREGORY, B. OF TOURS.

(A.D. 594.)

[Roman, Gallican, and Benedictine Martyrologies. Authorities :—A Life written by the clergy of Tours, "omnium quidem sanctorum," in Surius. Another Life by Odo of Clugni (d. 942), in Ruinart's edition of S. Gregory of Tours, and also in Surius. This meagre Life is almost entirely composed of anecdotes collected from the writings of S. Gregory, which he has abridged. It is only in the last chapters that anything occurs which is not found in the writings of S. Gregory. The best authority for the life of this remarkable man is himself; and, fortunately, he has given us some particulars about his own life.]

GREGORY of Tours came of a family as distinguished for its sanctity as for its nobility. His grandfather George was married to Leocadia, granddaughter of Leocadius, senator of Berri, who was the first of his family to embrace Christianity. Leocadius was closely related to Vettius Epagathus, who was a martyr for the faith.

George had two sons, Gallus and Florentius. Gallus became bishop of Clermont; Gregory of Tours wrote his Life. He is honoured as a saint. Florentius lived on his estates. He had one in Auvergne, another in Burgundy. His wife was Armentaria, granddaughter of S. Gregory, bishop of Langres. Gregory of Langres had two brothers, uncles of the subject of this memoir, S. Nicetius (Nizier), bishop of Lyons; and the other, a duke under Childebert II., and governor of Marseilles.

S. Gregory of Tours was born on S. Andrew's day, 539. He was named George Florentius, but afterwards, when made bishop, he adopted instead the name of Gregory, in honour of his uncle, the bishop of Langres. He was very young when his father died; he was brought up by his mother, towards whom he always manifested the most tender and respectful love.

He was educated by Avitus, archdeacon of Clermont, till he reached manhood, when his mother made over to him the estate in Auvergne, and retired to that in Burgundy. Gregory at once received Orders, but before he settled anywhere permanently he made several journeys to Burgundy, to visit his mother, who resided then at Chalons-sur-Saône.[1]

In 573 S. Euphronius, bishop of Tours, died, and S. Gregory was chosen to succeed him. Two months after he was ordained, he was attacked with bowel-complaint; he cured it by drinking the dust of S. Martin's tomb mixed with water; the lime, no doubt, corrected the acidity which disturbed his stomach. Meroveus, son of Chilperic, married his aunt Brunehild, widow of Sigebert. Chilperic, highly incensed, and completely under the influence of Fredegund, who wished to clear the way to the throne for her son Clothair, forced his son to separate from Brunehild, and be tonsured in the abbey of Anisole. Meroveus, suspecting that Fredegund was waiting an opportunity to put him to death, took refuge at Tours, at the tomb of S. Martin. In that asylum he asked to be communicated, and threatened to kill several of the servants of the bishop unless Gregory would give him the Holy Eucharist. Gregory consulted with Ragnmod, bishop of Paris, and they communicated Meroveus to save him the guilt of murder. Meroveus waited his opportunity of escaping to Brunehild, and casting to the winds his enforced monastic restraints. But as the roads were watched, he lingered on at Tours, telling the bishop

---

[1] On one of these journeys a storm threatened. Gregory pulled some relics out of his bosom, and held them towards the clouds. They parted, and no rain fell. Gregory could not help thinking, and saying to his companions, that it was quite possible the clouds might have been controlled by his virtues as much as by those of the relics. Shortly after his horse fell, and pitched Gregory on his head in the mud. This brought him to a more sober estimate of himself.

all the scandalous stories about his father which had come to his ears. Gregory told him that though these might be true, it was not proper for a son to proclaim his father's iniquities. Meroveus, shortly after, asked the bishop to consult the Sortes Sacræ for him. Gregory did so, and opened the Scriptures at the words, "The eye that mocketh at his father, and despiseth to obey his mother, the ravens of the valley shall pick it out, and the young eagles shall eat it" (Prov. xxx. 17).

Meroveus thought the verse inappropriate, but not so Gregory. He consulted the oracles again more solemnly. He laid the Psalter, the Book of Kings, and the Gospels on the tomb of S. Martin, and after three days of fasting besought that the fate in store for him might be disclosed. On opening the Book of Kings, he read, "Because they forsook the Lord their God, who brought forth their fathers out of the land of Egypt, and have taken hold upon other gods .... therefore hath the Lord brought upon them all this evil" (1 Kings, ix. 9). In the Psalter he found, "Thou dost set them in slippery places, and castest them down, and destroyest them. O how suddenly do they consume, perish, and come to a fearful end" (Ps. lxxii. 18, 19; A. V. lxxiii. 17, 18). On opening the Gospels he read, "Ye know that after two days is the feast of the passover, and the Son of Man is betrayed to be crucified" (Matt. xxvi. 2).

The texts were sufficiently dismal of import to depress the mind of the young prince, and he went away weeping. He escaped, and at the head of five hundred men made his way to the arms of Brunehild, but finding it impossible to escape his father and the implacable enmity of his stepmother, Fredegund, the unhappy prince either committed suicide, or, more probably, was assassinated by his stepmother's orders, and it was given out that he had killed himself.

A council was then assembled at Paris to try S. Prætextatus of Rouen, who was charged with having married Meroveus to his aunt. Forty-five bishops attended. The king himself appeared as accuser. The account of how Gregory conducted himself in this transaction has been already given (S. Prætextatus, Feb. 24, pp. 403-5), and need not therefore be repeated here.

Fredegund could not forgive S. Gregory for opposing her wishes with such dauntless courage, and rejecting so sternly her offered bribes. She stirred up Leudast, count of Tours, to vex the saintly bishop without showing him open violence. Leudast (Leudegast) was a native of Poitou, son of a slave girl. He was employed in the royal kitchen, but as his eyes could not stand the smoke, he was exalted to the bakehouse. He ran away two or three times, and in punishment had one of his ears cut off. He ran away again, and took refuge with Queen Marcoveva,[1] who accorded him her protection, and made him count of her stables. On her death he succeeded in retaining his place with Charibert. Charibert sent him to Orleans, with the title of count. When Orleans fell to Sigebert, Leudast joined the side of Chilperic, and Sigebert accordingly plundered his possessions. On the murder of Sigebert, Leudast returned to Orleans, but Meroveus prevented him from recovering his property. When Meroveus left, Leudast accused Gregory of having favoured the unfortunate prince. The count sent word to the king that the bishop had spoken disrespectfully of Fredegund, his queen, and had said she was a bad woman. It was perfectly true that she was wicked and unscrupulous, and it is possible that Gregory may have allowed some such a re-

---

[1] Marcoveva was daughter of a serf, a weaver. Her sister Merofleda was servant to Ingoberga, wife of Charibert. The king fell in love with Merofleda, put away his wife, and married her. Marcoveva was a nun. When Merofleda died, Charibert took her from her convent, and married her. S. Germanus excommunicated them. Marcoveva died before Charibert, *i.e.* before 572.

mark to have escaped him in private conversation. Chilperic was, however, getting tired of his queen, her beauty was losing its hold over him, and he gave ear to the counter-charges against Leudast made by the bishop and citizens of Tours. He sent to the city, and gave the inhabitants permission to choose a count for themselves. They at once elected Eunomius. Leudast, exasperated to the last degree, hastened to Paris, burst in on the king, and said, "Hitherto I have kept the city of Tours; now the office is taken from me, and this at a time when the bishop, Gregory, is plotting to deliver it over to the son of Sigebert."

"Bah! your disappointment has made you invent this tale."

"Not at all, sire! Moreover, Gregory dares to affirm that your queen is living in adultery with Bishop Bertrand of Bordeaux."

This was going too far. The king sprang at him, gave him blows on each ear, and kicked him vigorously out of the room. What the count had said rankled, however, in the breast of Chilperic, and he recalled Leudast, and asked what evidence he could produce. Leudast named Riculf, the subdeacon, Plato, the archdeacon, and a certain Gallienus, a friend of Gregory. The king sent Leudast to Tours to bring them before him. The ex-count bound Plato and Gallienus with chains, and carried them to Paris. Riculf continued to spread reports that Gregory had slandered the queen, and was in league with Gontram against Chilperic. The king summoned a council to assemble at Berni, near Soissons, to hear the charges against the bishop of Tours.[1]

Bertrand, bishop of Bordeaux, accused Gregory of having declared that he lived in adultery with the queen. Gregory answered that he had never imagined such a thing.

[1] Not Braine, as is generally thought, but Berni, where the king had a domain The date cannot be fixed. It was between 577 and 581

Chilperic said, "An accusation brought against my wife is an outrage upon me. If it please you that witnesses should be produced against the bishop, they are here. But if not, speak, I shall be satisfied with your decision."

The bishops decreed that the word of an inferior could not be valued above that of a bishop, and that Gregory should take oath he had not circulated this scandal, and should say mass at three altars to justify himself of the accusations. This he did readily. Then the bishops decided that Leudast, having brought this false accusation against Gregory, should be excommunicated, and otherwise punished, as the wisdom of the king decided. Leudast had, however, taken flight. Apparently Chilperic put his son to death, and certainly banished his wife. The clerk Riculf was tortured on the wheel, and hung to a tree by his hands tied behind his back.

Chilperic had a theological discussion with S. Gregory during the council, or just after it. The king fancied himself a theologian; he composed collects, hymns, and treatises on divinity, all great rubbish. These he had read to the bishop of Tours, who was candid enough to give his opinion of their worthlessness. The collects of Chilperic were intolerable. His hymns halted; he put short feet where there should be long, and long where the metre required short feet. A treatise on the doctrine of the Trinity, in which he argued against the word "person" as applied to each member of the Trinity, called for severer animadversion. "Give up this doctrine, O king," said Gregory, "and cleave to that which Hilary and Eusebius have taught."

Chilperic knew nothing of S. Hilary of Poitiers and S. Eusebius of Vercelli, and thinking that Gregory spoke of living persons, "I see," said the king, "this Hilary and this Eusebius are my enemies, I must have to do with them."

"They are saints," said Gregory, "and you cannot fight

against them. There are in truth three Persons, not corporally but spiritually, in one glory, one eternity, and one power."

The king, in a rage, said, "I will submit my treatise to wiser men than you, and they will approve it."

"He would be not a wise man but a fool who would approve it," answered Gregory, boldly. The king was furious, and showed it to Salvius, bishop of Albi, who spurned it from him, and wanted to tear it to pieces. Having met with such poor success in theology, Chilperic turned his attention to other matters.

The country abounded with deranged men, whose madness had taken a religious turn, and who led about troops of deluded peasants after them. One poor wretch who had gone mad after having been stung by a swarm of bees, ran through the Gevaudan and Velai with a woman named Mary, working miracles, and calling himself Christ. S. Aurelius, bishop of Le Puy, by a discreditable bit of dissimulation, got possession of the man, had him cut to pieces, and his wife tortured. It is pleasant to find S. Gregory of Tours behaving very differently towards another fanatic of the same type.

This poor wretch went about carrying a cross, from the arms of which hung little bottles full of oil, which he said was sacred. He pretended also to possess relics of S. Vincent and S. Felix of Gerona. He came to Tours one evening, when S. Gregory was at table, and invited the bishop to come out in procession and venerate the relics. Gregory declined. It was late. Let the relics be deposited during the night on an altar.

Next morning at daybreak the man came into Gregory's bed-room bearing aloft his cross, and threatening to report him to the king for having so ill received his bottles of oil and relics. Then he went into the bishop's oratory, said some prayers, hoisted up his cross again, and marched forth.

His language was ordinary, his pronunciation vulgar, and his ideas disconnected, so that Gregory did not form a high opinion of the man. The fanatic went on to Paris, where he arrived during the Rogation procession on the eve of the Ascension. The train of the man bearing his tall cross and jingling oil-bottles met that of the bishop of Paris, with his cross and tapers. Both processions chanted, both were large, and neither would yield to the other. The bishop bade him place his relics in one of the churches, and fall in with his episcopal procession. The fanatic began to rate him soundly, and without careful choice of expressions; whereupon Ragnbod had him arrested and examined. In a pouch at his waist were found roots of medicinal plants, moles' teeth, bones of mice, the claws and grease of bears. The bishop concluded that these were used for necromantic purposes, pitched them into the Seine, despoiled the man of his cross and oil-bottles, and had him thrust out of the gates of Paris. But he made himself another cross and began again his extraordinary practices; whereupon he was taken by the archdeacon of Paris, and cast, heavily chained, into prison. In the night he got out of the jail, and crept into the church of S. Julian, when he fell down asleep—or drunk, as Gregory thinks. At that time Gregory had come to Paris, and was lodged close to the church of S. Julian. The bishop rose in the middle of the night to go into the church and sing prime and lauds. But the smell in the church was so dreadful that he could not enter. A clerk, stopping his nose, ran in to the sleeping man, and tried to waken him, but was unable to do so. He was obliged to call three others to his assistance, and they dragged him out. After this the pavement on which he had lain was soused with water, and the floor was strewn with rosemary and other fragrant herbs, and after a while Gregory was able to enter and perform the accustomed offices. The poor creature did not wake till morning.

Gregory sent him to the bishop of Paris, readily pardoning him for the annoyance he had caused him. At that time other bishops were assembled in Paris, and Gregory obtained as a punishment for the man that he should be present whilst he and they were breakfasting, and whilst he related to the bishops the story of how he had found the man, and the trouble it had given him to sweeten the atmosphere of the church which he had polluted with his heretical presence, or disordered internal condition. One of the bishops, Amelius of Bigorre (Tarbes) fixing his eyes on the poor wretch, suddenly exclaimed that he knew the man, he was one of his serfs who had run away. He was pardoned, and Amelius took him back with him to Bigorre. Gregory gives interesting discussions he had with a Jew, with an Arian, and with a priest who denied the Resurrection, which we are obliged to omit from want of space. He wrote the Ecclesiastical History of the Franks; and this work is the most precious memorial we possess of the history of his times, obtaining for him the title of the Father of French History. Thierry says of him, "By an accidental but singularly happy coincidence, this period (500 to 650), so complex and of such mixed colour, is that of which original documents provide the most characteristic details. It met with a historian marvellously suited to describe it, a contemporary, an intelligent and saddened witness in the midst of this confusion of men and events, of crimes and catastrophes, in the midst of which the old civilization followed its irresistible declension. One must descend to the century of Froissart to find a historian equal to Gregory of Tours in the art of producing characters on his stage and painting them by means of dialogue. All that the conquest of Gaul had brought to clash on the same soil, races, classes, conditions, figure pell-mell in his narrative, always true and always animated."[1]

[1] Récits Mérovingiens, preface.

S. HILDA, V. ABSS.

(ABOUT A.D. 679.)

[Gallican Martyrologies on this day. York Kalendar on Aug. 25. The Horæ B.V.M., probably belonging to Coldingham (Harl. MSS. 1804), and the Durham Missal "ad altare S. Joh. B. et S. Margaretæ, ad ix altaria in eccl. cath. Dunelm" (Harleian MSS. 5289), on Nov. 17. Authority :—Bede, Hist. Eccl.]

THE monastery of Hartlepool was founded about the year 645 by Heiu, a Northumbrian lady, the first woman of her race who embraced conventual life. She received the veil from the hands of Bishop Aidan. After a few years she retired to a solitude, and Aidan replaced her by Hilda, a princess of the blood-royal and of the Deirian dynasty. She was grand niece of Edwin, the first Christian king of Northumbria, father of the queen who had shared the throne of Oswy. This illustrious lady seemed to be called by her genius and character, even more than by her rank, to exercise a great influence over religious and political movements in her time. Born in exile, during the sovereignty of Ethelfrid, among the West Saxons, where her mother died a violent death, she returned with her father, on the restoration of his race in 617. In her early youth she had been baptized, with her uncle King Edwin, by the Roman missionary Paulinus, which did not, however, prevent her from leaning during her whole life to the side of the Celtic missionaries. Before consecrating her virginity to God, she had lived thirty-three years " very nobly," says Bede, among her family and her fellows. When she understood that God called her, she desired to make to Him a complete sacrifice, and forsook at once the world, her family, and her country. She went immediately into East Anglia, the king of which had married her sister, and whence she designed to cross over to France, in order to take the veil either at Chelles, where her widowed sister was one day to devote herself to God, or in one of the monasteries on the banks of the Marne, which sprang from the great Irish colony of Luxeuil, and whither the Saxon virgins already began to resort. Gallican martyrologists commemorate Hilda as having been some time at Chelles; but Bede says nothing of the sort. He implies that she did not go thither, but only wished to do so, and before she left East Anglia for Chelles received her recall to Northumbria from Bishop Aidan. She was only a year in all away from her native province. Aidan gave her lands by the Wear, and there she spent a twelvemonth with a few companions, till Heiu retired from governing Hartlepool, when Aidan made Hilda superior of the monastery. Probably Heiu had not ruled very well, for we are told that one of the first things done by Hilda was to introduce order into the monastery.

Nine years later, when the peace and freedom of Northumbria had been secured by the final victory gained by King Oswy over the Mercians, Hilda took advantage of a gift of land granted her by that prince to establish a new monastery at Streaneshalch (the Beacon Headland), now Whitby. There, as at Hartlepool, and during the thirty years that she passed at the head of her two houses, she displayed a rare capacity for the government of souls, and for the consolidation of monastic institutions. This special aptitude, joined to her love of monastic regularity, and her zeal for knowledge and ecclesiastical discipline, gave her an important part to play, and great influence. Her society was sought by S. Aidan, and all the religious who knew her, that they might be guided by her clear judgment and wise experience. Kings even, and princes of her blood, or of the adjacent provinces, often came to consult her, asking enlightenment, which they afterwards joyfully acknowledged

themselves to have received. But she did not reserve the
treasures of her judgment and charity for the great ones of
the earth. She scattered round her everywhere the benefits
of justice, piety, peace, and temperance. She was ere long regarded and honoured as the mother of her country, and all
who addressed her gave her the sweet name of Mother, which
she well deserved. Not only in Northumbria, but in distant
regions, to which the fame of her virtue and enlightenment
had penetrated, she was to many the instrument of their
salvation and conversion. And in her two communities
especially she secured, during a rule of more than thirty
years, the supremacy of order, union, charity, and equality,
so much, that it became usual to say to the proud Northumbrians, that the image of the primitive Church, wherein
was neither rich nor poor, and where all was common among
the Christians, was realized at Whitby.

But the most touching particular of all in the enthusiastic
narrative of the Venerable Bede, is that which proves the
passionate tenderness felt for her by her daughters, especially
by the young girls whom she prepared for religious life in a
separate house, by the discipline of a novitiate establishment regularly constituted and attentively superintended.

Nor did the royal abbess confine herself to the government of a numerous community of nuns. According to a
usage then very general, but principally prevailing in the
Celtic countries, a monastery was joined to the nunnery.
And Hilda inspired the monks subject to her authority with
so great a devotion to the rule, so true a love of sacred
literature, so careful a study of the Scriptures, that this
monastery, ruled by a woman, became a school of missionaries and bishops. Bosa of York, Hedda of Dor-
chester, Oftgar of Worcester, S. John of Beverley, Bishop
of York, and Wilfrid, the disturber of her declining days,
issued from her nursery of great men.

S. HILDA.

Nov. 17.

The poor cowherd Caedmon was reared into an ecclesiastical poet under her care, and became the father of English poetry.

In 664, Oswy convoked the council of Whitby to regulate and terminate the dispute raised by Wilfrid. This saint was fired with ambition to bring the Northumbrian Church into conformity with Roman practices. When appointed abbot of Ripon by Alcfrid, he turned out the monks because they would not give up their customs for those which he wished to introduce. Chief among the differences was the time for the observance of Easter. The Celtic Church had their calendar out of gear, and observed the queen of feasts before the time when it was celebrated by the Roman Church.

Hilda was fifty years old when the gathering at Whitby took place. She and her whole community clung to the Celtic tradition, and the national party was headed by Colman, bishop of Lindisfarne, supported by S. Cedd, then only a monk. Alcfrid and the queen favoured Wilfrid and Roman observance. An account of the assembly has been given elsewhere. King Oswy decided in favour of Wilfrid; Colman protested, refused to recognize the decision, and returned to Lindisfarne, collected the bones of S. Aidan, and departed for Iona. Wilfrid triumphed. He was appointed bishop of Northumbria, and then, to show his scorn for the Anglo-Saxon bishops, went to France to receive ordination from the Bishop of Paris. On his way back he was shipwrecked. When he returned, he found that his conduct had roused disgust and opposition. King Oswy had appointed in his room the holy bishop Chad. The Northumbrians, though they observed the decree of Whitby as to the celebration of Easter, refused to have such a firebrand as Wilfrid among them as bishop. There can be little doubt that this, to a great extent, was due to the advice

of S. Hilda, who, as long as she lived, never relaxed her
opposition to Wilfrid. Chad was afterwards removed to
Mercia, and Wilfrid reinstated. But his violence and pride
made his presence intolerable, and S. Theodore, archbishop
of Canterbury, divided his diocese into three, A.D. 678, and
gave York to Bosa, one of the disciples of S. Hilda, who in
her monastery at Whitby, was now at a great age, but had
not lost her influence, or her antipathy to Wilfrid. Wilfrid,
incensed to the last degree, went to Rome to appeal to Pope
Agatho against this subdivision of his huge diocese into
workable parcels. It was done for the good of the Church,
but it offended Wilfrid's pride. S. Hilda, the abbess, and
S. Theodore, the archbishop, sent messengers to Rome to
complain of Wilfrid's insolence. The council of Rome confirmed the division of the diocese, but ordered the reap-
pointment of Wilfrid to one of the sees, that of York. King
Egfrid called a council, the pontifical bulls were read, but
instead of submitting, with the consent of Archbishop
Theodore, the king imprisoned Wilfrid, and refused to carry
out the orders of the Pope.

Hilda was dead before the strife ended. During the last
six years of her life she suffered much from fever. But
"during all this while she never failed either to return thanks
to her Maker, or publicly and privately to instruct the flock
committed to her charge." When dying, she called her
monks and nuns around her, at early cock-crow, and, after
exhorting them to preserve evangelical peace among themselves and towards all men, she passed by death to life
eternal.

S. JOHN OF BEVERLEY, ABP. OF YORK.
(See May 7.)

S. FERGUS, B.

(8TH CENT.)

[Dempster's Scottish Menology. Adam King's Kalendar. Aberdeen Breviary on Nov. 18. David Camerarius on Nov. 18. Authority :— The Aberdeen Breviary.]

FERGUS, an Irish bishop, came to the west of Scotland, and after founding three churches near Strogeth, went on into Caithness, where he founded churches at Wick and Halkirk. After that he visited Buchan, and built a church at Lungley. Then he went on to Glamis, and there he died. At Glamis is S. Fergus' cave and S. Fergus' well. At a council held in Rome in 721, under Gregory II., there were present Fergustus of Scotland,[1] and "Sedulius, bishop of Britain, of the Scottish race." Sedulius must have been bishop of the Strathclyde Britons, who submitted to the Pope in 703. North Wales submitted in 768, South Wales in 777. The name was probably Siedhuil or Shiel. Fergustus is probably S. Fergus Cruithneach, commemorated in the Donegal and Tallaght Martyrologies on September 8. Fergus, who died at Glamis, is said by the Aberdeen Breviary to have been formerly a bishop in Ireland, and so these two are probably the same.

S. HUGH, B. OF LINCOLN.

(A.D. 1200.)

[Roman Martyrology. Canonized by Honorius III. in 1280. Sarum Kalendar and Anglican Reformed Kalendar. Authority :—A Life by an anonymous writer in Pez, Bibliotheca ascetica, Ratisb. 1733, abbreviated in Surius; Roger of Wendover, sub. an. 1200.]

HUGH was the son of a Burgundian knight; he was de-

[1] " Fergustus Episcopus Scotiæ Pictus huic constituto a nobis promulgato subscripsi."

prived of his mother when very young, and at eight years old was sent by his father to a convent of Regular Canons, at no great distance from his home, to be educated for the religious life. "Every opportunity of joking and playing was denied him, and he was exhorted to a gravity beyond his years. His master said to him, 'Hugh, I bring you up for Christ. No jokes for you.'" He bent under this rigorous discipline, which would have crushed some young spirits, and became another Samuel, guileless, meek, loving, and obedient. When he was nineteen years old his master took him to the Grande Chartreuse, near Grenoble. The solemn grandeur of the situation of the monastery in its basin of green Alp, surrounded by sombre pine-clad heights towering up to perennial snow, impressed his boyish spirit with awe and admiration, and he entreated to be allowed to enter the Carthusian House. His companions endeavoured to dissuade him from embracing a life of such severity. But the impression of that Alpine scene could not be eradicated from his heart; he felt drawn to the mountain retreat, from the rich but monotonous plains of Burgundy; and, escaping from his convent, he made his way to the Grande Chartreuse, asked to be admitted, and with delight saw himself vested in the habit, and settled in the solitude of the mountains. Ten happy years were spent there, during which he heard the thunder of the avalanche, saw the gentians break out over the smooth sward, the Alpine rose blush on the rocks, the pasture sprinkled with the delicate snow-flake, the lily of the Alps; saw the evening glow in autumn turn the Grand Som to a pyramid of fire; and then his call came to leave all this world of loveliness for the dull commonplace of a Somersetshire valley, the prelude to a more hideous change—the desolate flats of Lincolnshire, where, in place of the dark blue sky and crisp air of the mountains, he would be called to endure the hazy sky and raw fogs of English fens.

S. HUGH OF LINCOLN. After Cahier.   Nov. 17.

King Henry II. had founded the first Carthusian house in England at Witham, in Somersetshire. It had not thriven under its two first priors, and he sent Reginald, bishop of Bath to the Grande Chartreuse to summon thence one thoroughly imbued with the spirit of the order, under whom the colony at Witham might be nursed into a thriving community. Hugh was chosen. He struggled to escape the charge; but when he saw that duty called him, he crushed his rebellious wishes, and, with a sigh and last look at the glorious solitude, descended the gorge that leads to the outer world, and set his face for doleful England.

On reaching Witham, Hugh set diligently to work to enlarge and improve the buildings; he carried the stones on his shoulder, and kneaded the mortar with his own hands. In the neighbourhood were landed gentry and nobles, who disliked the introduction of a new religious community into England; they were prejudiced against a rule which they regarded as excessive in its strictness. But the sweet face, the gentle courtesy, the halting English in which Hugh expressed his kind wishes, united to break down all dislike, and to win the hearts of everyone with whom he had dealings. The house of Witham began to fill with postulants; and harmony, activity, and devotion reigned in the holy community.

The see of Lincoln had been vacated in 1184 by Walter de Constantiis, who had been translated to Rouen. Henry II. kept it vacant for two years, receiving the revenues during the vacancy for his own use; but as he could not venture to leave the see in widowhood any longer, he bade the chapter elect, and recommended them to choose Hugh the Carthusian. Henry had conceived a great respect for the prior, and this respect was deepened by a recent incident, for, in a storm at sea, when crossing from Normandy, he had cried to heaven, "O God whom the prior of Witham serves, by his merits and intercession save me." He was not shipwrecked, and attributed his deliverance to the prayers of S. Hugh.

The chapter dutifully elected the king's nominee, but Hugh refused to accept the mitre on such an election ; it was not free ; if the chapter wished him, they must choose him unconstrained by the king's command. The chapter met again, and again elected the prior of Witham.

As bishop, Hugh was fearless in restraining the lawless, and in redressing wrongs. The royal foresters, or overseers of the royal chases, were tyrannical and insolent. They treated the unfortunate peasants in his diocese with injustice and cruelty. Hugh excommunicated the chief of them. Henry II. was angry, and remonstrated ; but Hugh was firm. Soon after, the king asked the bishop to give a prebendal stall to one of his courtiers. "No," answered the saint, "these places are to be conferred on clerks, not on courtiers. The king has the means of rewarding his own servants without burdening the Church with them."

Hugh zealously prosecuted the building of the transept and choir of his cathedral. The exquisite work, so pure and beautiful that it has scarce any to surpass it in England, was done under his supervision. He had a favourite swan, which he fed ; and when he walked by his moat the swan flew or swam to him, and put its head caressingly up his sleeve to be stroked. The swan disappeared at breeding time, when it went off to the fens, but returned invariably to the moat of the palace. As the return of the swan coincided on one or two occasions with that of Hugh from a Lenten retreat, it was thought by the superstitious that the coming of the swan was an infallible token of the return of the bishop.

S. Hugh opposed the raising of a subvention for the prosecution of war in France, when demanded by Richard I. He refused to have it levied in his diocese. The Cœur de

Lion was furious when he heard of this, and sent some men to Lincoln to arrest and eject the bishop. Hugh had all the bells rung as they arrived, and they were solemnly excommunicated. Seeing all Lincoln stirring, they felt themselves not strong enough to get possession of the person of the bishop, and withdrew. When Richard came to England, Hugh went to meet him. The king was angry with the bishop, and would not salute him. Then Hugh went up to Richard, and said, "Give me a kiss." "No," answered King Richard, "you have not deserved one." "I have," said Hugh; "for I have come a long way to see you. You owe me a kiss," and he pulled the king's cloak, and drawing him towards him, extorted the salutation which Richard had at first refused. The king laughed at his pertinacity, and gave way.

They began to talk together. "How stands your conscience?" asked the bishop; "you are my parishioner, and I must give an answer for it." "My conscience is fairly easy," answered Richard, "but I admit it is ruffled with anger against those who are hostile to my sovereignty." "Ha!" said Hugh, "is that all? And yet I hear daily complaints of the poor oppressed, the innocent afflicted, and the land crushed with exactions. Nor is that everything. I hear that you have not kept your marriage vows." The king started up, angry and aghast; and Hugh took his leave. "If all the bishops in my realm were like that man," said Richard, when he left, "kings and princes would be powerless against them." Hugh got the nickname of Hammerking because he had dealt both Henry and Richard some hard knocks.

Hugh was sent by King John on an embassy to Philip Augustus, to conclude a peace between England and France. He took the opportunity for revisiting the Grande Chartreuse. On his return, he fell ill of a quartan fever in London, and died there in peace. His body was translated to Lincoln, and is said to have wrought many miracles.

In art he is represented as a bishop with a swan at his feet, and holding a ciborium, above which is a host with a child in the midst of the wafer, as he is said to have been favoured with a vision of this sort to confirm his faith in the Real Presence.

THE PRESENTATION IN THE TEMPLE.
After a Fresco by Giotto at Padua.

November 18.

S. HESYCHIUS, *M. at Antioch*; A.D. 304.
S. ROMANUS, *M. at Antioch*; A.D. 304.
SS. ORICULUS, ORICULA, AND BASILICA, *MM. at Rennes*; 5th cent.
S. MAUDEZ, *Ab. in Brittany*; 6th cent.
S. MOMBOLUS, *Ab. at Lagny*; 6th cent.[1]
S. WYNNEN, *B. in Scotland*; A.D. 579.
S. ROMPHARIUS, *B. of Coutances*; circ. A.D. 586.
S. FRIGIDIAN, *B. of Lucca*; A.D. 589 (*see* March 18).
S. FLORINUS, *C. at Coblenz*.
S. ODO, *Ab. of Cluny*; A.D. 942.
DEDICATION OF BASILICA OF SS. PETER AND PAUL AT ROME; A.D. 1625.

S. ROMANUS, M.

(A.D. 304.)

[Roman Martyrology, Usuardus, Ado, Notker, &c. Greek Menæa and Menologies. Authorities:—Eusebius, "The Martyrs of Palestine," c. ii.; "On the Resurrection and Ascension of the Lord," lib. ii. A hymn of Prudentius, 10; and S. John Chrysostom, Orat. 43, 48.]

ROMANUS, a deacon and exorcist, a native of Palestine, and serving in the church of Cæsarea, was at Antioch, in Syria, when the churches were destroyed by order of Diocletian. When he saw men, women, and children crowding to the idol altars to do sacrifice he rebuked them. He was at once seized, and ordered by the judge to be tortured. When the tormentors were exhausted, Romanus called aloud, "Why do you cease, O tyrant? I have confessed with my mouth that Christ is the true King!"

The judge ordered him to be scorched, and his brows to be wounded in a manner not described. He went joyously

[1] A disciple of S. Fursey.

to his martyrdom, bearing a cross on his shoulder and crowned with his blood.

A pyre was heaped up, but the rain came down from the clouds which overspread the sky in such a drenching shower that the wet sticks and rushes would not kindle. The judge therefore ordered his tongue to be cut out. The Christians present received it when amputated, and treasured it as a precious relic. Curiously enough, Romanus was not thereby deprived of speech. The same thing was observed by Victor of Utica in certain sufferers in the Vandal persecution. After having had their tongues cut off they retained the faculty of speech. The same has been observed in cases of late years, where the tongue has had to be removed on account of cancer.[1] Romanus was able to answer the jailer, who asked him his name, and to profess his faith in Christ. He was, however, subjected to the rack, stretched to the fifth hole, and died under the torture.

According to a hymn of Prudentius, a child of seven, named in the martyrologies Barulas, suffered with him, but of this Eusebius, who was likely to know all the circumstances, says nothing in either of his accounts of the martyrdom of Romanus, and it is therefore probably a fiction.

S. MAUDEZ, AB.

(6TH CENT.)

[Gallican Martyrologies. Authorities:—A MS. Life written before 878, used by Lobineau and Le Grand. The Lections in the Breviaries of Léon; and the MS. Legendaries of Treguer, used by Albert Le Grand.]

S. MAUDEZ, Modez, or Mondez, was an Irishman. In Ireland he bears the name of Moditeus, but little or nothing is related of him. The reason is, that he left his native

---

[1] See Hon. E. Twisleton: "The Tongue not essential to Speech."

land at an early age. He was born in Ulster, and his father's name is said to have been Ardæus. This is probably the title Ard-righ, or chief king, taken as a name. The mother is called variously Getusa and Vernosa. He was the tenth son of his parents, and was given by them to God as a tithe of their offspring.

He came to Brittany, and placed himself in the monastery of Dol for a short time. He then went to Treguier, and visited S. Tugduval in the town of Cozgueaudet, or Lexobie, who gave him the abbey of Trecor, as a place of retreat under the holy abbot Ruelin. After some years he sought a solitary place on the shore of the sea near Plou Bihan, now called Iles-Modez, or the church of S. Maudez, but was pursued by such crowds that he fled to an island near Enez-Glaz, in the diocese of Treguier. It is said that the island abounded with serpents, and that S. Maudez drove them all into the sea. He died, and was buried in the island, but his relics were removed to Bourges in 878. A portion of the right arm is preserved in the church of Lesneven, a portion of the left arm in the church of Saint Jean-du-Doigt; some bones in the cathedral of Treguier. The earth of the island of S. Maudez is diligently collected and mixed with water, and given by Breton mothers to their children, hoping that as S. Maudez expelled snakes from the island, so the earth blessed by him will act as a vermifuge.

S. Maudez is S. Mawes in Cornwall.

S. ODO, AB. OF CLUNY.

(A.D. 942.)

[Roman, Gallican, and Benedictine Martyrologies. Authority:—A Life by John of Salerno, a companion of Odo. Another Life by Nalgod of Cluny, written in the 11th cent. A third Life by his disciple Godschalk existed in the Carthusian convent at Antwerp in the 16th cent. Where it now is, is uncertain.[1] The Life by John of Salerno in Mabillon, Acta SS. O.S.B. sæc. v. So also that by Nalgod.]

Odo of Cluny was the son of Abbo, a knight of Frank origin, in attendance on William, count of Aquitaine. As soon as he was weaned, he was given to a priest to be educated for the monastic life, and was dedicated by his mother to S. Martin. However, when he was aged about sixteen, his father changed his mind, and placed him with the count of Aquitaine; and he spent his time in hawking and hunting. But this was an age at which he was growing rapidly. He had not, perhaps, had sufficiently nourishing food at the parsonage, and his strength was not equal to the activity required of him. The hunting and hawking exhausted him greatly, and he was attacked with violent headaches, which troubled him till he was eighteen. He and his father, however, supposed these headaches came from S. Martin, who was angry at his votary devoting his time to secular amusements. Under this conviction Odo was taken away from the court of the count, and given a canonry at Tours, with minor orders. He read the old classic poets with great advantage and satisfaction, but one night after he had been studying Virgil, he dreamt that he saw a noble antique vase full of serpents, and was convinced by this that he would get more harm than good from these

---

[1] "Usuardi Martyrologium, cum additionibus . . . . opera Joannis Molani." Antwerp, 1582, p. 166 b.

authors. He therefore gave up reading them. As expurgated editions of the classic poets were not then accessible, it is quite possible that he was right. From Tours he went to Paris to study philosophy under Remigius of Auxerre, monk of the abbey of S. Germain, the first to open a public school in Paris, A.D. 900. One bitter winter day as Odo was going to hear mass with the rest of the scholars, he saw a poor man in rags, blue with cold, in the porch. He was moved with pity, and gave him his fur overcoat. After mass he went to his class, but was so cold that he could not endure it, and returned to his bed to snuggle into it and recover warmth. To his astonishment, as he got in, he found a piece of gold among the blankets—enough, and more than enough, to provide him with a new fur overcoat. Remigius died in 908, and probably about that time Odo left Paris and returned to Tours. There he was joined by Adegrin, a knight who was tonsured, and had received a canonry. Adegrin lived with Odo in the practice of every virtue. After a while, however, he retired to Beaume, and was shortly after followed by S. Odo, and was admitted by S. Berno, the abbot, to take the habit.

The great abbey of Cluny was founded in 910, and was committed to the care of S. Berno, who was obliged to govern six other monasteries at the same time. On his death, in 927, the government of three of these monasteries, Cluny, Massay, and Deols, devolved on S. Odo. He made Cluny his residence. He was a strict disciplinarian, and made conformity to the Rule of S. Benedict a point of supreme importance. When at Beaume he had got into trouble on account of not observing the letter of the rule of the monastery, and this impressed itself on his mind and made him strict with others. The occasion was this. At Beaume it was ruled that no monk should speak with one of the scholars except before witnesses, and that if a pupil should have occasion to leave the dormitory at night he should be attended by the master of the boys, and either another monk or another pupil, and that they should take a candle with them. One night a boy rose from his bed, woke S. Odo, who was master at the time, and announced his intention of leaving the dormitory for a few minutes. Odo at once roused from his bed another scholar, and the two gravely attended the youth on his excursion. As the lamp in the dormitory illumined equally the locality which was the goal of the boy's journey, S. Odo thought it unnecessary to light a candle for him. Next day, when the monks were ranged in solemn chapter, S. Odo was denounced for having infringed the rule by neglect in this particular, immediately on the conclusion of the reading of the martyrology.[1] S. Odo prostrated himself at the feet of the chapter, imploring pardon, and explaining that a light on this occasion had been wholly unnecessary.[2] He was sentenced by general acclamation and special judgment of the abbot to be excommunicated, and not to dare ask pardon again that day. Odo had to throw himself before the feet of the brethren with tears of compunction for his crime, before any of them would undertake to intercede for him, and obtain the removal of his sentence of excommunication.

On one occasion he acted most injudiciously. He had left the abbey and lodged one night in the castle of a nobleman, who was then away from home along with his wife. The daughter, however, entertained him, and sat all the evening with him. She confided to him that she was about to be married, and that she did not like to be given to a man whom she detested. Odo advised her to run away with him, and allow him to put her in a convent. Next morning she

---

[1] "Cæperunt illum graviter increpare, cur sine cereo transacta nocte post puerum isset."—Vit. a Joan. Sal.
[2] "In terram corruens veniam petiit, sufficere inquiens sibi posse dormitorii lucem."—*Ibid.*

galloped off with Odo, and he took her to a little oratory near the abbey of Beaume. Then he told Berno, the abbot, what he had done. The abbot was horrified. Odo had acted in a most improper manner. There was no knowing that the girl had a real vocation; all that was clear was, that she was obstinately set against the husband chosen for her by her parents. He bade Odo go to her, carry her daily some food, and satisfy himself by repeated interviews that the vocation was genuine. Odo was quite convinced, after a conversation or two, that she really wished to receive the veil; she was therefore put in a nunnery, and died a few years after in the odour of sanctity, though the rest of the sisters were not quite satisfied of her sanity.[1]

As abbot, the exhortations of S. Odo were directed towards the observance of the rule in its strictest severity. He was wont to enforce it on his monks by terrible examples. His biographer, John of Salerno, quotes some of his discourses and stories.

"The sin of deserting the habit of S. Benedict is most grievous. Some years ago the monks of S. Martin at Tours abandoned their distinctive habit,[2] and began to wear their tunics and hoods flowing and coloured, their shoes were also so shining and bright coloured that they looked like glass.[3] Instead of rising for lauds in the middle of the night, they left their beds at break of day. One night a monk, who was not asleep, saw two men enter the dormitory, one bearing a sword; the other pointed to each slumbering delinquent, and said, 'Strike!' He struck, and next morning all the monks were dead, except he who had seen the vision."

An awful example, no doubt, if true.

[1] "Ceteræ autem eam insanire putabant."—Vit. a Joan. Sal.
[2] "Nativa et assueta vestimenta."—*Ibid.*
[3] 'Calceamenta .... erant colorata et nitida, ut vitreum colorem viderentur assumere."—*Ibid.*

When the Normans harassed the French coasts the monks were often reduced to great straits. They were obliged to leave their monasteries near the sea, and take refuge with their relatives inland. This occasioned relaxation of discipline. When their old habits wore out, they made shift with such clothes as would be given them in charity. This was a great crime. Better have none at all than adopt a garb not sanctioned by S. Benedict. On one occasion, said S. Odo, a monk thus disguised was with a monk in proper habit. The former fell ill, and the latter saw in vision the soul of the unvested monk appear before the great throne set in heaven, on which sat S. Benedict, surrounded by an innumerable company of monks. And when the poor brother approached, and the monastic choir shouted that for his good deeds he deserved to be numbered with them, S. Benedict said, sternly: "Depart from me, I know you not, you wear no habit of mine." The monk, on waking, at once despoiled himself of his own garb, put it on the dying brother, and had the satisfaction of seeing in vision that on this occasion the Patriarch of Monks acknowledged his son. This story enforced the teaching of S. Odo, that "It does not suffice a monk to have only purity of soul, if he be without the exterior signs of a monk. . . . . Man may be an apostate from God in two ways, by falling away from the Creator either in faith or in works. Whoever leaves God in faith is an apostate; so also is he an apostate who departs from Him in works. Faith is no good without works, and works are profitless without faith. Therefore let no one be shocked at what I have said of the aforenamed brother: he could not receive pardon, or merit admission into heaven, till he changed his coat."

Another horrible crime committed by too many sons of S. Benedict was that they ate meat. "Once a monk arrived at daybreak at the house of one of his relations, and asked for something to eat. The reply given him was, that it was not yet breakfast time. 'Hey!' shouted the monk, 'here have I been riding all night long by orders of my abbot, and am I to fast now?' They replied that they had some fishes in the house; but he was indignant, and looking here and there saw a number of hens running about the floor. Then he took a stick and struck one on the head, and exclaimed, 'This is my fish, to-day!' Those who stood by were abashed, and said, reddening, 'Perhaps, father, it is permitted you to eat meat.' But he said, 'Chicken is not meat. Don't you know that birds and fishes were created together on the same day, and have one origin, as our hymn says?' This silenced them. But when the hen was cooked and set before him, he pulled off a piece of meat, and bit into it, and it stuck in his throat, and so he died."

When Odo was a monk at Beaume it is said that he was eating the crumbs he had made at dinner when the abbot gave the sign for grace. He shut his hand, which was full of crumbs, till grace was over, and was then in sore trouble of conscience what to do. To throw away the crumbs would be a sin, to eat them after meal-time would be also a sin. He looked perplexedly into his hand, and lo! the crumbs were changed into pearls. Abbot Odo urged with all his eloquence and earnestness the duty of eating crumbs that had been made. He related that a monk's eyes were once opened, and he saw the devil with a great sack on his shoulder, and was told it was full of the crumbs made by wasteful monks. Odo went with a few monks to a monastery which he was required to bring into better discipline. On Saturday evening, according to the rule of the Cluniac reform, the party he had brought were busily engaged at a tub, washing their drawers (subtulares). A monk of the old monastery passed through, and seeing them thus engaged stood still, and said, "Tell me in what rule did our holy father Benedict lay down that any monk should wash his drawers?" The Cluniacs kept silence, for this was a time when they were forbidden to speak, but they either hissed or groaned, for the angry monk exclaimed, "I was not created a serpent to hiss, or an ox to bellow, but a man to speak with human voice, and I say that you are fine fellows to come here teaching us to keep the rule of S. Benedict, and yet in defiance of his rule to be tubbing your under-linen on a Saturday night!" Next day, when the chapter met, all this was related before the abbot Odo. S. Odo was indignant. But he said, "To-day is the Lord's day. We will put off this matter till to-morrow, so as not to have discord to-day." But next day the wicked monk was taken ill, and in three days was dead without absolution.

A monk was ill, and it was necessary to bleed him, but it was against rule that one should be bled without special licence from the abbot. S. Odo was absent. The case was urgent, so the surgeon bled the sick man. Note the punishment for breaking the rule. The bandage slipped, the vein opened in the night, and the monk bled to death. The vigilance of S. Odo extended beyond the walls of Cluny. Thrice he visited Rome, whither he was summoned by Popes Leo VII. and Stephen VIII. He reformed the monastery of S. Paolo fuori mure, afterwards that of S. Augustine at Pavia, and that of S. Elias at Nepi, in Etruria. He introduced Cluniac discipline into the monasteries of Tulle, Aurillac, Bourg-Dieu, and Massay, of Fleury, Saint Pierre-le-Vif at Sens, of S. Allire at Clermont, S. Julian at Tours, of Sarlat and Roman Moutier. He encountered great difficulties in getting the monks to give up eating meat. At Fleury, when the monks heard he was coming to abolish their meat dinners, they took up arms to oppose his entrance.

He died at Tours, and was buried in the church of S. Julian. His relics were scattered by the Huguenots, but the head is preserved at L'Ile-Jourdain, in the diocese of Auch.

THE PRESENTATION IN THE TEMPLE.
After the Picture by Fra Bartolommeo in the Vienna Gallery.

November 19.

S. ABDIAS, *Prophet at Samaria.*
S. PONTIANUS, *Pope M. of Rome; circ.* A.D. 23
S. MAXIMUS, *P.M. at Rome; 3rd cent.*
S. CRISPIN, *B.M. of Ecija in Spain; circ.* A.D. 302.
SS. SEVERINUS, EXUPERIUS, AND FELICIAN, *MM. at Vienne in Gaul.*
S. FAUSTUS, *Deac. M. at Alexandria;* A.D. 304.
S. BARLAAM, *M. at Cæsarea in Cappadocia;* A.D. 304.
SS. AZAS AND COMP., *MM. in Isauria;* A.D. 304.
S. PATROCLUS, *H. at Colombiers in Berry;* A.D. 577.
S. BUDOC, *B. of Dol; end of 6th cent. (see* Dec. 9).
S. ERMENBURGA *or* DOMNEVA, *Abss. Minster,* A.D. 690.
S. JAMES DE SASSY, *C. at Chapelle d'Angilon in Berry; circ.* A.D. 865.
S. PAUL, *B. of Skalholt in Iceland;* A.D. 1211.
S. ELIZABETH OF HUNGARY, *W. at Marburg in Germany;* A.D. 1231.

S. PONTIANUS, POPE M.

(ABOUT A.D. 236.)

[Roman Martyrology. Usuardus, Ado, &c. Authorities :—Euseb. H. E. vi 29, Chron., Liberian Kalendar.]

ONTIANUS succeeded Urban on the throne of S. Peter in 230, when the Church was enjoying rest under Alexander Severus. Maximinus, the successor of Alexander, persecuted, and Pontianus was banished to Sardinia in 235, where he died, probably of old age and rough treatment, about a year after. His body was brought back to Rome by S. Fabian and laid in the cemetery of S. Callixtus.

S. MAXIMUS, P.M.

(3RD CENT.)

[Roman Martyrology. Usuardus, Ado, Notker, &c. Authority :—
S. Cyprian, Epp. 16, 44, 46, 50.]

MAXIMUS, a Roman priest, was arrested in the persecution of Decius. He confessed Christ in the midst of cruel tortures, and was then sent back to prison. Having been released, he fell into the schism of Novatus, but the letters of S. Dionysius of Alexandria and of S. Cyprian of Carthage were the means of bringing him back to Catholic unity. He is thought to have suffered under Valerian. A certain Maximus was then decapitated on the Appian Way, and it may have been the same man. He was buried near S. Sixtus.

S. FAUSTUS, DEAC. M.

(A.D. 304.)

[Roman Martyrology. Also on Oct. 4, with Caius, Eusebius, and others. Usuardus, &c. Authority :—A letter of S. Dionysius of Alexandria in Euseb. H. E. vii. 11.]

FAUSTUS, a deacon of Alexandria, accompanied S. Dionysius, the archbishop, in his exile, during the persecution of Decius. Eusebius tells us that afterwards, when Faustus was an old man, he was beheaded in the persecution of Dioclctian.

S. BARLAAM, M.

(A.D. 304.)

[Modern Roman Martyrology. By the Greeks on the 16th and 19th Nov. Authorities:—A Panegyric of S. Basil on the Martyr; another by S. Chrysostom; the Greek Acts in Lambecius, viii. 277; and a homily of Severus of Antioch, quoted by Assemani, i. 571.]

BARLAAM was a humble labourer in the neighbourhood of Antioch, in Syria. His zealous profession of Christ attracted the attention of the governor, who had him racked and scourged, and then ordered Barlaam's hand to be held over a burning altar, with hot coals and incense laid on his palm. If in the natural shrinking from pain he should shake the incense into the fire on the altar, it would be regarded as a sacrifice. Barlaam held his hand immovable, in spite of the agony it caused him, till his hand was wholly consumed.

S. PAUL, B. OF SKALHOLT.

(A.D. 1211.)

[Icelandic Necrology. Authority:—Páls Saga Biskups, written between 1216-1220 (Biskupa Sögur, formáli xxxiii.). The best edition of the Páls Saga is that in Biskupa Sögur, Copenh. 1858, t. i. p. 125-148, introduction, xxv.-xxxiv. An earlier edition with Latin translation, along with Hungurvaka and the Thattr af Thorvalldi vithförla, Copenh. 1778, p. 142-253.]

PAUL was the son of John Loptson, son of the illustrious Saemund the Wise, who made the collection of the elder Edda. His grandmother was Thora, daughter of King Magnus Barelegs of Norway. The mother of Paul was the sister of S. Thorlac. Paul was a man of wealth and rank.

He married Herdisa, and was educated in schools in England. He was handsome, had a remarkably sweet voice for singing, and was a poet and literary man. His talents and rank pointed him out as a suitable man to occupy the see of Skalholt on the death of Bishop Thorlac. It was arranged in the family that he was the most proper person to succeed his uncle, and as Bishop Brand of Holar was of the same opinion, he was sent to Lund in Denmark to be consecrated by Archbishop Absalom of Nidaros (Dronthjem) and Eric of Lund. He was consecrated in May, 1195, by Peter, bishop of Roskilde, acting for the archbishop Eric, who was blind. On his return to Iceland he gave a great banquet, and supplied the guests with wine as a beverage instead of beer—a piece of splendour and liberality hitherto unheard of. He brought with him two glass windows for his cathedral, and erected a tower of wood, in which he hung several bells. In the tower was an oratory dedicated to his predecessor Thorlac, which he had painted sumptuously.

He spent a winter in Skalholt before he was rejoined by his wife. Her coming led to the happiest results. "She was to him and to the diocese great support and strength, the like of which was not seen anywhere else whilst he was bishop. So great was her economy and management, that before she had been there many years, there reigned a superfluity of all things necessary, so that they could entertain at a time a hundred guests, besides their own servants, who numbered eighty men."

This excellent wife was drowned with one of her daughters in crossing the river Thiorsá. Paul buried them with great solemnity, and after that his daughter Thora, aged fourteen, managed the house. In 1199 S. Thorlac was canonized by popular acclamation at the national council, and Paul then translated his body. In the winter of 1202-3 he entertained John, a Greenland bishop, who gave him a recipe for making wine of crowberries, which had been taught him by King Swerrir. The following summer, however, was not fruitful in crowberries, and only one man in the neighbourhood was able to lay in a stock of home-made crowberry wine. Paul had 220 churches in his diocese, and 290 priests. He only preached on the greatest festivals, because he thought that too frequent preaching lost its effect on the people, and perhaps he was not altogether wrong. He had two sons, Lopt and Ketell, and two daughters; one, as already said, was drowned. He died in 1211.

S. ELIZABETH OF HUNGARY, W.

(A.D. 1231.)

[Roman Martyrology. Canonized by Gregory IX. in 1235. Authorities :—(1) "Libellus de dictis Quatuor ancillarum S. Elisabethæ," written in 1234; in Mencken, "Script. rer. Germ." ii. 2007-2034, slightly abbreviated, but nothing of importance omitted. "In Prologo continentur inanes laudum tituli et tædiosæ de virtutum Elisabethæ repetitiones; quas, pace Lectoris, omittimus." (2) "Epistola Conradi de Marburg ad Papam (Gregorium IX.) de vita S. Elisabethæ." The earliest account of the saint, but very deficient in details. In Leo Allatius, Συμμικτά, Colon. Allobrog. 1653, p. 269; and in Kuchenbecker, "Analecta Hassiaca," ix. 107. (3) "Vita S. Elisabethæ, auct. Theodorico de Apolda," author also of a Life of S. Dominic, written probably in 1289, the foundation of later biographies—a much overrated work; in Struve, Acta Literaria e MSS. ii. 1; Kollar, Vett. analecta, i. 885. (4) A Life of Ludwig IV., by Berthold, the chaplain of Ludwig, written in Latin, large extracts from which are incorporated in the "Chronica Pontificum et archiepiscoporum Magdeburgensium," in the Hannover Library, and the greater part in the Annales Reinhardtsbrunnenses (ab. 1026-1335), ed. Wegele, Thüringischen Geschichtsquellen, i. Jena, 1854. This was composed certainly before 1289, and was added to up to 1308-1315. A German translation was made by Friedrich Ködiz von Salfeld, ed. H. Rückert, Leipzig, 1851. Ködiz did his work between 1315 and 1323. (5) An old German rhyming Life of S. Elizabeth, originally composed by an unknown poet in seven books, of

which an excerpt was given by Graff, "Diutiska," i. p. 344-489.
Dronke published 193 more verses in the Anzeiger, vi. p. 54. With
the assistance of this poem a "Rhyming Chronicle of S. Elizabeth" was
written by Johann Röthe, according to Bodmer and Gräter, Bragur, vi.
2, p. 137. This rhyming chronicle is in Mencken, "Scr. rer. Germ." ii.
p. 2033-2102, and consists of 4500 verses. (6) "Hæc est forma de
statu mortis Landgraviæ de Thuringia," in Martene and Durand, Ampl.
Coll. i. 1245-56. (7) "Vita S. Elisabethæ, filiæ Andreæ Hungariæ,
auctore Cæsario Heisterbachensi" (d. 1240) is merely a recasting of the
narrative of the four maids of Elizabeth. (8) Johann Rothe (d. 1434),
"Chronik von Thüringen." Rothe was formerly monk at Eisenach,
afterwards chaplain to Anna, the Landgravin at Eisenach. In Mencken,
ii., the portion referring to S. Elizabeth, p. 1697-1729. (9) Wadding,
"Annales Minorum," Romæ, 1732, vols. i. ii. (10) Adam Bäring
(Ursinus) von Molberg, "Chronica Thuringiæ vernaculum" (1547), in
Mencken, "Scr. rer. Germ." iii., the portion referring to S. Elizabeth,
p. 1276-1287.]

HERMANN, landgrave of Thuringia and Hesse, was married
first to the daughter of the Elector of Saxony, and when she
died childless, secondly to Sophia of Bavaria, by whom he
had four sons—Ludwig, Hermann, Henry, and Conrad.
Hermann died young.

One day during the year 1211, as Hermann, landgrave
of Thuringia, sat among his minnesingers in his castle, the
Wartburg, the renowned poet Klingsor of Hungaria announced to him that on the self-same night Gertrude of
Meran, consort of Andrew II. of Hungary, would give
birth to a daughter, the destined bride of his eldest son,
Ludwig.[1] This daughter, Elizabeth, was at once demanded
in marriage for his son by the landgrave, and she was carried
in a silver cradle to the Wartburg, attended by the gallant
knight Walter von Vargila. The arrival of the baby-bride
was honoured with festivities, and as symbol of their union,

---

[1] The prophecy of Klingsor was delivered during the famous Wartburg Contest of
the Minnesingers, an account of which we have in rhyme by one of those present,
Wolfram von Eschenbach. An account is also given in the Life of Ludwig by his
chaplain Berchthold ; 465 lines are devoted to it in the Rhyming Chronicle.

the two little children were rocked to sleep in the same cradle.¹

The children grew up together from infancy in much love, regarding each other as brother and sister.

In the year 1215, Hermann the landgrave died at Gotha, and his body was brought to Eisenach, and buried in the church of S. Catherine. Ludwig, his eldest son, succeeded him, he was then fifteen, his little bride was only nine or ten years old.

The young landgrave was a boy of great promise. His chaplain Berchthold says of him, " He was a youth of nobleness of character and of delightful holiness. As he now came to the full bloom of youth, he seemed full of all virtues, great goodness, and mild compassion . . . . although in the first years of succeeding his father he had to endure much opposition and hostility, yet his natural virtue and sincerity did not suffer, for his mind was ever musing on heavenly things." The Rhyming Chronicle thus sums up his character, " In his childish years he began to bear himself right princely. He was a handsome youth, and did all things with prudence and advice. It grieved him to hear of any wrong. From his youth up he feared God, and was sternly set against evil. He loved the right, and he would not endure those who opposed it, but dismissed them from his court and favour. He who was deceitful, and lied, and misled people with false words, dared not face Ludwig."

Elizabeth was not kindly treated by Sophia, the mother of the young landgrave. She was prejudiced against the child, and thought her son might make a more advantageous match. The ladies of her attendance and the servants caught the feeling of their mistress, and behaved harshly,

---

¹ "Eine wirtschafft wart gemacht wol gespeyset und frölich gelacht betantzt wart dae und gesprungen und manch frölich lydlichen gesungen. Dae legten sy die Kinder bey zu einem vorspiell sold es sey."—Vita Rhythm.

even insolently, to the poor child. Ludwig stood chivalrously by her, and refused to listen to proposals for a dissolution of engagement. But he could not be always at home, and in his absence she suffered. Her heart clung with intense love to the handsome boy who was affianced to her. She had no one else to love; her mother had been assassinated in 1212; she had no friend in the Wartburg, and she turned instinctively to the Church, the home of the sorrowful. Adam Bäring says, " Elizabeth was perfect in body, handsome, brown complexioned, earnest in her conduct, modest in all her ways, kindly in speech, fervent in her prayers, and overflowing in her charity to poor people, peacefully disposed towards her attendants, considerate of her maids, and full of virtues and godly love at all times." At the same time Ludwig " was not too tall nor yet too short; he had a handsome loveable face, was cheerful, kindly, and modest as a young maid, clean in person and in his dress and habits, wise, provident, patient, manly, honourable, and truthful, and to his men very trusty, and to the poor charitable."

One feast of the Assumption, the Landgravin Sophia, with her daughters Agnes and Elizabeth and the young betrothed of Ludwig, went in state to the church of Our Lady at Eisenach to hear high mass sung by the knights of the Teutonic Order,[1] and gain the indulgences accorded on that day. Elizabeth of Hungary was sad at heart, having recently met with illusage, and feeling greatly her desolation. The noble ladies were richly dressed, and wore their coronets set with pearls and precious stones. As they swept into the church, Elizabeth looked up at a great solemn crucifix near the door. Instantly she took off her coronet, laid it on the bench, and

---

[1] "Dae sprach Sophia die lantgrevin . . . . Wir gehen gein Eysenach in die Stadt, dae man heut vil ablas hat, in der kirchen vnser lieben frawen ; dae wollen wir uns beschawen. Dae singen schöne messen die deutzschen herren."

fell on her knees before the Crucified. Sophia was angry and rebuked her. "Stand up! what mean you by falling down like an old worn-out horse on the ground, and casting off your coronet? Are you a silly child still, and is the crown too heavy for your temples? Stand up, and don't remain bowed like a common peasant." Elizabeth with tears in her eyes replied, "Dear lady, I pray thee let me alone; there stands the form of the sweet, merciful Christ, crowned with thorns, and I cannot pass Him with a chaplet of gold and pearls on my head." And she poured forth the burden of her heart in silent prayer. Her tears ran down her cheeks, and Sophia and her daughters had some difficulty in screening her from the crowd; for they had no wish that her grief at their ill treatment should become generally known.

When Elizabeth was ten years old she chose for herself a patron. It was customary in those days for children to put cards, or candles, on the altar, on which the names of saints and apostles were written, and then to draw card or candle, blindfolded, from the altar; the name written on what they had drawn was to be that of their patron. Elizabeth thrice drew S. John the Divine, and ever after she regarded him as her special guardian saint.[1] The landgravin not only ill-treated her, and repelled the love of the child, but she allowed her to be wounded at heart by sneers at her birth. "She may be a king's child," was said, "but her mother was a concubine,"[2]—a gratuitous insult based on no foundation of truth. It is not to be wondered at that Elizabeth dreamt she was visited by the spirit of her mother, to console the weeping child, and ask her prayers that God

---

[1] De Dictis iv. Ancillarum. "Unde cum secundum consuetudinem Dominarum, omnium Apostolarum nominibus vel in candelis vel in carta scriptis singulariter, simulque super altare mixtum compositis singulos sibi Apostolos forte eligentibus: ipsa Elyzabeth . . . . tribus vicibus beatum Johannen recepit Apostolum," &c. Ap. Menck. ii. p. 2013; cf. also de Rothe, Chron. Thuring. p. 1703.

[2] "Sy were eyn Konnigis kint, sy were eynes geburis tochtir."—Rothe, p. 1703.

might shorten the period of her purification and admit her into His rest.[1]

But Ludwig was always a comfort to her, when at home. The ancient German metrical Life gives a pretty picture of their love. "God looked upon her very sore sorrows and gave that the landgrave loved her dearly in his heart. And when he came to Eisenach, and they were alone together for a while, then he began to treat her very tenderly, and to console her as best he could. And he spake to her friendly words, and these helped her greatly. And when he was ridden forth over the fields after princely fashion, and went to any great city, where costly things are exposed for sale, then he bought her always something that pleased him or was rare—a pater-noster of coral (rosary),[2] or a picture, or a pretty little cross, or whatever he found which she was not likely to have seen before. And so he always brought her a present as token that he had been thinking of her. He never came empty, but always brought either a knife, or a bag, or gloves. And as the time came for him to return, she ran lovingly to meet him, and he took her on his arm, and he gave her what he had brought home for her."

On one occasion Ludwig had not returned, or sent her any little present. Elizabeth pined for his coming, but time passed, and there was no token that she was remembered. He was, in fact, busy, so deeply engaged at Reinhardtsborn that he could not go back to Eisenach. The malicious court ladies, and perhaps also Sophia and her daughters, began to hint to Elizabeth that Ludwig was tired of her, was going to send her back to Hungary, and look out for a wife who was not so devoted to works of piety and to the virtues of a cloister. The poor, solitary girl felt this keenly.

---

[1] "Diz geschach, alzo diz kint Elsebeth sibin jar alt war, do quam dy muthir deine kinde dez nachtis vor, unde sprach, Liebiz kint, ich ben gestorbin."—Rothe, p. 1701.
[2] Quite a novelty; as the rosary was first introduced by S. Dominic about 1210.

At last she could bear the suspense no more, and she confided her trouble to the trusty knight Walther von Vargila, who had brought her in her silver cradle from Hungary, and had received from her mother earnest exhortations to be a true champion to the little child. Walther at once rode off to Reinhardtsborn, and asked Ludwig humbly what his intentions were, for the poor little girl who loved him was unhappy among the harsh ladies of the Wartburg. Ludwig pointed to a great mountain, " Do you see that mountain ? Were it all of pure gold from base to crown, I would cast it away as waste drops before I would surrender my claim to Elizabeth. Let them say what they will, Elizabeth shall be mine."

" My Lord," said the trusty Walther, " what token shall I take back to the little maiden ? She has been looking out and longing for a present from you."

"Take this, which is for her," answered Ludwig, and he drew from his pouch an ivory looking-glass, on the back of which was carved a crucifix.[1]

In 1218, Ludwig was dubbed knight in S. George's Church at Eisenach, on S. Kilian's Day, by the bishop of Naumburg.[2] This was followed by a tournament and great festivities. Elizabeth looked on, and saw her young bridegroom conduct himself valiantly in the lists, bearing, no doubt, her colours, and doing battle for her honour. And now he was at home and she could pour out some of her troubles into his faithful heart. Jutta, a servant girl who was with her all her girlhood and till after she married, declared, on the death of S. Elizabeth, that "she endured heavy and open persecution from the relations, and vassals,

---

[1] Theodoricus, l. i. c. 7. " Proferensque de bursa sua dedit nobili illi quod penes se habebat speculum duplex, eneis inclusum sedibus, una parte simplex vitreum, et in parte altero ymaginem preferens crucifixi." But Vitar hyth. : " Sinen spiegell gab er Ime . . . . von helffenbein."

[2] " Do schyuete en der bischot von der Nuwinborg zeu ritter."—Rothe, p. 1703.

and councillors of her betrothed; they were always trying to induce him, by every means in their power, to repudiate her, and send her back to the king, her father. Flying from their contempt, she took refuge, as she was wont, in God alone, and in submitting herself wholly to His will and commending herself to His hands. But, in spite of all, and contrary to all anticipation, she had in her betrothed a secret consoler in all her sorrow and affliction."

As a little child, she had been driven to find playmates among the poor peasant girls; now, grown nearly to womanhood, finding only cold looks in the castle, she sought the grateful smiles on the faces of the sick whom she ministered to in their cottages.

In 1219, Archbishop Siegfrid of Mainz excommunicated Ludwig and his deceased father, about some trifling matter, apparently of boundaries. Ludwig was greatly incensed, assembled an army, and invaded the archbishopric, burned villages, defeated the troops of the prelate, and caused such devastations that the archbishop was obliged to come to terms with him and raise the ban from him and his father.

Next year, 1220, the Landgrave Ludwig celebrated his marriage with Elizabeth. He was then twenty years old, and she fifteen. The wedding was celebrated with great splendour, and lasted three days, with feasting, tournaments, dancing, and minstrelsy.

As soon as the festivities were over, she returned to her favourite occupation of looking after the poor. In plain clothes she visited the meanest cottages, sat by the sick on their pallets, and gave them the food and warm coverings she had herself brought them. Never weary in her holy work, never shrinking from the poorest beggar, never repelling the most ungrateful of those whom she assisted, she became an object of wonder and admiration to the suffering and needy of the whole neighbourhood. Shortly after the marriage,

S. ELIZABETH OF HUNGARY.

After the Painting by Hans Holbein (the elder). One of the wings of the Altar-piece of S. Sebastian in the Pinakothek, Munich.

Nov. 19.

Ludwig said to his wife, " Dear sister "—he had so called her since they were little children together—" your father is sending an embassy to congratulate us on our union, now I pray you lay aside that very plain dress, and appear before them in noble attire." " Dear brother," she answered, " I will do my best not to shame you." And she appeared in a silk suit embroidered with pearls, which she had not worn before, and in which her beauty shone refulgent. Her biographers suppose it was miraculously brought her from heaven, but there is no occasion for imagining anything of the sort; it was, no doubt, a rich dress given her at her wedding, perhaps by her husband.

Next year, she and Ludwig, attended by an escort of the noblest of the land, Count Henry of Schwarzburg, Henry of Stolberg, Meinhard of Mölburg, Rudolf of Vargila, and others, paid a visit to Andrew, King of Hungary. They were received with great honour, with feasts and tournaments; and when they returned, Andrew gave them "a newly-made coach filled with money and precious things."

When the whole party had returned from Hungary, Ludwig invited all to a banquet at Wartburg, after which they were to separate. Elizabeth, on her return, had gone at once to see her poor people, and when all were seated at the table she had not come in. She had been detained, listening to piteous stories, and now she was hastening up the rock on which the Wartburg stands, to be in time for the banquet. At the door of the hall she saw a poor naked wretch, haggard with hunger and cold, lying prostrate, and begging for something to cover him. He had heard that the good landgravin was returned, and had crawled up the steep path, and fallen at her gate. She had no money with her. She hastily promised to send him out food; but the poor man, showing his rags, entreated her rather to give him a wrap against the cold, for night was coming on.

Moved at his misery, she plucked off her silk mantle, cast it over him, and went into the hall and took her place at table. Ludwig looked at her, and said, "My sister dear, where is your mantle?" "Hanging up in my room," she answered, reddening. Then she bade one of her maids bring her one, and she ran and fetched her another mantle, and placed it over her shoulders, to the satisfaction of her husband.

The Landgrave Ludwig was guardian of Meissen for his nephew, Henry, a minor, the son of his half-sister Jutta by Albrecht, Margrave of Meissen. Directly that the margrave died, Ludwig entered Meissen, and arranged everything necessary for the government of the principality. Four years after, Jutta, much against her brother's will, married Poppo, Count of Henneberg, and this led to strife and mutual invasion of territories with sword and flame.

In 1223, Elizabeth gave birth to a son, and named him Hermann.

About the same time[1] Agnes, the sister of the Landgrave Ludwig, was married to the Duke of Austria, at Nürnberg. In 1224 Elizabeth bore her husband a daughter, at Wartburg, and it was baptized Sophia. The child was afterwards married to the Duke of Brabant. Next year she had another daughter, which was also named Sophia, after her grandmother. She became eventually a religious, and died at Kitzingen. It is touching to see in the naming of the two little girls after their grandmother, the efforts made by Elizabeth to soften the harsh woman whose animosity had embittered her life, and who still resided in the Wartburg to be a thorn in her side, and to attempt to make mischief between her and her husband. One day Elizabeth had a very sick leper carried into the castle and laid on her husband's bed; he was from home, and she could thus be at

[1] John Rothe says 1223, but Bäring, 1227.

S. ELIZABETH—THE MIRACLE.

hand to nurse the dying man, who was in such a condition from disease that no one else could be got to nurse him. Unexpectedly Ludwig returned from Naumburg. His mother rushed to meet him, and angrily bade him follow her and see what Elizabeth had done—she had actually brought infection to the room of her husband. Ludwig accompanied his indignant mother to the chamber, she drew back the curtains, threw off the clothes, and said, "See what Elizabeth has dared to do." "I see only Jesus Christ ministered to in the person of His sick member," answered the landgrave.[1]

In 1225 Ludwig went to meet the Emperor Frederick II. in Apulia, to which he came from Sicily, but returned almost directly to Germany. This was a year of great distress. Heavy gales beat down the corn, and shook the grain out of the ears; then followed rain, and the wheat rotted on the sodden fields. Many died of starvation. Elizabeth opened her granaries on the Wartburg, and gave corn to the poor, and sent it to those too weak to climb the steep rock. She built a hospital at the foot of the castle rock, in which she nursed twenty-eight sick folk. The steward and others complained that she was wasting the stores. They told her husband, on his return, of what she had done. He bade them in no way hinder her. The people were feeding on roots, hay, berries; they had devoured their horses and asses; it was necessary to empty the granaries to save life. One day, says the legend, as he was walking up the steep path to the castle, he met Elizabeth with her lap full of loaves. "What have you there?" he asked, and, drawing her mantle away, he saw that her lap was full of roses. Looking up, he beheld a cross shining in the air over her head.[2]

---

[1] The story has, of course, been improved into their really finding Christ on His Cross in the bed. But it is easy to see how such an answer of the landgrave may have furnished material for the fabulist.

[2] An old myth of Freya, the Goddess of Nature, whose lap is now filled with corn,

Her attendant, Irmentrude von Hörselgau, says, "Under the castle of Wartburg there was a great house in which she placed many infirm persons, who could not get to the distribution of general alms, and in disregard of the laborious ascent and descent, she visited them daily, consoling them and talking to them of patience and the health of the soul, and she satisfied each according to his fancy with drink or food. Even did she sell her ornaments in order to support them; and although she was scrupulous about fresh and pure air everywhere else, yet she did not revolt from the offensive odours which hung about the diseased in the heat of summer, and which her servants could not endure, and grumbled at. She had, moreover, in the same house many poor little children, whom she took good care of, and treated them with such gentleness and sweetness that they were wont to call her Mother, and when she entered the house they crowded round her; and among these she showed special love to the scrofulous, infirm, weak, and deformed, taking their little heads in her hands and rocking them on her bosom. And she brought little boys as an amusement little crocks, pewter rings, and other trifling treasures for children, and as she rode from the town to the castle, she had all these toys in her mantle. One day by accident they fell down from the rock on a stone, and although they fell on a stone, yet none were broken, and she was able to distribute them uninjured among the boys."[1]

When she heard of poor women being confined, she hastened to visit them, and lend or give them things they might be in need of. She was careful not to give in profu

---

and then with chips of wood, and then with flowers, according to the season—the wood for fuel in winter. This myth, lingering on in the memory of the people, has attached itself to numerous saints. S. Nothburga had loaves and chips; S. Elizabeth of Hungary, S. Elizabeth of Portugal, S. Germaine Cousin, loaves and roses. Same story of S. Zita, S. Casilda, S. Verena, S. Roselina, S. Rose of Viterbo, S. Martha of Troyes, S. Diego of Alcala, S. Louis of Toulouse, &c.

[1] De Dictis iv. Ancillarum, pp. 2017-8.

sion in money, so as to make the people beggars, but with wise discretion, giving scythes or reaping-hooks to poor men in order that they might work for their living. She delighted in being godmother to the poor children, so as to be able to claim spiritual relationship with them.

One day when the great fair was being held at Eisenach, Ludwig went to the market-place for amusement, and saw there a poor pedlar with a box, selling thimbles, needles, drums, flutes, black-lead, brooches, and spoons. The landgrave asked him whether he earned much from his pack. The pedlar answered, "Gracious sir, I am ashamed to beg, and I am not strong enough to do field-work. If I might go in peace from one of your towns to another I should earn, with God's help, enough from this pack to do comfortably." The prince was moved with compassion, and said to the pedlar, "Very well, you shall have my permission, and you may trade in all my territory freely." Then he said to his chamberlain, "Give him ten shillings and my letters of free conduct." And turning to the pedlar, he said, "I will go shares with you in your pack. Swear to be true in your reckoning with me. Lay out the money in wares; I will hold you safe from molestation, and at the end of the year you return to me, and we will share profits." The chapman was delighted, he promised to be faithful to his sleeping-partner, and went on his way. At the end of the year the pedlar came with his account to the Wartburg, and the profits were so considerable, that the landgrave was able to clothe all his court with his share. Every year the profits increased. The chapman could no longer carry his pack, he was obliged to buy an ass, and he laid his wares in two panniers. He became more venturesome, and went to Venice, bought "gold rings and brooches, head-gear, ribands, precious stones, goblets, ivory looking-glasses, tablets, table-knives, adders' tongues, coral rosaries (pater-nosters) and the like." On his way back he passed through the territories of the Prince Bishop of Würzburg. Some Franconians, coveting his goods, which they wanted to give to their wives and sweethearts, and could not afford to buy, waylaid him as he left Würzburg, and robbed him of his packs and ass. He arrived at Eisenach very doleful, and told his lord and comrade[1] all his misadventure. The landgrave said to him, "My dear comrade, don't trouble yourself about our pack, and look nowhere for it."[2] Then he gathered together his knights and retainers, and suddenly fell on the estates of the bishop of Würzburg, burning villages, and desolating the land. The bishop asked what was the reason of the onslaught. Ludwig replied that the pack and ass of his comrade were stolen; and he should burn and destroy till the ass was restored, with the two panniers, and everything in them, just as the pedlar had packed them. The ass and all the property of the company were speedily produced and returned. So Ludwig went back with them to Eisenach in triumph.

One festival, Ludwig was looking from a window in Eisenach at the peasants dancing in the market-place. A slim young woman, the wife of a humble tradesman in the town danced so gracefully and looked so beautiful, that the prince said, "It is a pleasure to see her dance." "If you like," said an attendant, "I will carry her off to your castle for you." Ludwig turned sharply upon him, flaming with indignation and shame. "Man," said he, "as you value my favour, not another word of this sort. Leave the poor innocent thing alone. Woe to the ruler who, instead of being the refuge of his people from those who do them wrong, is the wrongdoer himself." As Ludwig went through his courtyard one night, a lion which had been kept caged

---

[1] "Quam kegin Ysenach zcu syme herrin vnde gesellin trurig."—Rothe.
[2] "Myn libir geselle, betruwe dich nicht vmme vnsirn kram, vnde zeuch ouch nergin."—*Ibid.*

met him. The beast had broken forth. Ludwig raised his fist, threatened him, and the lion crouched at his feet. The attendants who ran up at his call had much difficulty in chaining the lion again.

About five years after her marriage, Elizabeth fell under the influence of a man who was to darken the rest of her life, and whose baleful power over her timid, yielding spirit blighted all its best and noblest aspirations. This was Conrad of Marburg, an inquisitor, apparently a Franciscan, who was commissioned by the Pope to hunt out and destroy such heretics as the pleasant Thuringian land was found to harbour.

It is necessary to give an outline of this man's life, that the character of the director may be thoroughly appreciated, who, when once he got Elizabeth in his iron grasp, never released his hold till he had crushed the trembling, pure life out of the fragile body. Conrad of Marburg[1] was, there can be no question, of low birth. In 1212, eighty heretics were burnt alive at Strassburg, and Trithemius mentions Conrad as "inquisitor apostolicus" who gave them over to the flames. But earlier accounts of this persecution do not mention him, and Trithemius probably mistook. Certainly, however, Conrad was at that time, and later, inquisitor in Lower Germany. Conrad, a native of Marburg, one of the castles and estates of the landgrave, pushed himself into notice with Ludwig, and his asceticism and zeal attracted the reverence of the simple prince, who had not the faculty to see, behind this mask of religion, the baseness, envy, and cruelty which made a hell of this infamous man's heart. Berthold, the chaplain of Ludwig, says that his master held Conrad in such honour that he allowed the friar to present to all the livings to which he had nomination. Berthold says, "He preached throughout the whole of Germany with

[1] See Dr. C. L. Th. Henke, "Konrad von Marburg," Marb. 1861.

apostolic commission, and an innumerable crowd of clerks and people followed him; for they all held him to be a saintly and upright man, some following him with love, others trembling. He assured the Landgrave Ludwig that it was a less sin to kill sixty men than to appoint improperly to a living." Ludwig in a weak moment gave consent to Elizabeth's vowing perpetual obedience to this man as her director, little dreaming that by so doing he was condemning her soul to the rack, and her body to death. In 1227, Pope Gregory IX. was in communication with Conrad, praising his zeal in the extermination of heretics, and, in a glow of enthusiasm over the energy with which they had been tortured and butchered, designating Conrad as his "dilectus filius." He gave him a commission to proceed against German priests guilty of immorality, and afterwards constituted him Visitor of German monasteries and convents. A letter of the Pope in 1231 praises the success Conrad had achieved in rooting out heresy in Germany, and extending to him further and fuller liberty to act against all unhappy wretches suspected of holding independent views. He was urged to devote himself solely to persecution, not to pause and rest on his laurels after the most wholesale massacre, but to nerve his arm for fresh destruction. All those who harboured heretics, who gave a cup of cold water to a suspected person, were involved in a common condemnation, and threatened with similar extermination. Whosoever gave him a hint where to catch a heretic, or a harbourer of such, was to be rewarded with indulgence for three years, with remission of all sins, and freedom from obligation during those three years to do penance for them, however heinous they might be. Twenty days' indulgence was granted by the Pope to all who should listen to one sermon of Conrad's against the heretics. In 1233 the Pope further commissioned him to extend absolution to murderers and incendiaries on condition that they armed themselves to destroy heretics in their neighbourhood or their own families. Conrad wrote exultingly to Gregory IX. of havoc wrought amongst the heretics at Leiden and Stedinger. In 1232, "innumerable heretics," says the Erfurt chronicler, "were burned by him." On the 5th May, 1232, he sat and gloated over the agonies of four poor wretches writhing in flames at Erfurt. At this time, says the Gerstenberg Chronicle, "many knights, priests, and other honourable persons were seized, some recanted, others were burned behind the castle of Marburg, amongst them a poor woman; wherefore the place is still called the Heretics-beck." Such were the tender mercies shown to his native place. It was precisely at the time when Frederick II. was in hostility with the Pope, and his son Henry had been instigated by Gregory IX. to take up arms against his father, that the inquisition in Germany became an alarming power, and Conrad was able to give full rein to his natural ferocity and vindictiveness. For whoever sided with the emperor against his rebel son became involved in excommunication, suspected of heresy, and marked for ruin. In his excommunication of Frederick, launched from Perugia, the Pope had denounced as equal in infamy, the Cathari, the Paulicians, the poor men of Lyons, and the emperor. Conrad, "supported by the esteem of the Pope," says the Trèves Chronicle, "became so bold, that he treated king and bishop as common folk." He associated with himself two others, worse than himself, Conrad Tors and Hans the One-eyed and One-handed. Both these men had been formerly heretics, but had changed from the persecuted to the persecuting form of faith. The first was now a Dominican. In 1231 he had assumed on his own authority to be judge and executioner, and at the head of a rabble had committed many poor creatures to the flames on the smallest suspicion. "Better," said he, "that a hundred innocent persons be burned than that one guilty one should escape." Even knights and nobles had been araigned before Conrad Tors, who made this agreement with the bishops and judges, "We will burn the rich people, and you shall divide their lands, the bishops one half, the temporal authorities the other half."[1] Conrad of Marburg took these two wretches under his protection, and associated with himself also a fanatical girl of twenty, named Alaidis, "femina vaga," who had quarrelled with her family, and whose relations with Conrad perhaps ought not to be inquired into too closely. Another of his allies in his bloody work was a jail-bird named Amfried; and there were others of the same stamp, forming the inquisitorial army marching under the protection of Papal authority.

The fear of this host fell on all the country. They arrested whoever they chose, and many innocent persons, to save their lives, confessed themselves to have been heretics, but to be open to conviction, and ready to do penance. Conrad shaved their heads, and ordered them to be kept under surveillance. Whoever denied the imputation was burned at once, on the same day, without appeal. The Archbishop of Mainz wrote to Pope Gregory a letter of remonstrance. The terror inspired by these ruffians caused false evidence to be given, and innocent persons to be denounced. The trembling victims were asked, he said, to name their fellow heretics, and when they were unable to do so, a list of names was read, and the victims cried out which were guilty.[2] Thus the Counts of Sayn, Arnsberg, and Solms, and the Countess Lotz were accused. Thus, said the archbishop, the wife, in her terror, denounced her husband, the servant his master, the master his servant. Those with shaved

---

[1] Annales Wormatienses.
[2] "Nescio quem accusem, dicite mihi nomina, de quibus suspicionem habetis," &c. Letter of Archb. Siegfried to the Pope in Alberici Chronicon.

heads were bribed by the intimidated people to tell them the secret of escape. Other Dominicans and Franciscans threw their energies into the grand crusade and butchery, and the whole of North Germany trembled. But it had become unendurable. King Henry held a Diet at Mainz on July 25, 1233, and Count Henry von Sayn appealed to the assembled princes and bishops against the Papal Inquisitor. Conrad of Marburg had summoned him for trial, and had threatened to storm and plunder his wealthiest castles with an army of women.[1] The count claimed to be a good Catholic, and all the bishops present attested that he was so. Conrad was present and defied them. He bore the papal authority to try heretics, and the count was denounced to him. The archbishops of Mainz, Cologne, and Trèves in vain endeavoured to dissuade the papal inquisitor from proceeding against a man of unblemished orthodoxy. Conrad at once began to preach in Mainz his crusade, and to declaim against the Diet, the Archbishop Siegfried, and King Henry, to collect a horde of fanatics about him, absolve murderers and incendiaries who joined him, and arm them for a massacre. The mob threatened the count of Sayn. He appealed to the Diet for protection; the archbishop was obliged to appear before the mob and assure them that the count was a good Catholic.

Conrad left Mainz to return to Marburg. On his way, on July 30, 1233, he and his companion the Franciscan Gerhard were waylaid and killed by some nobles who had been insulted and shaved by him, or had relatives similarly disgraced. According to Trithemius the murderers were the Lords of Dernbach. He fell on his knees, and in abject terror begged for mercy. They sternly answered that he

---

"Quem affirmabant equitasse in cancro, dicentes nisi confiteretur, quod castra sua, quæ erant peroptima, ipsi cum veteribus muliebris vellent auferre et inquirere."
- Annal. Worm.

should meet with the mercy that he had shown to others, and was cut down. His brothers in arms met a similar fate. Tors was killed in Elsass by the knight of Mülnheim, whom he had accused of heresy, and dragged before his tribunal. Hans with the One Eye was hung at Friedberg.

When Gregory IX. heard of the murder of Conrad, and of the scandals and atrocities committed by his inquisitor, he said, "The Germans have ever been mad, and therefore it befitted them to have mad judges." But later he changed his mind, and wrote in October, 1233, to the bishops of Germany, and to the archbishop of Mainz, and the bishop of Hildesheim, describing Conrad of Marburg as a second Thomas à Becket, deserving canonization, and requiring the murderers to be put under the ban, and an interdict laid on the places that harboured them; and urging that the persecution of heretics should not be relaxed by the untimely death of Conrad. No punishment was, however, accorded to the murderers. King Henry refused to proceed against them in the Diet held at Frankfort in 1234, and one bishop even urged that the body of Conrad should be exhumed and burnt as that of a heretic and criminal.

Conrad of Marburg has found a certain amount of veneration, and is even designated as "the Blessed," but he has not, as yet, been formally canonized.

It has been necessary to sketch the history of this man, that the reader may have a correct idea of the character of the director whose influence was to weigh on, and indeed crush the life of Elizabeth. He had been allowed, as has been said, to become the director of Elizabeth, and even to impose on her a vow of implicit obedience to his will.

During the long absences of Ludwig from home Conrad gradually extended his authority, till he domineered over the meek landgravine with unbounded insolence. One instance alone need be given to show the pride and violence of the man. Conrad had to preach at Eisenach one day, and he expected Elizabeth and all her ladies in waiting to be present. But the margravine of Meissen, her husband's half-sister, was coming that day. There had been so much ill-feeling between Jutta and Ludwig that Elizabeth thought it doubly necessary for her to be ready to receive the margravine in person on her arrival. Conrad, marking the absence of Elizabeth and her ladies, sent a message to her that he renounced his charge of her conscience. She hastened next day to him, threw herself at his feet with all her ladies, and implored his pardon. This he only granted on condition that they should strip to their shirts, and be lashed with his knotted scourge. They shudderingly submitted, as, gloating his eyes on their bare shoulders, he beat them without more mercy than he had displayed to heretics dancing in the flames of their pyre.

Pope Honorius III. had urged Christendom to make another effort to recover Jerusalem. Frederick II. was to lead the crusade. It was preached throughout Germany; the most liberal promises were made to those who joined. Honorius died in 1227, and Gregory IX. succeeded him as the crusaders assembled. Ludwig, the landgrave of Thuringia, was persuaded by the bishop of Hildesheim, and a large sum of money offered him by the emperor, to take the cross. He did not, however, tell his wife for some time, and kept concealed the cross marked on his habit; but when the time approached when he must be making his preparations to depart he broke the news to her, saying that he went for the sake of Christ, and to recover His tomb from the hands of infidels, and that it would be unseemly were he to remain behind, when the emperor and so many princes were going to the East. She bowed to the inevitable, but with a presentiment of evil. He arranged all that was necessary for the well government of his land during his absence,

and then departed with his troops to Smalkald, accompanied
by his brothers Hermann and Conrad, his mother Sophia,
his beloved wife and little children. As he left Elizabeth,
he showed her his ring. "Dear sister," said he, "look at
this signet ring, with the Lamb of God engraved on the
stone. Should this be brought you, it will be a token of
my death. Then God bless you and the fruit of your womb.
Then forget me not, sweet sister, in your prayers to God."
So he parted from her and his children, his mother and all
whom he loved, on S. John the Baptist's day, 1227. Frederick II. was at Melfi, in Apulia, awaiting the arrival of the
soldiers of the cross. The long expected crusade was to
start in August. To a great extent it was a failure. Few
came from England, fewer still from France; the main
strength of the enterprise lay in the Germans, who came over
the Alps under the landgrave of Thuringia and the bishop
of Augsburg. The German host arrived in Apulia, and their
emperor, leaving his wife Yolande at Otranto, joined them
at Brindisi. He rode thither in the heat, against the wishes
of his physicians, who feared the worst from his imprudence,
since his health was giving way. As it was, the constitutions
of the northern men could not bear the heat of an Italian
summer; they were more than a week engaged in freighting
their ships with provisions and water; the power of the sun
was so great that they thought it must melt even solid metal;
Brindisi was an ill-chosen trysting-place, being most unhealthy. The badness of the air, and the rain that fell, killed
off many of the crusaders. The bishops of Angers and Augsburg died; and the landgrave fell ill at Otranto. The surviving warriors set sail, Frederick and Ludwig among them.
But, after remaining at sea for three days, the emperor fell
ill, and, unable to endure the roughness of the waves and
the unhealthy season, put back. The nobles of the East,
who surrounded him, advised him to delay his voyage, as his

health was shaken. He put about, and returned to Otranto. They had set sail from Brindisi on the feast of the Nativity of Our Lady (September 8); Frederick was with the landgrave for a while in his ship, till they reached the islet of S. Andrew, when they parted. The sickness of Ludwig came on him at Otranto, and when the expedition put to sea he lay in his bed with death before his eyes. The patriarch of Jerusalem ministered to him the last sacraments, and when the unlucky expedition put back to Otranto with the sick emperor, it brought with it also the body of the landgrave. Before he died he removed his ring, and gave it to a trusty knight to bear to Thuringia and give to his mother, without mentioning to anyone else what had befallen him, so that the news might not reach Elizabeth suddenly, but that his mother might be able gently to break it to her. His last thoughts were on her.

The crusade seemed a total failure. The fighting-men who reached the Holy Land, when they heard that the emperor was incapacitated by ill-health from heading them, returned to Europe. Gregory IX. was furious. The emperor sent a deputation to explain to him the reasons of the failure. Gregory would not listen, but gathering about him as many bishops as he could collect, he excommunicated the recreant crusader, and despatched his violent sentence to all Christian kingdoms.

The harbinger of bad news arrived in Thuringia, and the dowager landgravine Sophia went to Wartburg, to the Lazar-house, and sent to the castle for Elizabeth, and when she came made her sit at her side. Then said Sophia to her, "Dear daughter, you must pluck up good courage, and not be too grieved at the misfortune that has befallen your lord, my son, for all has fallen out according to the ordinance of God." Elizabeth did not understand that he was dead, but supposed he had been taken prisoner, and she answered, "Is my brother then a captive? Surely, with God's help and the assistance of his friends, he can be recovered." Then said her mother-in-law to her, "Be patient, my dearest daughter; take this little ring which he has sent you, for he is indeed dead."

When she heard this, Elizabeth turned white, then red, and then springing up, ran to the top of the house, as if out of her mind, gasping, "Dead, dead, dead!" It was all she could say. The ladies hasted after her, held her, and forced her to sit down, and tried to console her. After a while she began to cry, her hands sank on her lap, and she sobbed, "Lord God! Lord God! he is dead, and all the world is dead to me," and then she moaned, "I am a poor, desolate widow. He alone can comfort me, Who forsaketh not the fatherless and the widow."[1]

No sooner had the landgrave Henry heard of the death of his brother than he determined to seize the government of the principality for himself. Ludwig's son, Hermann, was a child of only four years old. Henry's counsellors advised him to take means that the child should not come to maturity, and to secure Thuringia for himself and his children. Henry drove Elizabeth from the Wartburg without compunction, without allowing her even money to maintain her position. She went sorrowfully forth with her three little children, followed by some of her faithful attendants.

It was a sad procession that descended the rocky path from the castle to the town of Eisenach. Elizabeth carried her baby in her arms; one of the maids led the two other children by the hands. Other servants carried bedding or

---

[1] "Dae sprach ire Swiger, Er ist todt. Dae wurde sy bleich vnd darnach rodt. Dy arm fylen ir in den Schos. Dy hende sy in einander schlos. Ach herre Got, herre Got, sy sprach. Nu ist mir alle dy welt toedt."—Chron. Rhym. "Do sy daz gehorte, do stunt sy uff, vnde ging snellis gehins obir daz muer huez hene vnde ted also ab sy nicht mer redelichkeyd hette, vnde sprach, Gestorbin, Gestorbin, Gestorbin! Do gingin er dy Frowin nach, vnde satztin sy nidir, vnde trosten sy."—Rothe, p. 1718.

S. ELIZABETH DRIVEN FROM THE WARTBURG. Nov. 19.

clothes in their arms, or the little trifles they valued, and which they had been allowed to take with them. The dowager landgravine Sophia stood weeping at the castle gate. Henry and Conrad had given peremptory orders that Elizabeth and all her servants and ladies in waiting were to be sent forth, and to take with them nothing that they could not carry, and that no one in Eisenach or in the whole land of Thuringia should give them shelter or food if they did not at once leave the country. Henry feared lest Elizabeth, by staying in Thuringia, should rally around her a strong party and oppose him in his design of securing the principality for himself. Rudolf of Vargila, son of her old friend Walther of Vargila, was away, banner-bearer to Frederick II. in his crusade. Hermann, Truchsess of Schaltheim, Henry, Marshal of Ebersburg, Meinhardt of Mölburg, and all the chief nobles and allies of her husband were in Apulia or in the East. Now was the time for the landgrave Henry to rid the country of her and her son, before the return of the crusaders. Elizabeth went into the town and sought shelter from some of the citizens. They dared not receive her. At last she found shelter in an outhouse of an inn, where the taverner kept his crockery, and which adjoined the pigstye.[1] There she spent the night, but her rest was broken by the skittle-playing and the noise of the drinking men, who cursed and swore, and dashed the skittle-balls against the walls of the outhouse. After midnight, when all grew stiller, and the bells of the Minorite church began to tinkle, she went forth to the dimly-lighted church, and heard the friars sing Te Deum in their matins. The song of praise she thought she could join in, in spite of all her troubles. Next day she sought hospitality at the doors of the burghers of Eisenach, but met with refusal everywhere. They dared not receive her lest

---

[1] "Intravit pauperem domum in curia cujusdam cauponis, et in qua erant vasa et supellex ipsius cauponis, et in qua fuerant porci illius."—De Dictis iv. Ancill.

they should incur the vengeance of the landgrave Henry. She was obliged to pawn some of her jewels to provide food for herself and her children; and then, finding herself rejected everywhere, she went to the church, and seated herself there with her children. It was bitterly cold, and the night was creeping on. She knew not where to lay the heads of her little ones that night. The parish priest in pity opened his house to her, and gave shelter for some days to the outcasts. Her jewels were pawned one by one to nourish the little family. At last orders came from the landgrave that she was to be lodged with a burgher and his wife, who had always been ill-disposed towards her, sneered at her piety and charities, and had been known for their ill-temper. It was a very small house, and they were cramped for room in it. This did not tend to make the host and hostess more amiable. They insulted her, abused her, and at last, unable to endure their coarseness and violence, she went out and took refuge again in the outhouse of the inn, saying, sadly, "I would gladly fly from men, if I only knew whither to go."

Sophia, who was at the Wartburg, sent her down some things, such as she thought she might need, but secretly, because Henry was a violent man, and was determined that his commands should be obeyed. It was she, probably,[1] who sent a messenger to the abbess of Kitzingen, to advise her of the condition of Elizabeth, and to entreat her to receive the homeless landgravine.

During Lent she was one day long praying in the church, leaning against the wall, with her eyes fixed on the altar, but without seeming to see anything. She rose at last and returned to the wretched dwelling behind the tavern; there she began to stagger and her colour to go. The attendants made her eat something, as she was very weak, but she would not

[1] "Ich gleube das dysc betschafft thete, ire Schwieger Sophia dy sy nicht schmehete. Sondern mit ir in den gezeitin, hette gros mitleidenn."—Chron. Rhym.

take much, and Ysentrude von Hörselgau, seeing how exhausted she was, made her rest her head on her lap. Elizabeth lay long thus, her eyes looking out of the window at the wintry sky, and Ysentrude noticed that an occasional smile, and then a sad shadow fleeted over the patient face. Presently Elizabeth, in a kind of dream, said, "And Thou, Lord, desirest to have me with Thee, and I long to be with Thee, and never to be separated from Thee." When she came to herself Ysentrude asked her what she meant by the exclamation, and Elizabeth said that she was in a kind of waking dream, and thought she saw Christ in the pale blue wintry heaven bending towards her, and comforting her for all her sorrows. He turned as to depart, and then sorrow filled her heart, but He looked again at her, and said, " If thou desirest to be with Me, so do I will to be with thee." And this it was, probably, which drew the exclamation from her lips.

Her nerves had been overwrought.

The tavern was a place of great discomfort, on account of the drinking and shouting during the night, and the noise of the skittles, which were played close to the pigstye and the outhouse.

When all her jewels were gone, and she had nothing more to pawn, she spun for her livelihood.[1]

One day during the winter Elizabeth was going along on the stepping-stones at the head of the Messerschmieds Gasse, which was then unpaved and in mud. An old woman met her, a beggar whom she had often relieved, and wished to pass. As Elizabeth could not step aside without sinking into the slush above her ankles, the woman struck at her, thrust her off the stepping stone, and upset her in the mud, so that Elizabeth was obliged to return to where she lodged and wash her clothes.

---

[1] "Do vorsatzte dy heilige frowe ere phande, daz sy sich generete, vnde span vnde erbeite waz sy kunde."—Rothe, p. 1729.

But the abbess of Kitzingen sent two waggons to fetch the landgravine, her children, and faithful attendants, and they were conducted out of Thuringia into Franconia. Kitzingen is pleasantly situated on the Main, with the range of the Steigerwald rising blue on the horizon above the fertile plain. It is a picturesque old town, with its ancient walls and gates, its four churches and rathhaus.

The storks returned, and began their hatching on the chimneys of the town, the lily of the valley bloomed and scented the air in the woods beyond the Main. Spring had returned, after a winter of sorrows, to bring some comfort and peace to the sorely tried heart of the patient Elizabeth.

The bishop of Bamberg now sent for the landgravine.[1] He offered her his castle of Pottenstein, and to maintain her as befitted her rank, till some arrangement could be arrived at for the future. The offer was too kind and considerate to be refused. She left one of her little daughters, Sophia, with the abbess of Kitzingen, to be there brought up for the monastic life, and departed with her little son and her other daughter for Pottenstein. He could scarcely have chosen for her a more suitable retreat. In a quiet valley of the clear Wiesent, where the narrow glen between fantastic limestone spires and crags opens into a green basin, lies the little town of black timbered and white plaster houses, crowned by the castle from which the town takes its name, perched on groups of dolomitic limestone, roofed with red tile. Now the poor ruins are converted into cottages reached by the arched roadway that leaps from one rock to another. The little church lies below the castle. The writer was in it one spring day when the newly gilded saints were being set up in preparation for Whitsunday in the renovated rococo reredos. Among them S. Elizabeth was not forgotten, the

---

[1] He was Egbert of Meran, her uncle, brother of her mother, Gertrude of Meran, and S. Hedwig.

gentle saint who had prayed daily in that church and received the bread of life from that altar.

The bishop was anxious to get her married again to some powerful noble or prince, who could maintain the claim of her little boy against his uncles. He represented to her how helpless she was, and what a great advantage it would be to her to secure a protector for herself and her children. But Elizabeth shrank from the thoughts of a second marriage. "I promised," she said, "that I would never belong to any-one but Ludwig. I made the promise to God and to my lord when he was alive, and I cannot fail my word."

That year the body of Ludwig was brought back to Germany. His bones were in a costly shrine adorned with gems.[1] When the retinue stayed a night on their way back, they laid the body in the church, a vigil was held, and early next morning a mass was sung, and to each church where the shrine rested they gave a piece of silk. And so, in time, they came to Bamberg. When the bishop heard of the approach of the mournful train, he sent in all haste to Pottenstein for S. Elizabeth, that she might be in the cathedral city to meet the body of her lord and husband. When the shrine arrived, the bishop, with all his knights, men-at-arms, clergy, and choir went forth to meet it, and accompanied the remains of the landgrave to the minster, with burning tapers, mournful chanting, and muffled tolling of bells. Elizabeth followed the coffin weeping, with her children. She prayed to God, "Lord, I give Thee thanks that Thou hast consoled me by bringing back to me the dear bones of my husband. Thou knowest how greatly I have loved him, and yet I do not repine at his being taken from me. O Lord, I would give the whole world to have him back, that we two might trudge together begging our bread;—and yet, if contrary to Thy will, I would not buy him back with one hair. And

---

[1] He was boiled to get the flesh off his bones before he was enshrined.

now I commend him and myself to Thy grace; and Thy will be done."[1] The knights and nobles who returned from the ill-starred crusade with the body of their prince surrounded her, and heard with indignation her sorrowful story. She begged them to stand as a wall round Ludwig's son, and protect his rights. Next day the mournful cortége went on its way towards Reinhardsborn, where it was to be laid.

Nearly all the nobles of Thuringia and crowds of knights and country people flocked to Reinhardsborn to do honour to their late prince. The dowager landgravine attended, the landgraves Henry and Conrad dared not remain away. The bishop of Bamberg, the bishop of Naumburg, and many abbots were present. Elizabeth came in the train of her uncle.

After mass had been sung, and the bones placed in their last resting-place, the knights and nobles of Thuringia and Saxony held a consultation together, while the two landgraves Henry and Conrad sat with their mother and some of their followers in the hall of the abbey. Great indignation was expressed at the way in which Elizabeth had been treated. Rudolf of Vargila acted as their spokesman. He was the son of Walther, who had brought Elizabeth in her silver cradle from Hungary to Thuringia. He was a gallant knight like his father, and inherited his office of butler (*Schenk*), an honourable title in Germany. He had been wounded in his arm by an arrow in the battle of Tennstedt in 1213, fighting against Otto IV., and had never after recovered the use of his arm. He entered the hall before the brothers and addressed them:—" It is not well, my lords, that you have been advised to commit an act of injustice. Who will build on your favour, when you thus treat the blood of your brother, who was so full of goodness to you? I am ashamed to speak before so many, and greater men than I, but I have been

[1] De Dictis iv. Ancill.

asked to express the common feeling. Your brother ventured his life for God and to win His grace, and you cast away his desolate orphans and his weeping widow. It is the duty of a knight to defend the unprotected and weak with all his chivalry and power, and you with violence have thrust these little ones and this lady into poverty and insult. And they are those who have never wronged you, but who claim of you protection and succour as their nearest of kin and natural protectors. Your conduct is against God and right, against law, and against your own honour and integrity. All these lords say this to you through my mouth. Nay, sirs; the Great God in Heaven casts this reproach in your teeth."[1]

When the dowager landgravine Sophia heard this she burst into loud weeping, rose up, and wrung her hands. Her ladies drew her back to her seat. Elizabeth also began to cry, and the women present sobbed. "For God's sake," said the knight of Vargila, "cease your weeping, and do you princes listen to me a little longer. Do right now to this tearful widow and to the orphan infants of your brother. Turn from the evil counsel that has been offered you, and make amends for the wrong done."

Then spoke the bishop of Bamberg and the other nobles. Henry and Conrad, red with wrath and shame, were obliged to ask pardon of Elizabeth, and promise to treat her better for the future. They agreed to take her back to Wartburg, and give her a proper retinue, and yield the town of Marburg, and whatsoever was agreed in the marriage settlement should be her dower.

She remained for a while in Wartburg, but it was not likely that the proud brothers, writhing under their castigation, could endure her presence long, or that her mode of life would agree at all with their manner of living. It was settled that

---
[1] I have followed the speech in the Rhyming Chronicle.

she should retire to Marburg, where she should occupy the castle, and exercise sovereign rights over the town and neighbourhood. A sum of money was also given her, and this she wanted at once to distribute among the poor. But Conrad, her director, forbade this, very sensibly. He bade her keep the money and distribute it as needed, and use what was necessary on her own household. But when she settled at Marburg he constituted himself her treasurer, received and kept all the money that was paid to her, and allowed her only a certain sum for her charities and general expenses. If she ventured to give alms without his being told of it he slapped her face or beat her with a stick.[1]

On Good Friday, when the altars were stripped, Elizabeth went with Conrad and some witnesses into a chapel of the church of the Franciscans, and having laid her hands on the bare altar she made solemn renunciation of her parents, her children, her kindred, of the pomps and vanities of the world, of her own free will, of all her worldly goods and earthly possessions, and placed herself wholly under the guidance of Conrad. He used his authority over her occasionally with discretion. When she wished to go and beg from door to door for her sick and poor, he forbade it. He sometimes forbade her nursing the most revolting cases of disease, lest she should take infection; but for all that, his rule was mischievous. She had in her every element of nobleness, a great, pure, and loving nature. All he sought was to crush her into feeble, helpless, imbecility.

The unfortunate princess had fallen under the despotic sway of a man of no birth, who had raised himself by his talents, and now exulted in humiliating, brow-beating, and trampling on a lady of royal birth, whose sorrows and isola-

[1] "Renuntiaverat omnibus in manus suas; nec volebat sustinere quod illa ori proprio subtraheret, tantum quod deficeret ut aliis erogaret. Unde sæpe ex tali accusatione multa verbera sustinuit a Mag. Conrado et alapas."—De Dictis iv. Ancill. p. 2023.

tion had broken her spirit, and who was without protectors to defend her from his insolence. She was afraid of the man, yet she dared not break from his thraldom. "O God!" she cried to her maids, "if I fear a mortal man so greatly, how terrible must the Lord and Judge of all the earth be!" He used her religious fears as a means of installing himself in absolute command over her purse and actions. Once he ordered her to go to Altenburg, to a convent, that he might consider whether to shut her up with some recluses. The nuns, hearing of her arrival, asked Conrad if she might be allowed to go inside their walls, that they might see her. "Let her enter if she will," he answered. Taking this as his consent, Elizabeth visited the nuns. Conrad at once produced the book of rules he had drawn up and made her swear to, by which she was forbidden to do anything without his express command, under pain of excommunication. And though Irmingarde, her attendant, had not entered the hermitage, but had stood without, Conrad bade both her and her mistress kneel down, and a Brother Gerard to beat them with a thick cudgel, whilst he looked on in grim satisfaction, mumbling "Miserere mei Deus." The tender shoulders and back of Elizabeth bore the bruises for over three weeks.[1]

The two children of Elizabeth were taken from her; her son Hermann, aged six, was sent to the castle of Kreutzburg, on the Werra, dangerously near his ambitious and unscrupulous uncles. Sophia, the daughter, was betrothed, though still a child, to the son of the duke of Brabant.

Elizabeth met with great discomfort at Marburg. To what this was due does not transpire. The citizens certainly re-

[1] "Et licet Irmengardis foris stetisset, quia tamen foris accepta clave ostium aperuerat claustri, dixit ei, ut prosterneret se cum beata Elyzabeth, et percepit fratri Gerardo, ut bene verberaret eas cum quadam virga grossa satis longa. Interim autem Mag. Conradus : Miserere mei Deus, dicantabat. Et dixit præfata Irmengardis, quod post tres hebdomadas habuit vestigia verberum et amplius beata Elyzabeth, quia acrius fuerat verberata."—*Ibid.* 2029.

sented her presence among them, but whether this was due
to her mode of living, or to the influence of the landgrave
who fomented hostility against her, does not appear certain.
Probably Henry Raspe, the landgrave, had much to do
with this. An attempt was made to get her to return to her
father in Hungary, but she refused. It is clear that Henry
wished her absence, and resented the interference of the
nobles in her favour; but it is also probable that her poor
mode of living, and especially her degrading subjection to
Conrad of Marburg, who was intensely hated for his cruelty,
and for his interference in political matters, tended to pro-
mote dissatisfaction.

She was forced to leave Marburg and take refuge in a
little village, where she found a poor building in dilapidated
condition in which to take shelter. The roof was off, and
the only place where she could obtain shelter was under
the stone stairs. There she fitted up a rough habitation,
wattling a screen of green boughs to shut off the open side
from the weather. She suffered greatly in this miserable
kennel from rains, sun, and the smoke, which made her eyes
water. There, however, she remained till a little timber
and plaster house had been erected for her outside Marburg. She then had a large hospital attached to it in which
she could nurse the sick. She sold all that remained to her
of jewels and silks which had been brought with her from
Hungary, to provide for the support of her sick people. She
took into her hospital the most helpless and neglected cases,
and attended to their necessities with the utmost gentleness
and patience. The sick children especially demanded and
obtained her tenderest solicitude. One poor scrofulous boy,
covered with sores, she would take in her lap, lay his head
on her breast, and soothe him in his fretfulness under pain.
She sat up with him at night, and carried him about in her
arms from place to place.[1]

"Dixit (Irmengardis) quod quendam puerulum scabiosum et monoculum una

S. ELIZABETH WASHING BEGGARS.

Nov. 19.

There was a poor leprous woman in a piteous condition of neglect, eaten up by disease, so that she caused general disgust, and no one could be found to attend to her. Elizabeth moved her to the hospital, dressed her ulcers, washed her, made her take medicine from her hand, combed her hair, and put her into a clean bed at the end of the court away from the rest of the patients. She made the old woman's bed every day, chatted cheerfully with her, and comforted her with her sympathy when depressed or in pain. She stroked the poor creature's face, disfigured with sores, and nursed her with such devotion that she was able at last to send her away restored to tolerable health. One day there was a lack of towels for the poor who were being bathed. There were some linen hangings over the wall of her room. Elizabeth pulled them down and tore them up for bath towels.[1] "How fortunate it is that we've this to fall back on," said she. "It may seem so to you," said her maids, "but we shall miss the hangings."

One day she gave alms to a great crowd gathered in expectation of receiving it. After the able-bodied beggars had retired, in the evening a number of the older, feebler, and those with children remained. They had come from far, and intended to sleep under the hedges and about the court of the hospital, wherever they could get a little shelter, and return leisurely next day.

It was evening, and full moon. Elizabeth had a fire lighted for them in the open air under the trees, hot water prepared that they might wash; then bread was served out to them, and something to drink. Late on into the night she heard

---

nocte sex vicibus ad requisita naturæ deportabat ad lectum portans frequenter ipsum tegebat. Pannos etiam ipsius pueri defœdatos ipsa lavabat jocundissime, eidem blandiendo loquebatur."— De Dictis iv. Ancill. 2027.

[1] The "linen pattern" of carved oak panelling is a relic of the old painted linen hangings which adorned rooms. Tapestry took the place of linen in the best rooms only.

them singing round the fire under the full moon, and was pleased. "I told you," she said to her maids, "that it was our duty to make the poor creatures merry."

She went to Werden in Westphalia on one occasion, for what reason does not transpire. Whilst there she heard of a poor tramp's wife being on the eve of her confinement. She had her lodged in a barn adjoining the house where she was staying, a fire lighted, a feather bed provided for her, with pillows and plenty of coverings. The woman gave birth to a boy, and he was baptized by the name of Elizabeth by the desire of the landgravine, who visited the poor mother every day, and provided everything necessary for her during four weeks. Then the woman was given a cloak and a pair of shoes by the saint, and twelve deniers of Cologne. Elizabeth gave her moreover a tunic, and took the sleeves off the fur dress of her servant, for a wrap to keep the baby warm. She stocked the tramp's basket with flour and cold bacon,[1] and went to bed, understanding that the tramps were going next day. She woke early and prepared to go to church to hear matins before daybreak. But before she started, she said to her maid, "It has occurred to me that I have got something in my bag which may be of use to the child and its mother. Run to the barn and bring her to me." The servant went as directed, but though she found the youthful Elizabeth whimpering, his parents had walked off in the shoes given them: they had taken the cold bacon, but abandoned the babe. When Elizabeth (the elder) heard this, she said, "Run at once and bring me the little child, lest it should suffer from neglect." She went with it to a soldier's wife, who was a motherly body, and had a baby at her breast, and gave her the child, then saw the magistrates and requested them to catch and bring back the undutiful parents.

---

[1] "Jussisset de pellicio ancillæ ejus manicas tolli, ut puer involveretur ; lardum et farinam dari cum præcepisset," &c.—De Dictis iv. Ancill. p. 2026.

They were caught before they had gone very far, and brought before the burgomaster, who judged that for their ingratitude they should be deprived of the shoes and cloak S. Elizabeth had given them, and should be required to take charge of the babe. Elizabeth was asked if this decision approved itself to her judgment. "Do what you think just," she said. The cloak was taken from the weeping mother's shoulders, and the shoes from her feet. Elizabeth gave the cloak " to a certain devout virgin in the town, who straightway vowed chastity to the Lord, and that she would serve the Lord in a religious habit." The shoes were given to a widow. Elizabeth, however, so pitied the disappointment of the poor tramp, her red feet, constrained to walk on the snowy roads, and her thin gown, that she secretly gave her another pair of shoes and a fur cloak.

Apparently young girls were very ready at that period to take religious vows on them at the smallest provocation. The cloak of Elizabeth determined the state of life of a "devout virgin," a mistake she made with a pair of scissors decided the vocation of another.

Elizabeth found that some beggars after they had received their bread or penny, pocketed it, and putting on an anxious, supplicating face, came up a second time, as though they had not been already served. She soon found them out, and ordered that in future all who wanted bread should sit in a row on the grass and receive their food in turn. And it was announced that any woman or girl who left her place during the distribution should have her hair cut off, to brand her ever after as an impostor. One day whilst the bread was being doled out, a pretty young girl, with long, light, very beautiful hair, came up and went among the beggars. Elizabeth was down on her at once, got her head fast and seized her scissors. In vain did the girl scream and protest that she was not a beggar, she had come there accidentally to see a friend. Elizabeth did not believe her—the beggars were most audacious in their indifference to truth; whilst her maids held the girl, she cut off her beautiful locks of spun gold, and only let the girl go when cropped like a boy.

Then, when the mischief was done, Elizabeth found out that she had punished the poor girl for a fault of which she was innocent. "It cannot be helped," said the landgravine, dolorously. "However, this good may come of it, that the girl will not be so often dancing with the men. Girl!" said she, suddenly turning to the weeping maiden, who was piteously contemplating her golden locks lying on the turf, "have you never thought of a better life than that of dancing and merrymaking, and looking out for a husband?"

"I cannot dance and make merry, and I am not like to catch a husband with my head in this condition," said the girl. "Then," said the saint, "while your hair is like this, live with me and serve me." So the maiden was taken into service by Elizabeth, and in time the influence of the landgravine effected such a change in her that she became a Grey Sister.

Elizabeth wore an unbleached habit, as a token that she had renounced the world. It became very ragged, and she patched it as best she could, so that there were insertions of all sorts of shades on her sleeves. Her cloak not being long enough, she added a strip, but it was of a different colour. In cold weather she heaped her bed coverings over her sick people, if she heard their teeth chattering; and to keep herself warm she pulled out the two feather-beds from under her, set them up sideways, and lay between them. "It is something like a coffin," she said, laughing, to one of her maids who looked to see what she was doing.

When not attending to the sick she occupied herself with spinning, and sold what she had spun for the benefit of the hospital.

A blind boy—blind from his birth—who lived in Marburg, found his way to the hospital, and went into the chapel. Elizabeth entered the church at midday, and found the blind boy there groping along the walls, and asked him what he was doing. He replied, "I want to go to the dear lady who comforts the poor people. I have said my prayers in this church, and am now feeling about it to find how wide and how long it is, as I cannot see."

She said to him, "Would you like to see?"

He answered, "If it had been God's will I would gladly have seen, but from childhood I have been deprived of sight." Then she was full of pity, and said, "Pray to God to enlighten you, and I will pray with you."

When she said this, the boy thought she must be Elizabeth, and he fell on his face before her and said, "Oh gracious lady! have pity on me." She knelt by him and prayed, and he obtained his sight, and had eyes that saw the light like other men.[1]

Her father heard in Hungary that she had been badly treated by her brother-in-law, and he sent the count of Banat and some knights to Thuringia to see her and bring her back to Hungary, if she desired it. They arrived, went to Marburg, and were directed to the hospital. They found Elizabeth seated at her door, spinning wool. When the Magyar noble saw her, he crossed himself and said, "Whoever before saw a king's daughter reduced to spin?" He tried to persuade her to return with him, but she refused to do so. She wished to remain by her poor and sick, and be laid near her husband.

When Elizabeth was ill and laid up in her bed, which was often the case, her busy hands worked still at the distaff, and when that was taken from her, she occupied her fingers in pulling out the hemp for future use. She also gained a

[1] Theodoric of Apolda and Rothe, p. 1736.

little money by the sale of fishes which she caught. A
hermit, Henry, son of the count of Weibach, sold them for
her in the town. The money she offered at the altar. This
manual labour was not a caprice, but a necessity. Henry
Raspe, her brother-in-law, had paid her down five hundred
marks, and this she had spent in erecting her hospital, or in
alms. He declined to do more for her. If she would live
at the Wartburg with him and his noisy, insolent followers,
well and good, she should then be fed at his table and enjoy
such an annuity as he saw sufficient, but as she chose to
reside elsewhere he washed his hands of her. She had two
reasons for refusing to stay at Wartburg—the uncongeniality
of her mode of life with that of his knights, and the knowledge that he kept open house, and lived in lavish profusion,
on the money ground by taxation from the much suffering
Thuringian peasants.[1]

Her health was declining; she needed nourishing food,
tender nursing, and gentle treatment. Conrad made her fast
with redoubled rigour, became more brutal in his assaults
with fist, and knotted rope, and stick on her back, as the
bones showed more sharply outlined through the pearly skin;
and, most cruel proceeding of all, removed from her Ysentrude and Jutta, her two faithful attendants, ladies by birth,
who had been brought up with her from childhood, and
whom she loved as sisters. He drove from her every other
servant whom she had brought with her from Wartburg,
everyone who loved her, and whom she cared for. Jutta
had been with her from earliest infancy. She was only five
years old when placed with the little Elizabeth, aged four.
They had grown up together: Jutta shared all her joys and

[1] "Mortuo marito, non fuit permissa uti bonis mariti sui, præpedita a fratre mariti sui. Poterat quidem sustentationem habuisse cum fratre mariti sui, sed de præda et exactione pauperum, quæ sæpius in curiis principum sunt, noluit victum habere, et elegit abjecta esse et ope manuum ejus velut quæstuaria victum acquirere."—De Dictis iv. Ancill. p. 2028.

sorrows, and talked to her of the past, the troubles of childhood, the brief joys of her married life, and of the little children from whom she was parted, and to whom her heart clung so tenaciously that she had to pray to God to moderate her love for them. Elizabeth parted from Jutta and Ysentrude with bitter tears.[1] Conrad supplied their places with creatures of his own—coarse, heartless old women, full of spite and bad temper, who delighted in hurting her by their malicious speeches, and bringing her into trouble with the tyrant who was destroying her health and happiness.[2]

There can be little doubt that Elizabeth's faithful attendants groaned under the despotism of this vile man, and advised her to shake off the intolerable yoke he laid on her neck, and take some more discreet and humane director.[3]

One would have been inclined to suspect Conrad of secretly conspiring with the landgrave Henry to cause the death of Elizabeth. He did kill her by his ill-usage, but it is not necessary to adopt such a violent explanation of his conduct. We must rather see in him the man of no generosity of mind, puffed up with pride, cruel by his profession of inquisitor, enjoying the mean satisfaction of torturing the helpless woman whom he hated because of her virtues and yielding meekness. The coward is always cruel. When he found she took a delight in giving alms of money, he forbade her doing so. Then she gave

[1] "Magister Conradus multipliciter temptavit ejus constantiam, frangens ejus in omnibus voluntatem et sibi contraria præcipiens. Deinde ut plus eam affligeret, singulos sibi dilectos de familia ab ea repulit, ut de quolibet pro se doleret, et tandem me Ysentrudem ei prædilectam ab ipsa expulit, quæ cum multo gravamine et infinitis lacrymis me dimisit. Ultimo Gudam sociam meam, quæ ab infantia ei fuerat com morata, quam specialissime dilexit, ab ea repulit, quam ipsa beata Elyzabeth cum lacrimis ac suspiriis dimisit."—De Dictis iv. Ancill. p 2023.

[2] "Adjunxit ei austeras fœminas, a quibus multas oppressiones sustinuit, quæ etiam captiose se habentes erga ipsam, sæpe detulerunt eam Magistro Conrado de non servata obedientia quando pauperibus aliquid dabat," &c.—*Ibid.*

[3] *Ibid.* p. 2029, where it is not exactly stated that the maids advised this, but it is suggested.

loaves, and found satisfaction in that. He forbade her that pleasure. Then she gave crusts away; when he heard of that he stopped it. Gregory IX. wrote to her to confirm her in her submission to Conrad, and to Conrad to keep hold on her. There was no escape for her. Offensive things were said of her relations with him. It was openly asserted that she was the mistress of Conrad. Her cheek burned, but she could not break from under his iron thraldom. She was made to wash up dishes, and scrub the floor; she submitted.

At last her health, which had long been failing under this usage, gave way. She died apparently of decline, struggling against the languor which oppressed her, as her strength gave way, and only taking to her bed at the last extremity.

She did not repine; she lay quiet, praying, and lost in dream. One day she began to sing faintly, but very sweetly. A little bird had perched on the window-sill, and had twittered so merrily that it had stirred a musical chord in her heart, and she sang in response to the bird.

On the night of her death, about midnight, she meditated a great deal on the words of Holy Scripture, and on sermons she had heard. After vespers silence fell on the hospital and the little cottage, for all slept save the nurse who attended her. Elizabeth was so quiet that the woman thought she slept, but presently heard her again singing. When midnight approached, she said: "Now comes the hour when the Mother Maid Mary brought the child Jesus into the world, and the star appeared in the East to guide the Wise Men to His cradle. He came to redeem the world, and He will redeem me. And now is the time when He rose from the grave and broke the prison doors of hell, to release the imprisoned souls, and He will now release me."

Afterwards she said, "I am very weak, but I have no pain," and then she laid her head on her pillow, and went off so gently that the maid who was by her thought she had

MARBOURG.—CHURCH OF S. ELIZABETH. TOMB AND RETABLE.

HIGH ALTAR, CHURCH OF S. ELIZABETH.

Nov. 19.

fallen asleep. One consolation she did enjoy on her deathbed—relief from the presence of her tormentor. Conrad was too ill to visit her.

Elizabeth died on November 19th, 1231, when only twenty-four years old, and was buried in the hospital church, four days after. Many sick persons were believed to be restored to health at her tomb, and Siegfrid, archbishop of Mainz, sent an account of these miracles to Pope Gregory IX., who canonized her on Whit Sunday, 1235, four years after her death. Siegfrid translated her body next year in the presence of Frederick II. and the children of Elizabeth, assisted by the archbishops of Cologne and Bremen, and many other prelates.

Her body was richly enshrined in the church dedicated to her at Marburg, which was begun in 1235, and was completed in 1283. Philip, landgrave of Hesse, the Reformer, put a stop to the pilgrimage to these relics by secretly burying them in a place now known to none. The beautiful shrine, however, still remains. The Carmelites of Brussels boast of possessing some of her bones, some more are in a shrine in the Electoral Treasury at Hanover. Conrad of Marburg made himself so detested by his cruelty in persecuting heretics that he was waylaid along with his follower, Brother Gerard, and murdered, as already related.

The unhappy Hermann, son of S. Elizabeth, was poisoned by his uncle, when at the age of eighteen, and likely to become dangerous (A.D. 1240). Henry was then about to marry the daughter of the duke of Austria, and was plotting with Pope Gregory IX. against Frederick II. It was therefore necessary for him to rid himself of the youth, whose right to the principality of Thuringia he could not contest.

The story of loaves transformed to roses (see p. 425) belongs to Elizabeth of Portugal, not her namesake of Hungary.

November 20.

SS. Amplius and Caius, *MM. at Messina in Sicily.*
SS. Octavius, Salutor, and Adventor, *MM. at Turin; circ.* A.D. 286.[1]
S. Dasius, *B.M. at Dorostorum in Mysia.*
S. Agapius, *M. in Palestine;* A.D. 306.
SS. Narses, *B.M.* and Comp. *MM. in Persia;* A.D. 343.
S. Benignus, *B. of Milan;* A.D. 472.[2]
S. Sylvester, *B. of Chalons-sur-Saône;* A.D. 526.
S. Maxentia, *V.M. near Senlis; circ. 6th cent.*
S. Authbot, *C. at Vaucourt near Arras; circ.* A.D. 690.
S. Hippolytus, *B. of Bellay in France;* A.D. 776.
S. Edmund, *K.M. at Bury St. Edmunds in Suffolk;* A.D. 870.
S. Humbert, *B.M. of the East Saxons;* A.D. 870.
S. Gregory the Decapolitan, *C. at Constantinople; 9th cent.*
S. Bernward, *B. of Hildesheim;* A.D. 1022.
S. Felix of Valois, *C. at Cerfroid, near Meaux;* A.D. 1212.

S. AGAPIUS, M.

(A.D. 306.)

[Roman Martyrology; also March 24 and Aug. 19. By the Greeks, with S. Timothy, B. of Gaza, on May 21; but also Greek Menæa on Nov. 19. Also, along with two Dionysii, two Alexanders, Timolaus, Romulus, and Paisius or Publius, on March 15 and 19 and May 17. Alone on July 22, in the Neapolitan Kalendar. Authority:—Eusebius, in his account of the Martyrs of Palestine, cc. 3, 6.]

IN the second year of the persecution of Maximian, Urbanus, governor of Palestine, acting under express orders from the emperor, proceeded with great severity against the Christians.

Timothy, bishop of Gaza, was tortured and then burned to death over a slow fire. With him were arrested Agapius

---

[1] Mentioned in a sermon attributed to S. Ambrose, but really, in all probability, by S. Maximus, bishop of Turin. [2] Or A.D. 477.

and Thecla, who were condemned to be thrown to the beasts, but were not at once given over to be devoured. They were detained till the arrival of the emperor, when the people were to be gratified with sport in the amphitheatre. Then six young men, named Timolaus, a native of Pontus, Dionysius of Tripoli, Romulus, subdeacon of Diospolis, Paesis and Alexander, two Egyptians, and another Alexander from Gaza, bound their hands together, and presented themselves before Urbanus, confessing themselves to be Christians. They were at once cast into prison. A few days later a second Agapius was arrested, and also another Dionysius, who endeavoured to convey food to the martyrs in prison. These eight were beheaded on one day at Cæsarea, and are commemorated on that day, March 24, in the Roman Martyrology, and in the Greek Menæa, on March 15, 19, and May 17.

But the first Agapius, who was taken with Thecla, was reserved for the birthday of the emperor in the fourth year of the persecution. Maxentius was present in Cæsarea. The two martyrs had been paraded with malefactors several times, and brought to the arena, but the magistrates had refrained from exposing them to the beasts, either from compassion or from hopes of breaking their constancy.

Now, however, Agapius was brought into the amphitheatre and placed in the arena together with a slave, accused of having murdered his master. The slave showed so much courage in fighting the wild beasts, that the whole theatre roared its applause, and the emperor pardoned and released him. Agapius was then brought forward, and was offered his liberty if he would renounce Christ. With a loud voice he cried that he would rather die; and a bear being let loose, he rushed towards him, and was hugged and mangled. He was carried, still breathing, to prison. Next day stones were attached to his feet and he was cast into the sea.

SS. NARSES, B.M., AND COMPANIONS, MM.

(A.D. 343.)

[Roman Martyrology. Greek Menæas, Menology of Basil (Prologue). Authority :—The genuine Chaldee Acts, published by Assemani, Act. Mart. Orient. i. pp. 97 and 226.]

NARSES, bishop of Sçiarchadata, in the province of Beth-Garma, in Persia, was arrested in the persecution of Sapor II. Sçiarchadata was then the first see under the metropolitan chair of Beth-Seleucia. With Narses was arrested his disciple Joseph. When they were led before the king, he said to Narses, "Your grey hairs and the bloom of your pupil's youth incline me to favour you. Consult your safety, do homage to the sun, and I will confer on you rank and reward." Narses answered, "I am fourscore years old, and have served my God from infancy, and how can I then desert Him to adore the creature of His hands?"

The king threatened him with death. Narses said, calmly, "Not if I should have to suffer seven deaths would I yield to your will."

Sapor then ordered them to execution. At the place where they were to suffer, Narses cast his eyes about on the crowd assembled to see him die, and Joseph said, "See, my father, how the people are assembled looking for thee to dismiss them with thy blessing." Narses embraced his disciple, and then both submitted their necks to the sword of the executioner.

Many others suffered about the same time. John, metropolitan of Beth-Seleucia, sentenced by Ardschir. Isaac, priest of Hulsar, was stoned to death. Papas, priest of Herminum, suffered at Gabala. Uhanan, a young clerk, was stoned to death by some renegade women. Guhschiatazades, an eunuch, was sentenced by Ardschir to be killed by the hand of Vartran, a Christian priest, who had shrunk from martyrdom, and had done sacrifice to the sun. There are other martyrs commemorated by the Greeks and named in the same Acts.

S. MAXENTIA, V.M.

(DATE UNCERTAIN.)

[At Beauvais on Nov. 20 and Oct. 24. Irish and Scottish Martyrologies on Nov. 20.]

AT Beauvais on October 24 is venerated S. Maxentia, who, it is pretended, was a Scottish (Irish) virgin, who settled there with S. Barbanus, her valet, and S. Rosebia, her maid, and there received the crown of martyrdom. They are purely apocryphal personages. However, Maxentia has been identified with Maxellenda, and Maxellenda with Mo-Easconn, an Irish saintly bishop.

Easconn is commemorated by Ængus the Culdee, on November 19, as "Maximus the great champion."

In the Felire of Ængus on November 20, we have "I invoke Escon with Froechan, a noble vessel with a fine mouth." The note on Escon (*i. e.* the uncleansed) is to the effect that he was so called because he was unbaptized till aged thirty. The Scottish martyrologists, finding a Maximus on this day, and Maxentia on the same day at Senlis, adopted the Gallican story, and changed the sex of the old bishop.

S. EDMUND, K.M.

(A.D. 870.)

[Roman Martyrology. Notker, Wandelbert, Sarum, York, Hereford, and Anglican Reformed Kalendars. Authority :—A Life by Abbo of Fleury, written by command of S. Dunstan. Abbo died in 1004, he wrote in 980. The Life is in Surius.]

THE Anglo-Saxon Chronicle says, under date 870, "This year the army (of Danes) rode across Mercia, into East Anglia, and took up their winter quarters at Thetford. And the same winter King Edmund fought against them, and the Danes got the victory, and slew the king, and subdued all the land, and destroyed all the minsters which they came to. The names of their chiefs who slew the king were Hingwar and Hubba."

The Danes arrived in 866, when Edmund was king of East Anglia, Burhred of Mercia, and when Osbert had been deposed in Northumbria, and Ælla, who was not of the kingly house, had been set up instead. The first winter the Danes spent in East Anglia. In 867 they crossed the Humber and took York. In 868 they entered Mercia and extended their ravages as far as Nottingham. In 870 they invaded East Anglia, with which hitherto they had maintained peace, having probably been bought off by Edmund. A battle was fought, and in it Edmund fell. This is all that can be counted historical in what we are told of Edmund. But legend has greatly improved the story.

Roger of Wendover tells a story, founded probably on old ballads, to account for the invasion by the Northerners.

"There was, not long ago, in the kingdom of the Danes, a certain man named Lodbrog (Hairy-breeches), who was sprung from the royal race of that nation, and had by his

S. EDMUND. After Cahier. Nov. 20.

wife two sons, Hingvar and Hubba. One day he took his hawk and went unattended in a little boat to catch small birds and wild-fowl on the sea coast and in the islands. While thus engaged he was surprised by a sudden storm, and carried out to sea, and after having been tossed about for several days and nights, was at last carried in sore distress to the English coast, and landed at Redham, in the province of Norfolk. The people of that country by chance found him with his hawk, and presented him as a sort of prodigy to Edmund, king of the East Angles, who, for the sake of his comely person, gave him an honourable reception. Lodbrog abode some time in the court of the monarch, and as the Danish tongue is very like English, he began to relate to the king by what chance he had been driven to the coast of England. The accomplished manners of King Edmund pleased Lodbrog, as well as his military discipline and the courtly manners of his attendants. Emulous of the like attainments, Lodbrog asked permission of the king to remain in his court, and having obtained his request, he attached himself to the king's huntsman, whose name was Bjorn, that he might with him exercise the hunter's art. But such was the skill of Lodbrog, that he was always successful in hunting or hawking, and being deservedly a favourite with the king, Bjorn became jealous of him, and giving way to deadly hatred, he one day, when they were hunting together, attacked him and slew him, and left his body in a thicket. This done, the wicked huntsman called off his dogs with his horn, and returned home. Now Lodbrog had reared a certain greyhound in King Edmund's court, which was very fond of him, and, as is natural, when the huntsman returned with his own dogs, remained watchful by his master's body.

"Next day, as King Edmund sat at table, he missed Lodbrog from the company, and anxiously asked his attendants what had befallen him; on which Bjorn, the huntsman, answered that he had tarried behind in a wood, and he had seen no more of him. But as he was speaking, Lodbrog's dog came into the hall and began to wag his tail and fawn on all, and especially on the king; who, on seeing him, said to his attendants, 'Here comes Lodbrog's dog; his master is not far behind.' He then began to feed the dog, hoping soon to see his master. But he was disappointed, for when the greyhound had satisfied his appetite, he returned to keep his accustomed watch over his master's body. After three days he was compelled by hunger to return to the king's table, and Edmund, greatly wondering, gave orders to follow the dog when he left the hall, and watch whither he went. The king's servants fulfilled his commands, and followed the dog till it led them to Lodbrog's lifeless body. On being informed of this the king was greatly disturbed, and directed that the body should be committed to a more honourable sepulchre. King Edmund then caused diligent inquisition to be made touching the death of Lodbrog; and Bjorn the huntsman was convicted of the crime, and by order of the king, the captains and wise men of his court passed sentence on him. The judges unanimously agreed that the huntsman should be put into the boat in which Lodbrog had come to England, and should be exposed on the sea without sail or oar, that it might be proved whether God would deliver him."

Roger of Wendover goes on to tell how Bjorn was wafted across to Denmark, and there was examined by torture by Hubba and Hingvar, sons of Lodbrog, who recognized their father's boat. Bjorn, under torture, declared that Lodbrog had been put to death by Edmund, king of the East Angles. The Danes accordingly assembled an army and invaded East Anglia, to avenge on Edmund the murder of their father.

The Norse story does not agree with this at all. According

to the Sagas, Ragnar Lodbrog was seized by Ælla, king of the Northumbrians, and was thrown into a dungeon full of serpents, in which he sang his dying song, the famous Krakumal. His sons, they say, were called Eirekr, Agnarr, Ivar, Bjorn Ironside, Hvitserkr and Sigurd Worm-in-the-eye.[1] Matthew of Westminster tells the tale, as does Roger of Wendover; both drew from the same source.

Edmund encamped at the royal vill of Haelesdune, when Hingvar and Hubba landed at Berwick-on-Tweed, and ravaged the country on their march through Northumbria. In 870 Hingvar entered East Anglia, and was attacked by Edmund whilst his force was divided from that of Hubba. Both sides suffered severely. Hubba joined Hingvar at Thetford, and the united army attacked Edmund again. His force was far outnumbered. He was routed, and he and Humbert, bishop of Elmham, were taken in a church; Humbert was despatched with the sword. Edmund was tied to a tree, and the Danes shot at him with their arrows, till they were tired of the sport, when he was decapitated, and his head flung into a thicket of the forest of Haelesdune (Hoxne). Next year, says the legend, when the Danes retired, the king's body was recovered and his head was sought in the wood. As those searching called in the wood to one another, asking where was the head, they heard a voice calling, "Here! here! here!" and found it proceeded from the head, which lay among the brambles, guarded by a great grey wolf. It was buried at Beodricsworth, afterwards called Bury S. Edmunds.[2] Sweyn, in 1014, was about to burn and

---

[1] The Thattr af Ragnars Sonum says that Ingvar, who invaded Northumbria and fought Ælla, "had two brothers, sons of a concubine, one called Yngvar, the other Husti: and these two put King Edmund to death by order of Ingvar."—Fornm. Sögur, i. 354.

[2] Roger of Wendover and Matthew of Westminster took their narrative of the martyrdom of S. Edmund from the Passion by Abbo of Fleury. He, however, does not tell the story of Lodbrog and Bjorn.

pillage the abbey of Bury, when he was suddenly struck ill
and died, and this was attributed to the interposition of the
saint.

S. BERNWARD, B. OF HILDESHEIM.

(A.D. 1022.)

[Roman Martyrology on Oct. 26. Molanus, in his additions to
Usuardus, Aut. 1583, on Nov. 20, under the name of Bertuald. Surius
on Nov. 20, which was the day of his death. Authority :—Thankmar,
"Vita Bernwardi Hildesheimensis episc." Thankmar was priest of
Bernward, sent by him to Rome in the matter of the contention about
Gandersheim. He is partial, no doubt, for he gives only his master's
side of the question. His statements are borne out by the "Annales
Hildesheimensis," ad ann. 1001, 1002, 1007, in Pertz, Mon. Scr. Germ.
t. i. p. 92 sq. Thankmar's Life of Bernward is in Pertz, t. v. p. 765—
775, and in the "Acta Sanctorum" for October, t. xi. p. 996—1024.]

THE abbey of Gandersheim, on the river Gander, a confluent of the Seine, stood on the borders of the ancient
diocese of Hildesheim. It had been founded in 856 by
Ludolf, duke of Saxony, for his daughter, Hathumod, who,
at the age of twelve, was made abbess, under the supervision
of Altfrid, bishop of Hildesheim. Bishop Altfrid and Hathumod died the same year, in 874. Altfrid had been a munificent benefactor of the abbey, and his successors in the see
continued to feel a lively interest in the abbey, which they
regarded as an ornament to the diocese. Bishop Wigbert
completed all the buildings except the church ; and on the
death of Gerburg, the second abbess, instituted her successor.
Bishop Otwin invested Gerburg II. with the office of abbess,
as his predecessors had done before him ; and when nuns
desired to be veiled, the ceremony was invariably performed
by the bishops of Hildesheim.

But in 993 Bernward became bishop of Hildesheim, and
at this time S. Willigis was archbishop of Mainz. Gander-

sheim became a bone of contention between them during several years, causing scandal, expense, and riot; and, as usual, a woman was at the bottom of the mischief. This woman was Sophia, daughter of Otho II.,[1] who had set her mind on taking the veil in the abbey of Gandersheim, with the purpose of becoming eventually its abbess. Osdag was at the time bishop of Hildesheim—a venerable prelate, very old and very holy, but only a bishop; and the Princess Sophia, as she was about to renounce the world, chose to do so royally, and receive the veil from no ecclesiastic lower than an archbishop.[2] She signified to Willigis of Mainz, primate of all Germany, that she chose him to perform the ceremony. Willigis readily assented to the request, regardless of the fact that he was invading the diocese of another. There was this plea he might have alleged to extenuate his conduct, that Pope Agapetus II. had by bull exempted the abbey of Gandersheim from episcopal jurisdiction, and made it dependent on the Holy See alone. But the abbesses had never acted on this bull; they had invariably applied to the bishops of Hildesheim to perform all the ecclesiastical functions that they required.

The Princess Sophia was to renounce the world and all its pomps and vanities on the feast of S. Luke. Bishop Osdag, before the day, visited the archbishop of Mainz, and asked him by what authority he was about to invade the diocese of Hildesheim. To avoid a scene and a scandal, the old bishop made this inquiry in private. Willigis, who seems to have been ignorant of the bull of Agapetus, insolently replied that he regarded Gandersheim as within the limits of his own

---

[1] Otho II., by his wife Theophania, the Byzantine princess, had three daughters: Sophia, abbess of Gandersheim; Adelheid, abbess of Quedlinburg; and Mathilda, who married Ezo, Count Palatine.

[2] "Secundi imperatoris Othonis filia fomes, ut pace omnium dicam, hujusmodi dissentionis dum a suo episcopo, domino videlicet Osdago, sacrum velamen accipere spernit, Willegisum appetit; indignum æstimans, nisi a palligero consecrari, quod ipse annuit."—Thankmar, c. 21.

diocese, and that on the day appointed he would be on the spot, and, in defiance of Bishop Osdag, would veil the princess and those who were about to renounce the world with her, and exercise in Gandersheim the plenitude of his archiepiscopal authority.

When S. Luke's day came, and the Emperor Otho III. was present with his mother, the Empress Theophania, the bishops of Paderborn, Minden, and Worms, both Osdag and Willigis appeared on the scene, and a loud and angry altercation ensued in the very church, as to which had rights therein. Suddenly Osdag bade his servants plant his throne in the middle of the apse, and seating himself thereon, he proclaimed to all that he had taken his rightful position in the church, and that he would maintain it. Willigis was furious, and violence would have ensued had not the empress intervened with the other bishops, and effected a compromise reluctantly submitted to. Willigis was to say mass at the altar; both were to hold the veil, and together cover Sophia with it; but Osdag was to perform the rest of the ceremony. Willigis had his throne drawn also into the apse, and "that day," says Thankmar, "the unusual thing was done, never before seen by us, of two bishops sitting together at the side of the altar, both vested in their full pontificals."

Now when it came to the veiling of the nuns, in the middle of the mass, Bishop Osdag rose, and turning to the emperor, asked him if he gave his consent to the renunciation of the world by his sister. Then he asked all the rest concerned; and when he had received a reply in the affirmative, he demanded of the Princess Sophia, and after her of the other candidates, whether they would take the oath of obedience to the see of Hildesheim, to him and to his successors. When they had taken the required oath, he announced publicly to clergy and people that the archbishop had neither right nor jurisdiction within those walls, and that he could not venture to minister therein unauthorized by the bishop of Hildesheim.[1]

So matters ended, and rested till the quarrel broke out again, when Bernward, whom we have already mentioned, was bishop of Hildesheim. This Bernward was son of Dietrich, count of Sommerschenburg by the daughter of Adalbero, Count Palatine. His mother's brother was Folkmar, afterwards bishop of Maestricht. He was educated by Thankmar, master of the school at Hildesheim, who survived him and became his biographer.

Bernward was a man with a love of art. He painted, and also wrought in metal with greater skill than many a smith whose life is spent in his art. Several specimens of Bernward's work remain. He cast the bronze gates, sixteen feet high, himself, for his cathedral, in 1015. They are unsurpassed as specimens of early metal work. The subject of the bas-reliefs on them, designed and executed by himself, is the First and Second Adam. In the cathedral square stands at the present day his brazen pillar, fourteen feet high, bearing, in bas-relief, twenty-eight representations of the events of our Lord's Life and Passion, winding round it like a scroll, from the base upwards, after the manner of those of Trajan's column. The date of this is 1022. In the treasury of S. Michael's is a crucifix twenty inches high, covered with gold plates, set with precious stones, and ornamented with filigree, made by the bishop. In the same treasury are two silver crosses and one of silver gilt, and two candlesticks of a mixed metal;[2] also a gold chalice set with jewels, all the

---

[1] Wulfher, author of the Life of S. Godehard of Hildesheim, d. 1038, says : "Vix obtentu regis ejusque matris licentiam ab eodem episcopo (Osdago) obtinuit (Willigisus) ut ibi (Gandersheimii) in natali S. Lucæ Evangelistæ missam celebraret archiepiscopus et prædictæ Sophiæ velationem simul cum eo ageret ; de cæteris vero velandis virginibus noster præsul suo jure provideret."

[2] Silver with some other metals united with it. They bear the inscription : " Bernwardus præsul candelabrum hoc puerum suum primo hujus artes flore non auro non

handiwork of Bernward. He is known to have made other
objects, which were lost in the Thirty Years' War, when
Hildesheim was occupied by the Swedes. He was moreover diligent in providing copies of the Gospels. At Hildesheim is still preserved a book of the Four Gospels, beauti-
fully written and illuminated for Bishop Bernward, and dates
1011. It bears the inscription, "I Bernward had this codex
written out, at my own cost, and gave it to the beloved saint
of God, Michael. Anathema to him who alienates it." This
is written with his own hand. Another book of the Gospels
contains a portrait of him in pontifical vesture, but without
mitre, kneeling before an altar.

He built and endowed monasteries and churches, and
fortified the town with strong towers. He was a good man,
chaste, pious, and abstemious, and is regarded as a saint.

Willigis, archbishop of Mainz, was born at Schöningen,
near Helmstadt, and was the son of a wheelwright. His
talents procured his advancement. He became canon of
Hildesheim, and was appointed chaplain to the Emperor
Otho II., and had the good fortune to be raised to the pri-
matial see of Mainz by the emperor in 975, and Benedict
VII. sent him the pall. The story goes that when he arrived
at Mainz, and proceeded in procession to the minster to be
installed, he noticed that the haughty burghers, impatient at
the idea of being ruled by a man risen from the ranks, had
chalked cartwheels on every hoarding and blank wall, and
urchins derisively span along the street on hands and toes,
after the fashion of a wheel. On reaching the cathedral,
Willigis noticed a blank shield hung over the throne. He
asked its purpose, and was told that the arms of the reigning
archbishop were always emblazoned thereon. "Go," said
Willigis to a servant, "fetch me a painter, and bid him

---

argento et tamen ut cernis conflare jubebat." They were found buried with him
when his body was taken up in 1194.

decorate the shield with a white cartwheel, and inscribe under it as my motto, 'Willigis, remember whence thou art sprung!'" It is certain that the city of Mainz, after the death of Willigis, out of gratitude for the many advantages it had gained through him, adopted this shield as its arms, and his white cartwheel on a field gules remains the coat of Mainz to this day.

However humble may have been Willigis on the first day of his elevation, his humility speedily evaporated when he felt his power as a prince of the empire, primate of Germany, and lord with power of life and death, making war and concluding peace, over a vast territory.

The proverb, "Set a beggar on horseback, and he will ride to the devil," bade fair to be exemplified in the case of Willigis.

Otho II. had confided to him the education of his son, and when his pupil had come to the throne, under the title of Otho III., Willigis seized the reins of government during the minority of the prince, between 983 and 989.

Relying on his influence with the emperor, and inspired with jealousy of Bernward, who was a favourite with Otho III.,[1] Willigis resolved on reasserting his claim to the abbey of Gandersheim, and of thereby at once extending his authority, and insulting and humiliating his young rival. Sophia was not long in affording him an opportunity.

If we may trust Thankmar, under the aged abbess Gerburg II., the discipline of the convent had become greatly relaxed. A bevy of young nuns, nursed in the lap of luxury, as Thankmar says, and unrestrained by a superior too old to attend to her duties, were likely to follow their own caprices.

[1] "Hanc iram et indignationem archiepiscopi adversus venerandum præsulem creavit maxime præcipua familiaritas domini Imperatoris, qua illum speciali devotione pietatis ceteris familiarius percoluit . . . . ob hoc animositatem et invidiam plurimorum in se commovebat, apprime quoque Moguntini episcopi, qui indignabatur aliquem præter se familiaritatis locum apud imperatorem habere."—Thankmar.

Sophia set the abbess at defiance, and, in spite of her remonstrances, left the cloister for the more congenial palace, and spent from one to two years there, intriguing with the faction of Willigis, and living in such a manner as to cause ugly scandals to circulate.[1] When these stories reached the ears of Bishop Bernward he remonstrated with her, and urged her to return to the quiet of the life she had vowed in her cell at Gandersheim. Sophia listened at first impatiently, then refused to listen at all, forbade the bishop access to her, and flew to the archbishop, to pour into his ear a torrent of wrathful and malicious speeches against the bishop of Hildesheim, who had dared to rebuke a princess of blood royal. "I renounce all allegiance to Bernward," said the furious woman. "You, archbishop, veiled me; neither I nor the convent of Gandersheim belong to the diocese of Hildesheim; and if you ask for proofs, I can find them. There are plenty at Gandersheim who will swear to this."

Then Sophia returned to her abbey, and did her utmost to incite the nuns to rebellion against the bishop.

Bernward, hearing that this was going on, thought it his duty to visit the abbey. He was received with studied discourtesy, even with insult.

Now it happened that the church, which had been greatly enlarged and beautified, needed consecration. Gerburg being too old to manage affairs, Sophia had taken the arrangement of the consecration into her own hands. Without consulting the bishop, she sent to Archbishop Willigis, and requested him to dedicate the church. He was only too glad to have the opportunity for reasserting his claim, and he fixed the day of the Exaltation of the Cross, A.D. 1000, for the ceremony. The abbess sent a messenger to Bishop Bernward,

---

[1] Sophia, domina Gerburga invita multumque renitente, ad palatium factione Willegisi se contulit : ibique annum vel biennium commorata, dissolubilis vitæ tramitem incedens, varium de se sparsit rumorem."—Thankmar.

inviting him to the dedication, and informing him of the day.

However, shortly after, Willigis postponed the ceremony for a week, till S. Matthew's day, probably because he knew that in that week Bernward could not attend; he would be engaged, according to his turn in court, in other duties.

On the day first appointed, the bishop of Hildesheim arrived at the abbey, and found nothing prepared, except some retainers of the abbess, ready to resist him by force should he attempt to consecrate the church.

The bishop entered the sacred building, and said mass before a large congregation, as the people from the neighbourhood flocked in when they heard that their diocesan was there.

The nuns stood in their stalls, sullen and contemptuous. It was customary then on solemn days for the people to make offerings of bread (oblationes); these were blessed by the priest or bishop, and were then distributed among the congregation. When blessed they were termed Eulogiæ, and were given to those present, and sent to those absent, as tokens of love and intercommunion. The rite still subsists in some French churches. The benediction and distribution of the *pain bénit* is a peculiar feature of the ritual in the diocese of Paris.

This blessed bread is, of course, quite distinct from the Host. It is, like the Greek *antidoron*, a relic of the ancient agape, or love feast, following the celebration of the Eucharist.

When the deacons and subdeacons went to the nuns of Gandersheim for their oblations, they refused to give anything, and when the bread presented by the people had been blessed, and some of it was offered to them, they flung the pieces away, with curses loudly expressed upon the bishop.[1]

---

[1] "Oblatas incredibili furore et indignatione projiciunt, sæva maledicta episcopo ingerunt."—Thankmar.

Bernward, ashamed of the noise and indecency of the nuns, burst into tears, and " charitably attributing this conduct to the ignorance, rather than the malevolence, of these furious women," he finished the mass with broken voice, blessed the congregation, and departed.

In the meantime Sophia was living with Archbishop Willigis on the most familiar terms,[1] and using all her arts night and day to incite him against Bishop Bernward.

As the bishop could not attend at Gandersheim on S. Matthew's day, he commissioned Eckhardt, bishop of Schleswig, driven from his see by the incursions of the Slavonians, to represent him, and remonstrate with the archbishop.

On the vigil of S. Matthew's day Willigis arrived at Gandersheim with the bishops of Paderborn and Verden, Duke Bernard of Saxony, and a large body of followers. On the morrow at dawn, appeared Bishop Eckhardt and a party from Hildesheim of clerks and monks, and after saluting the archbishop and the duke, announced that the bishop of the diocese was detained at court, and could not attend, but that he expressed his surprise that the archbishop should invade his diocese, and undertake to consecrate a church beyond the bounds of his proper jurisdiction; and in all fraternal charity he requested him to desist.

The archbishop blazed forth into fury, and vowed that he would certainly perform the consecration on the following day, which was a Sunday.

But when on that day the archbishop appeared in the church, Bishop Eckhardt and the clergy of Hildesheim made such strenuous opposition, that the matter was referred to a synod to be held on S. Andrew's day, and Willigis bade the bull of Pope Agapetus II. be read aloud to all the people.[2]

---

[1] " Sophia illi assidue cohærens et cohabitans, hæc interdiu noctuque ambigebat." —Thankmar.

[2] Thankmar disingenuously disguises the fact, saying that he caused some previously unheard of privileges accorded to the convent to be rehearsed.

The bishops of Verden and Paderborn, who were unaware before that Willigis was acting in opposition to the bishop, took Eckhardt aside and urged that Bernward should make appeal to the emperor and the Pope, for that otherwise, in the absence of Otho III. in Italy, there was no one to oppose the archbishop, and prevent his carrying matters through with a high hand, and establishing a precedent which it would be difficult afterwards to upset.

Bernward took the hint, and started as soon as possible for Rome.

He hastened south over the Brenner, down the valley of the Adige past Trent, and arrived at Rome on the 4th January, 1001, having left Hildesheim on the 5th November. Considering that it was winter, and the passes were deep in snow, he had certainly accomplished his journey with great speed.

When the emperor heard that Bernward was approaching Rome, he went out to meet him, kissed him, and made him take up his abode as his guest in the palace. Silvester II.—the learned Gerbert—was then Pope. Otho had appointed his kinsman and chaplain Bruno, to the throne of S. Peter, under the title of Gregory V. He had been driven from Rome by the turbulent citizens acting under the consul Crescentius. Gregory was replaced by the arms of the emperor, and the anti-Pope John XVI., set up by Crescentius, was mutilated and insulted by his rival,[1] and Crescentius put to death by the emperor.

Gregory V. died, it is said by poison, and Otho III. appointed the learned Gerbert in his room. Rome broke out into revolt, but was again crushed into submission by the young emperor. Bishop Bernward arrived when Otho was

[1] Pope John XVI. had his eyes put out, his nose and tongue cut off, and in this state, it is said by the command of the hardhearted Pope himself, he was paraded through the streets on an ass with his face to the tail, and with a wine-bladder on his head. An heroic monk of Calabria, S. Nilus, in vain implored that such ignominy might not be offered by one consecrated prelate to another. His voice was not listened to by the Pope, flushed with success.

master of Rome, and Silvester II. was acknowledged as Pope by the reluctant and sullen Romans.

The day after Bernward arrived, the Pope summoned him to his presence, and listened to his tale. The disturbances at Gandersheim had already reached his ears, and therefore Bernward found the Pope prepared for what he had to say, and eager to address himself to remedy a scandal. In the meantime the synod convoked by the archbishop of Mainz, for S. Andrew's day, had met at Gandersheim. He had brought with him the bishop of Paderborn, a number of Hessian and Thuringian ecclesiastics, and some from that portion of Saxony which belonged to his arch-diocese. Eckhardt of Schleswig appeared on behalf of the absent bishop of Hildesheim, and read a formal prohibition to the archbishop to intrude upon the cure of another prelate who was absent, and carrying his appeal to the feet of the emperor and the Pope.

When the archbishop heard this, his countenance blackened with rage, and he burst into a furious command to Eckhardt to hold his tongue, and go look after his own sheep in the wilderness.

"My diocese," answered Eckhardt, "is depopulated by the invasions of barbarians, my city deserted, my church desolate. I have no longer a see, and am become the servant of the church of Hildesheim."

The archbishop then summoned witnesses to swear that Gandersheim was in the diocese of Mainz. But the bishops present interfered, knowing that Bernward was with the emperor and Pope, and argued that in his absence it was unlawful to receive such oaths. Eckhardt again raised his voice and renewed his protest. Willigis roughly ordered him to keep silence, or he would order his servants to eject him from the church. This led to a tumult. Eckhardt, and all the clergy of Hildesheim who were present rose, and protesting that they refused to acknowledge the synod, withdrew, leaving in the church only Archbishop Willigis and his own creatures.

Witnesses were called to swear to the boundaries, but no agreement was come to. Some swore that the river Innerste, which flows by Lauterbach, was the limit of the diocese of Hildesheim, others that it was bounded by the Oder, which enters the Leinne at Nordheim. The archbishop summed up in his own favour, and pronounced that the monastery belonged to the arch-diocese of Mainz, and threatened with excommunication whoever should reject his authority or interfere with it, in the district of Gandersheim.

A report of what had taken place at the synod was at once forwarded to Bishop Bernward. At this time Henry, duke of Bavaria, afterwards emperor, was with Otho in Rome. He was a pious man, and felt keenly the scandal this miserable contest was causing, and he joined with Bernward in urging the Pope to put an end to it. By his advice, Silvester summoned a synod of twenty Roman prelates, and some from Tuscany. Bishops Siegfried of Augsburg, Henry of Würzburg, and Hugh of Zeitz, there, with the emperor, attended also.

The assembly was held in the church of S. Sebastian. After the Gospel had been read, and benediction given, Bernward rose from his seat, and stepping forward, briefly narrated his case before the Pope, the emperor, the duke of Bavaria, and all the bishops present. The Pope then asked the council what judgment they gave. The bishops requested permission to retire and consult in private. Permission was accorded, and on their return, Silvester again asked them their decision. They replied, that no bishop had a right to enter another diocese and hold a synod there, or perform any ministrations therein without the consent of the bishop of the diocese; nor could such a gathering as that held by Willigis at Gandersheim be termed a synod.

"By what name do you then designate it?" asked the Pope.

The council replied, "We entitle it a schism conciliating discords."

Silvester asked, "Are its decisions, then, to be rejected?"

The council answered, "By authority of the canons and of the holy fathers they are to be annulled."

Then Silvester announced, "By my Apostolic power and the authority of the assembled holy fathers, we dissolve, break, and annul all that has been decided and established by Archbishop Willigis and his confederates at Gandersheim, in the absence of his brother bishop Bernward." He added, "Our brother, the bishop Bernward asks that the investiture of which he has been despoiled by the archbishop, may be restored and confirmed to him. What say you to that, my brethren?"

The council replied, "There is no necessity for restoring an investiture of which the archbishop was incompetent to deprive him. But because he beseeches this, if it please the emperor, let the staff of your Apostolic Holiness restore and confirm it to him."

The Pope replied, "Be it done, according to your pleasure." And he put his staff in the hand of the bishop, saying, "We restore and confirm to you the convent of Gandersheim with its adjacent farms and boundaries, and by the apostolic authority of SS. Peter and Paul I forbid any one from interfering with you therein, except so far as the canons permit."

This done, the Pope asked the council what further steps should be taken. The council replied, that a synod should be appointed to be held on June 22, at Pöhlde, near Herzberg, in Saxony, under the presidence of Frederick, cardinal priest, a Saxon by birth, who should be sent thither as legate from the Holy See, to communicate the decision of the council and of the Pope to the bishops of Germany.[1]

Bernward did not at once leave Italy. The revolt of Tibur and afterwards of Rome detained him. He was unwilling to desert the emperor at a season of difficulty. But when Tibur was reduced and Rome had submitted, he took his departure, bidding farewell to the young emperor, who was so speedily to fall a victim either to the climate of Rome, or to the poison of the vengeful widow of Crescentius. Bernward, laden with relics, crossed the S. Bernard pass, was hospitably received at Agaunum by Rudolf, the Burgundian king, and arrived at Hildesheim on April 10th, 1001, being Maundy Thursday.

Frederick, the papal legate, arrived in Germany with the pomp and retinue befitting his office, and on the day appointed for the synod appeared at Pöhlde. He was received with anything but obsequiousness by the archbishop of Mainz, who knew the tenour of the paper he brought from Rome. The entry of the legate into the conclave was received with hooting and groans from the archbishop and his party. No proper seat was provided for the legate, and Bernward and the archbishop of Hamburg had to make room for him between them. It was with difficulty that the storm of curses and yells could be controlled.[2] When at length silence was obtained, the legate began by urging all present to peace and charity, and then having exhibited his credentials, he presented a letter from the Pope to the archbishop of Mainz. Willigis refused to touch or look at it.[3] The

[1] Thankmar, the biographer of Bernward, accompanied the bishop to Italy; his account of the council is graphic, it is that of an eye-witness.
[2] "Archiepiscopus et qui ci favebant, mira indignatione et execratione illum spernabant; quum ad concilium ventum est vix dici poterit, quanta seditione et tumultu agitetur. Nam nec locus sessionis Vicario Apostolici idoneus conceditur; horribilis strepitus ingeminatur, jus fasque contemnatur, canonica disciplina annullatur."—Thankmar.
[3] "Epistolam papæ . . . . profert, publiceque recitari precatus, quam cum archiepiscopus tangere vel videre dedignaretur," &c.—*Ibid.*

Vicar Apostolic then ordered it to be read publicly. It contained a rebuke to the archbishop for his conduct in the matter of Gandersheim. At a signal, the doors of the church were thrown open, and the armed retainers of the archbishop burst in, shouting, and threatening Bernward and the legate. The conclave broke up in tumult, and was adjourned to the following day by the legate, who strove to make himself heard above the din of arms. The archbishop left the church, but the legate pertinaciously followed him, and bade him attend the adjourned synod next day, on pain of being put under the ban of excommunication. The archbishop scornfully ignored the summons, and departed for Mainz at the head of his servants and adherents.

At the hour appointed the legate took his place in the church, and when he learned that the archbishop had left Pöhlde, he interdicted him from the execution of his office in the following terms:—"Because thou hast withdrawn thyself from the synod, and hast been disobedient to the commands of the Roman Pontiff, by the authority of the holy apostles Peter and Paul, and their vicar, Pope Silvester, know that thou art suspended from all sacerdotal functions till the feast of the Nativity, and that thou art summoned in person to appear before the Pope."

The indignant legate then sped back to Rome, and laid an account of the treatment he had undergone before the Pope and the emperor. Both were filled with indignation, and issued orders to the German bishops to appear in Rome, not only to hold a synod, but also, attended by their vassals, to assist the emperor in constraining the turbulent Italians. Shortly after his return, Frederick, the legate, was appointed to the see of Ravenna.

At Hildwardshausen was a convent of nuns ruled by Rotegard, aunt of Bernward. This nunnery had been given by the emperor to the bishop of Hildesheim, and in the same year he went there to consecrate the church. But the archbishop sent his servants beforehand, and they removed all the preparations made for the ceremony, resisted the bishop, prevented him from entering, and beat his servants. Bernward, unable, or unwilling to force his entrance, went thence to Gandersheim; but Sophia hearing of his approach summoned the vassals of the archbishop to her assistance, and when Bernward arrived he found an armed multitude prepared to dispute his passage.

The bishops of North Germany, determined if possible to bring this scandalous strife to an end, summoned a synod at Frankfort, to meet directly after the Feast of the Assumption. The archbishops of Cologne and Trèves were invited to attend, and appeared on the appointed day together with Willigis of Mainz, Rhietar of Paderborn, Robert of Spires, Beringar of Werden, and Eckhardt of Schleswig. The last named, together with Thankmar, the priest, Bernward's biographer, represented the interests of the bishop of Hildesheim, who was ill.

Willigis, irritated at the absence of Bernward, along with some of his party as hot-blooded as himself, angrily demanded that Bernward should appear in person; but Thankmar succeeded in pacifying them by assuring the council that the bishop was really ill and unable to attend. Willigis refused to abandon his pretensions over Gandersheim, and the council separated, after having ruled that neither the archbishop nor the bishop should exercise episcopal functions therein till after the diet which was convoked for the octave of Pentecost in the ensuing year, at Fritzlar.

When the time approached for Bernward to depart for Rome to attend the council summoned for Christmas Day, he found himself unable to make the journey through continued sickness, and he was obliged to despatch in his place his old schoolmaster, Thankmar, to whom we are indebted for all the particulars of the Gandersheim contest. Thankmar met the emperor at Spoleto, and tarried with him till the 27th of December, when the council met in the city of Todi. Only three German bishops had come, those of Augsburg, Liége, and Zeitz, though several others, especially Heribert of Cologne, had started to attend it. Willigis contemptuously refused even to send delegates to plead his cause. Bernward was represented by Thankmar. The Pope invited Thankmar to explain the case. He flung himself on his knees before the emperor and the Pope, and implored them to defend his master's cause, the cause of justice and of canon law. He narrated the whole story, and was followed by Frederick, bishop of Ravenna, who gave a lively picture of the insults and outrages to which he had been subjected at Pöhlde. His narrative elicited murmurs of indignation from the assistant Italian bishops on the audacity, the defiance, and insubordination of the archbishop of Mainz, and they demanded his immediate excommunication. But the German prelates urged delay till archbishop Heribert of Cologne should arrive, and the council was prorogued till January 6, 1002. But by that day no more bishops had come out of Germany, and the assembly was again postponed to the morrow. As on that day they had not appeared, no final decision was arrived at.

On January 13 Thankmar departed for his own country, laden with presents from the emperor. A few days later Otho III. died, poisoned by Stephania, the widow of Crescentius, who had nursed her revenge, and with subtle malignity had woven her spells round the young emperor till he had fallen a victim, first to her beauty and then to her vengeance. She became his mistress that she might obtain the chance of poisoning him. He died at the age of twenty-two on January 23, 1002.

The death of Otho prevented the assembly of the diet at Fritzlar.

Italian poison, which had freed Rome of the presence of a barbarian emperor, speedily relieved it also from that of a German and virtuous Pope. Silvester II. died May 12, 1003. The cup was mixed for him also by Stephania, according to popular belief.[1]

Otho dying childless, the succession to the throne was disputed. Henry of Bavaria claimed it as the nearest of kin, and was supported by the clergy on account of his piety, and munificence towards the Church. The other competitors were Hermann of Swabia, and Eckhardt of Meissen. But Henry's party was considerably strengthened by the adhesion of Willigis. Eckhardt, his most dangerous opponent, lost his life before he could carry his projects into execution.

Henry was crowned at Aix-la-Chapelle, and Hermann resigned his pretensions. On August 10 Henry II. arrived at Paderborn, and there his wife Cunegund was crowned by Willigis. In the meantime, Gerburg II., abbess of Gandersheim, had died, and Sophia was elected in her room. She sent at once to Willigis, and he instituted the new abbess, without Bernward being in a position to resist, for she had wrung from the emperor permission to have the ceremony performed by the archbishop.

Henry, who had been distressed at the contest before he was emperor, now that he was in power used his best endeavours to bring about a conciliation between Willigis and Bernward. In 1007 the emperor celebrated Christmas at Pöhlde, surrounded by his princes lay and ecclesiastical. He took the opportunity to urge on Willigis to submit the matter of Gandersheim to his arbitration. The archbishop

---

[1] "Veneficio ejusdem mulieris etiam Papa Romanus gravatus asseritur; ita ut loquendi usum amiserit."—Ann. Saxo.

felt it was not to his interest to oppose the king. Henry then announced that the consecration of the church at Gandersheim should take place on the 5th January next ensuing, and the veiling of the nuns on the following day, the Feast of the Epiphany, and he invited both Willigis and Bernward to be present and hear his award.

On the appointed day the emperor arrived, and Bernward was required to say mass. When mass was ended, the king went forth with the archbishop and bishop and addressed the people. He said that he recognized the church and the adjacent farms as belonging to the bishop of Hildesheim.

Willigis, shamed at his past pertinacity, thrust his pastoral staff into the hand of Bernward, and said, " Beloved brother, I renounce all right over this church, and I give to you this pastoral staff which I hold, as a testimony before Christ, the king, and our brethren, that neither I nor my successors can have any right here."

Thus the wretched contest had been brought to an end by the king, before whose face, as Thankmar says, all strifes melted away, and foes became friends. For the rest of his days Willigis remained on the best terms with Bernward, probably heartily regretting the impetuosity and ambition which had caused such discord, and had brought upon himself not a little reproach.

Willigis died in 1011, and is regarded as a saint. From the lessons for his festival in the diocese of Mainz (February 23) every allusion to the Gandersheim affair is carefully excluded. It is the same with a life of the saint existing in MS. in the Mainz Cathedral library. Bernward has greater claims to a place in the Kalendar, which he occupies on October 26. He died in the odour of sanctity about A.D. 1022, and was canonized by Pope Celestine III. in 1194.

S. FELIX OF VALOIS, C.

(A.D. 1212.)

[Roman Martyrology on Nov. 4 and 20; also that of the Trinitarians. Declared Venerable by Alexander VII. His feast transferred from Nov. 4, the day on which he died, to Nov. 20, by Innocent XI. in 1679. The Trinitarians pretend that he and S. John of Matha were canonized by bull of Urban IV. in 1260, but the bull does not exist. Authority:—Francis a S. Laurentio, "Compendium Vitæ SS. Johannis et Felicis."]

FELIX was born in 1127; his origin is obscure. He derived his designation from inhabiting the forest of Cerfroid, in the province of Valois. The Trinitarians have made great efforts to convince themselves and the world that he was of the royal race of Valois, but with most limited success. He was joined in his retreat by John of Matha, and together they founded an order for the redemption of captives. Felix, though seventy years old, readily fell in with the plan of his enthusiastic companion, and they started together for Rome in the winter of 1197-8 to obtain approbation of their scheme. Innocent III. lodged them in his palace, and approved the foundations of the Order, which he commended to the Holy Trinity, and of which he appointed John of Matha superior-general. Eudo de Sully, bishop of Paris, and the abbot of S. Victor were commissioned to draw up the rules for the new society, which were confirmed by the Pope on December 17, 1198. The mother house of the order was established in the wood of Cerfroid. The order grew so rapidly that in forty years six hundred monasteries are said to have belonged to it. S. Felix directed those in France, while S. John resided at Rome, or made journeys into Barbary to redeem captives. S. Felix died on November 4, 1212.

November 21.

Presentation of B. Virgin Mary in the Temple.
S. Rufus, *Disc. of S. Paul;* 1st cent.
SS. Celsus and Clemens, *MM. at Rome.*
SS. Demetrius and Honorius, *MM. at Ostia.*
S. Maurus, *M. in Istria.*
S. Gelasius, *Pope of Rome;* A.D. 496.
S. Columbanus, *Ab. at Bobbio in Italy;* A.D. 615.
S. Pappolus, *B. of Metz;* circ. A.D. 600.
S. Albert, *B.M. of Liége;* A.D. 1192.

PRESENTATION OF B.V. MARY.

[Greek Menologies and Menæas. Commanded by Sixtus V. in 1585 to be observed throughout the Western Church.]

THE presentation of the B. Virgin Mary in the temple, at the age of three, is the subject of a picturesque fable in the Apocryphal Gospel of James and the Pseudo Matthew. It is thus told in the former :—

"When the child Mary became two years old, Joachim said, 'Let us conduct her to the temple of the Lord that we may render the vow which we vowed, lest perchance the Lord refuse us, and our gift become unacceptable.' And Anna said, 'Let us wait till the third year, that the child may not require its father and mother.' And Joachim said, 'Let us wait.' And the child became three years old, and Joachim said, 'Call the undefiled daughters of the Hebrews, and let them take a lamp apiece, and let these be burning, that the child may not turn back, and its heart be taken captive from the temple of the Lord.' And they did thus until they came up into the temple of the Lord. And the priest received

her and kissed her, and said, 'The Lord hath magnified his name in all generations: with thee at the end of days the Lord will manifest his redemption to the children of Israel.' And he set her upon the third step of the altar, and the Lord God bestowed grace upon her, and she danced about on her feet, and all the house of Israel loved her."

In the Gospel of the Pseudo Matthew: "When Anna had weaned her in her third year, Joachim and his wife Anna went together to the temple of the Lord, to offer sacrifices to God, and placed the babe that was named Mary in the chamber of virgins, wherein virgins continued day and night in the praises of God. When she had been set before the gates of the temple, she went up the fifteen steps at such a rapid pace that she did not look back, nor ask for her parents, as is usual in infancy. Her parents, therefore, being anxious, and each asking after the infant, were alike astonished, till they found her in the temple, so that even the priests marvelled."

S. GELASIUS, POPE.

(A.D. 496.)

[Roman Martyrology. Florus, some copies of Usuardus, Ado, &c. Authorities:—Anastasius Bibliothecarius, and the writers of S. Gelasius.]

GELASIUS, of Roman birth, but of African family, succeeded Felix II. on the throne of S. Peter in 492. He signalized his assumption of power by exiling all the Manichæans he could detect in Rome, and burning their books before the basilica of S. Maria Maggiore. He demanded of the Emperor Anastasius that the name of the patriarch Acacius should be expunged from the diptychs of the Constantinopolitan Church, so that the celebrant at the altar might not even pray for rest to the soul of a bishop who had not only disregarded the excommunication of the Roman pontiff, but had presumed even to cast back the sentence of excommunication on the successor of S. Peter. Gelasius wrote to Euphemius, patriarch of Constantinople, who had advised moderation, and the forgetting of old offences when the parties who had quarrelled were dead:—"Do you call it condescension to admit among true bishops the names of heretics and excommunicated persons, and of those who communicate with them and their successors? Is not this, instead of descending (like our Lord) out of heaven to redeem, to plunge ourselves instead in hell?"

He summoned Euphemius, for giving such unchristian advice, to meet him before the throne of Christ.

He cast his excommunication over the Emperor Anastasius, he flung it against the Vandal king who persecuted the Church in Africa, but as Thrasimund was an Arian, and not in communion with the Catholic Church, the king received the sentence with indifference. He attacked the heresies of Eutyches and Nestorius with his pen. He is said to have been very generous to the poor, and very severe against simony. He dedicated the church of S. Euphemia in the Tiburtine city, the basilica of SS. Nicander and Eleutherius on the Via Lavicana, and the basilica of S. Mary on the Via Laurentina. He wrote hymns in imitation of those of S. Ambrose. He was a learned man. In a synod held at Rome he passed a sentence of condemnation on various apocryphal works which were by some regarded as canonical; such as the story of Paul and Thecla, the Itinerary of Peter, the Apocryphal Gospels, and—curiously enough—also the Ecclesiastical History of Eusebius.

S. COLUMBANUS, AB.

(A.D. 615.)

[Usuardus, Ado, Surius, on Nov. 23; Roman Martyrology on Nov. 21. Cistercian Martyrology on Nov. 28. Dempster's Scottish Menology on Nov. 21 and 22. The Translation of S. Columbanus on Aug. 31. Authorities :—A Life by Jonas, abbot of Bobbio, who died about 665, in Mabillon, Acta SS. O.S.B. sec. ii. Also a Metrical Life by Frodoard (Flodoard), canon of Rheims, afterwards monk. This is perhaps the nephew of Flodoard of Rheims who wrote the "Annals and History of the Church of Rheims;" but Flodoard composed in hexameters the lives of the Roman pontiffs, and this life of S. Columbanus may therefore possibly be by him. Mabillon, however, is inclined to attribute it to his nephew. Published also in Mabillon, after the Life by Jonas. In compiling the following Life occasional use has been made of M. de Montalembert's "Monks of the West."]

COLUMBANUS was a native of Leinster, and seems to have been of a respectable family. Of the precise date of his birth we are not informed. According to some accounts it was about 559, but according to others it was several years earlier. He received a good classical education, and resolved early to embrace an ascetic life. But the good looks and winning ways of the Irish girls were a snare to him. He tried to forget their bright eyes by toiling (desudavit) at grammar, rhetoric, and geometry, but found that at least syntax and the problems of Euclid were a less attractive study than pretty faces, and that the dry rules of rhetoric failed altogether before the winsome prattle of light-hearted maidens. He consulted an old woman who lived as a recluse. She warned him that if he wished to maintain his purpose of self-conquest he must fly to a region where girls are less beautiful and seductive than Ireland. "Save thyself, young man, and fly!" His resolution was formed; he decided on going away. His mother attempted to deter him, prostrating herself on the threshold of the door; he stepped over her, left the province of Leinster, and placed himself under the tuition of the venerable Sinell, son of Moenach, abbot of Cluaininis in Lough Erne. Sinell made Columbanus compose a commentary on the Psalms whilst under his tuition. After awhile, Columbanus went to Bangor,[1] where he remained under the abbot Congall. But this first apprenticeship in the holy war was not enough. The adventurous temper of his race, the passion for pilgrimage and preaching,[2] drew him beyond the seas. He heard incessantly the voice which had spoken to Abraham echoing in his ears, "Go out of thine own country, and from thy father's house, into a land that I shall show thee." The abbot in vain attempted to retain him. Columbanus, then thirty,[3] left Bangor with twelve other monks, crossed Great Britain, and reached Gaul. He found the Catholic faith in existence there, but Christian virtue and ecclesiastical discipline ignored or outraged—thanks to the fury of the wars and the negligence of the bishops. He devoted himself during several years to traversing the country, preaching the Gospel, and especially giving an example to all of the humility and charity which he taught. His little community accompanied him. If one of the members lapsed into vice, all the rest simultaneously, burning with charity, fell on him, and beat him back into the paths of virtue.[4] Not a harsh word was uttered by one of them; they had all things in common.

Arriving, in the course of his apostolic wanderings, in Burgundy, he was received there by King Gontram, of all the grandsons of Clovis the one whose life appears to have

[1] In Carrickfergus, not Bangor in Wales.
[2] "Scottorum quibus consuetudo peregrinandi jam pene in naturam conversa est."—Walafred Strabo, De Mirac. S. Galli, lib. ii. c. 47.
[3] The received text of Jonas says "twenty," but one copy of the Life has "thirty," and this is most probable.
[4] "Si quempiam ex his labi in vitium reperissent, simul omnes æquo jure negligentem correptionibus cædere studebant."—Jonas.

been least blamable, and who had most sympathy with the monks. His eloquence delighted the king and his lords. Fearing that he would leave them, Gontram offered him the ancient Roman castle of Annegray, now in the commune of Faucogney (Haute Saône). He lived there the simplest life with his companions, on the bark of trees, the wild herbs, the bilberries in the firwoods, and whatever the neighbours would give, out of charity. Often he separated himself from his companions to plunge alone into the forest. There, in his long and close communion with bare and savage nature, every living creature obeyed his voice. The birds came to receive his caresses, and the squirrels descended from the tree-tops to hide themselves in the folds of his cowl. He expelled a bear from the cavern which became his cell; he took from another bear a dead stag, whose skin he used for shoes for the brethren. One day, while he wandered in the depths of the wood, bearing a volume of Holy Scripture on his shoulder, and meditating whether the ferocity of beasts was not better than the rage of men, he saw a dozen wolves surround him. He remained motionless, repeating the words, "Deus in adjutorium." The wolves smelt his garments, and passed on their way without molesting him. He pursued his, and a few steps further on heard the voices of a band of Swabian robbers who wasted the country. He did not see them; but he thanked God for having preserved him from the maw of the wolf and the less merciful hand of man.

At the end of some years the increasing number of his disciples obliged him to seek another residence, and by the help of Agnoald, a minister of the Frank king, whose wife was a Burgundian of high family, he obtained from Gontram the site of another strong castle, named Luxeuil, where there had been Roman baths, magnificently ornamented. On the ruins of this seat of luxury the monks founded their ascetic colonists, these eschewing water, planted themselves in the ancient baths.

Luxeuil was situated on the confines of Austrasia and Burgundy, at the foot of the Vosges. Disciples collected abundantly round the Irish colonizer. He could soon count several hundreds of them in the three monasteries which he had built in succession, and which he himself governed. The noble Franks and Burgundians, overawed by the sight of these great creations of work and prayer, brought their sons to him, lavished gifts upon him, and often came to ask him to cut their long hair, the sign of nobility and freedom, and admit them into the ranks of his army. Labour and prayer attained here, under the strong arm of Columbanus, to proportions up to that time unheard of. The multitude became so great that he could organize that perpetual service, called "Laus perennis," which already existed at Agaunum, on the other side of the Jura and Lake Leman, where, night and day, the voices of monks, "unwearied as those of angels," arose to celebrate the praises of God in an unending song.

Rich and poor were equally bound to agricultural labour. The toil of the hands was the sovereign receipt for spiritual languor and bodily sickness. When he issued on one occasion from his cave in the depths of the forest, and came to Luxeuil, he found a large number of monks in bed with influenza colds. He made them get up and go to the barn and thrash out wheat. The violent exercise opened their pores and expelled the fever. A monk named Theudegisl cut his thumb whilst reaping, and wanted to knock off work. Columbanus removed the blood with a little saliva, convinced himself that the wound was not serious, and made the man finish the work.

An article of his rule ordained that the monk should go to rest so fatigued that he would be ready to fall asleep on his way to bed, and should rise before he had slept off his weariness. It was at the cost of this excessive and perpetual labour that the wilderness which had spread over the ruins of Roman civilization was restored to cultivation and life.

Twenty years passed thus, during which the reputation of Columbanus increased and extended afar. But his influence was not undisputed. He displeased one portion of the Gallo-Frank clergy by the intemperate zeal with which he attempted, in his epistles, to remind the bishops of their duties, ostensibly by his obstinate adherence to Celtic peculiarities of tonsure and costume, and of the observance of Easter.

At a period when the most trifling ecclesiastical peculiarities were ranked as heresies of magnitude, such a divergence from established custom could not fail to serve as the opportunity for his enemies, and to weaken and embarrass his success. The details of his struggle with the bishops of Gaul remain unknown; but the resolution he displayed may be understood by some passages of his letters to the council which met to examine his conduct with respect to the observance of Easter. This was the council, apparently, held at Sens in 601, attended by Betharius, bishop of Chartres. The council was summoned in consequence of letters written by Pope Gregory the Great to Brunehild, to Virgilius of Arles, and others, to urge the extirpation of simony. S. Columbanus was invited to it to explain his conduct, and abandon his eccentricities. He did not attend, but he wrote to the council a letter, in which he requested the bishops not only to consider the question of Easter, but also the canonical observances which they themselves were guilty of neglecting. "I am not the author of this difference; I have come into these parts a poor stranger, for the cause of the Saviour Christ; I ask of your holinesses but a single favour, that you will permit me to live in silence in the depths of these forests, near the bones of seventeen brethren whom I have already seen die. I shall pray for you with those who remain with me, as I have done these twelve years . . . If God guides you to expel me from the desert which I have sought, I will say with Jonah, 'Take me up and cast me forth into the sea; so shall the sea be calm.' But before you throw me overboard, it is your duty to follow the example of sailors, and try first to reach the land; perhaps it may not be an excess of presumption if I suggest that many men follow the broad way, and that it is better to encourage those who follow the narrow way that leads to life than to throw stumbling blocks in their path."

Whatever was the result of this letter, or the decision of the council, S. Columbanus persevered in his paschal computation, and still annoyed the Gallican clergy by so doing. For the purpose of being protected from their attacks he had recourse to the then Pope, whether Sabinian or Boniface the third or fourth is uncertain, and sent him copies of his letters to Pope Gregory on the subject of Easter. He requested him to be allowed to follow the tradition of his forefathers, and said that he had no wish to disturb others in the observance of their customs.

A much more severe persecution awaited him, excited against him by the wicked queen-dowager Brunehild, the widow of Sigebert of Austrasia, and mother of Childebert, who became king of Burgundy and died in 596. Childebert left two sons, Theodebert, king of Austrasia, and Theodoric or Thierry, king of Burgundy, who succeeded him under the tutelage of their grand-mother. Brunehild lived with Theodebert, until, at the request of the nobles of Austrasia, he banished her. Then she fled to Thierry, by whom she was kindly received. Gregory of Tours has praised the beauty, good manners, prudence, and affability of Brunehild, and Gregory the Great congratulated the Franks on having so good a queen. But Brunehild, in her thirst for rule, endeavoured to divert her grandsons from political interests by leading them into the pursuit of sensual pleasures. From fear of having a rival in power and honour near the throne of Thierry, she opposed with all her might every attempt to replace the concubines she had given him by a legitimate queen, and when, finally, he determined on espousing a Visigothic princess, Brunehild, though herself the daughter of a Visigothic king, succeeded in disgusting her grandson with his bride, and made him repudiate her at the end of a year.

S. Desiderius, bishop of Vienne, who had advised the king to marry, was murdered by the ruffians whom Brunehild had laid in wait for him.

However, the young Thierry had religious instincts. He was rejoiced to possess in his kingdom so holy a man as Columbanus. He went often to visit him. Irish zeal took advantage of this to reprove him for his disorderly life, and to seek a lawful spouse, that the king might have a successor on his throne from an honourable queen, and not from a concubine. The young king promised amendment, but Brunehild easily turned him away from these good intentions. Columbanus having gone to visit her at Bourcheresse, she presented him the four sons of Thierry by his concubines. "What would these children with me?" he asked. "They are the sons of the king," answered the queen, "strengthen them with thy blessing." "No!" answered the abbot, "they shall not reign, for they are of bad origin." From that moment Brunehild swore war to the death against him. She despatched messengers with orders not to allow the monks to quit their monastery, and an injunction that others were not to give them hospitality, or offer them gifts. Columbanus went to Epoisses to see the king and appeal against this command. Thierry promised to remove the ban, and Columbanus returned to Luxeuil.

Theodoric continued his disorderly life, and Columbanus

wrote him a severe letter, threatening to separate himself from communion with the king unless he set a better moral example. This highly incensed Thierry and Brunehild, and the bishops who were angry at the paschal usages of the saint fanned their wrath. Thierry went to Luxeuil, and reproached Columbanus for refusing to allow the queen-dowager to cross the threshold of the monastery. The abbot replied that he must defend the rule of his monastery. He threatened the king with divine vengeance if he interfered with him, and Thierry, as superstitious as he was licentious, was frightened and withdrew. Shortly after, Columbanus was taken to Besançon, and was required to remain there till he learned the king's pleasure. Columbanus, finding means of escape, returned to Luxeuil. Brunehild and Thierry, apprized of his return, sent soldiers to remove him. And this, his final departure, took place in the twentieth year from his arrival in the Vosges, A.D. 610. The king gave orders that the saint and the Irish monks who were banished with him should be sent back to their own land.

They were conducted across France to Nantes, where they were placed on board a vessel destined for Ireland. At the mouth of the river the ship encountered the bore, which carried it over the banks and left it astrand. The superstitious sailors attributed this misfortune to the presence of the monks in their vessel, and refused to put to sea with them as passengers. Columbanus and his disciples were therefore left behind, and they returned to Nantes, whence the abbot addressed a letter to his monks at Luxeuil, bidding them obey Attalus, the abbot appointed in his room, and should difficulties arise on account of the paschal question, to leave their monastery and come to him rather than accept the Roman computation. Columbanus then took refuge with Clothair II., son of Chilperic, king of Soissons and Neustria. This son of Fredegund, faithful to his mother's hatred for Brunehild and her family, gave a cordial reception to the victim of his enemy, and at his request provided him with an escort to Theodebert, king of Austrasia, through whose states he desired to pass on his way to Italy. On his road the Frank chiefs brought their children to receive his benediction. Theodebert, now at war with his brother Thierry, received Columbanus with great cordiality, and endeavoured to persuade him to settle under his protection. But the saint would not be detained. He had spent sixty years of labour in the vain attempt to reform kings and nations who called themselves Christians, and now he resolved on turning to a new field of labour—mission-work among the heathen. He accordingly embarked on the Rhine below Mainz, and ascending the Rhine and Lammat to the Lake of Zürich, remained for a while at Tuggen.

A strange tale is told of a huge vat of beer, offered to the God Woden, which burst at the mere breath of Columbanus. S. Gall, his companion, set the temples at Tuggen on fire, and threw the idols into the lake. The monks were compelled to fly; and Columbanus left the pagans of that district with a most unapostolic malediction, devoting their whole race to temporal misery and eternal perdition.[1] They retreated to Arbon, on the Lake of Constance; there they heard of a ruined Roman city at the head of the lake, named Brigantium (Bregentz). At Bregentz Columbanus found a ruined church dedicated to S. Aurelia, which he rebuilt. But the chief objects of worship in the re-paganized land were three statues of gilded brass. S. Gall broke the idols and threw them into the water. The narrative of this mission has already been given at large in the life of S. Gall, and need not be repeated here in anything like

---

[1] "Fiant nati eorum in interitum ; ergo ad mediam ætatem cum pervenerint stupor ac dementia eos apprehendant, ita ut alieno ære oppressi, ignominiam suam agnoscant conversi."—Vit. S. Galli, ap. Pertz, ii. p. 7.

detail. The apostles found the Suevi and Allemanns worshippers of Woden, and stubborn in their opposition to the Gospel.

During his sojourn at Bregentz, Columbanus went to see King Theodebert, who was still at war with his brother the king of Burgundy. Knowing by his visit to Thierry that the power of the latter was sufficient to overwhelm the Austrasian kingdom, he counselled Theodebert to abandon the unequal contest and take refuge in the cloister. His advice provoked an outburst of laughter. " Such a thing is unheard of," said the courtiers, " that a Frank king should become a monk of his own free will." " Well," said the saint, " if he will not be a monk voluntarily, he will be made one by force." So saying he returned to Bregentz. The battle of Tolbiac ruined the hopes of Theodebert, who was forced to assume the monastic habit, and was shortly after put to death.

The whole of Austrasia had fallen by the defeat and death of Theodebert into the hands of Brunehild and Thierry, and the banks of the Upper Rhine, where their victim had found a refuge, had passed under their sway. It was no longer safe for Columbanus to remain there, and accompanied by a single disciple, Attalus, he crossed the Alps and sought refuge with Agilulf, king of the Lombards.

He arrived at Milan in 612, after having spent but one year at Bregentz. While at Milan, Columbanus wrote against the Arian heresy with which the Lombards were infected. The schism of the Three Chapters was still distracting the North of Italy, although the chapters had been condemned by the Council of Constantinople in 553. The bishops of Istria and Africa refused to acknowledge this condemnation, because they thought it threw discredit on the Council of Chalcedon. The Lombards sided with the Istrian prelates, and were therefore involved in their schism. Gregory the

Great wisely let the matter drop—it was a tempest about a trifle; but Boniface IV. was not disposed to allow the question to sleep and expire. He stirred it up again, and Agilulf and his queen, Theodelinda, engaged Columbanus to write to the Pope in defence of the Three Chapters. Evidently little acquainted in his own person with the point at issue, Columbanus rushed into the controversy with his usual impetuosity. Whilst appealing in a series of extravagant and obscure apostrophes, to the indulgence of the Pope for "a foolish Scot," charged to write on account of a Lombard, a king of the Gentiles, he acquaints the Pontiff with the imputations brought against him and the chair of S. Peter, as fautors of heresy, and urges him to prove his orthodoxy by excommunicating his detractors. Pope Vigilius, he says, prevaricated; he was the cause of the whole scandal.[1]

Rome he acknowledges as the head of all churches, saving only the prerogatives of Jerusalem. He warns the Pope not by his perversity to lose his high privileges and dignity. For power was his only so long as exercised aright—the keys were only his to lock and unlock justly.[2]

He tells Boniface that the Irish were orthodox believers, constantly adhering to the faith and apostolic tradition, which they had received from their forefathers, and that they never had among them heretics, Jews, or schismatics. "I confess that I lament over the bad reputation of the chair of S. Peter in this country. I speak to you not as a stranger, but as a disciple, as a friend, as a servant. I speak freely

---

[1] "Vigila itaque quæso, Papa, vigila quia forte non bene vigilavit Vigilius, quem caput scandali ipsi clamant, qui vobis culpam injiciunt."
[2] "Roma orbis terrarum caput est ecclesiarum, salva loci Dominicæ resurrectionis singulari prærogativa. Et ideo sicut magnus honor vester est pro dignitate cathedræ, ita magna cura vobis necessaria est, ut non perdatis vestram dignitatem propter aliquam perversitatem. Tamdiu enim potestas apud vos erit, quamdiu recta ratio permanserit. Ille enim certus regni cœlorum claviculcrius est qui dignis per veram scientiam aperit, et indignis claudit. Alioquin, si contraria fecerit, nec aperire nec claudere poterit."

to our masters, to the pilots of the vessel of the Church, and I say to them, Watch! and despise not the humble advice of the stranger . . . . Pardon me if swimming among rocks, I have said words offensive to pious ears. The native liberty of my race has given me this boldness. With us it is not the person, it is the right, which prevails. The love of evangelical peace makes me say everything. We are bound to the chair of S. Peter; for, however great and glorious Rome may be, it is this chair which makes her great and glorious among us."

Agilulf bestowed on Columbanus the land of Bobbio, among the Apennines, between Genoa and Milan. Columbanus founded there a monastery. Despite his age, he shared in the builder's labour, and bent his old shoulders under beams of firwood, which he transported from the mountain slopes on which they were felled to the spot where his abbey rose. Bobbio was his last stage. Thierry died, Brunehild and the four sons of Thierry fell into the hands of Clothair II., who tortured to death the aged queen, and executed her two eldest grandsons. Clothair, on becoming sole king of Austrasia, Burgundy, and Neustria, sent Eustace, abbot of Luxeuil, to Bobbio, to recall Columbanus to France. But the old abbot refused the call; he answered it in a letter full of advice.

He was now very aged. On the opposite bank of the Trebbia to his abbey of Bobbio, he had found a cavern in a rock. This he transformed into a chapel dedicated to the B. Virgin. There he passed the remainder of his days in prayer, visiting his monastery only on Sundays and festivals, and there he died on November 21st, 615, when over seventy-two years old. He was buried at Bobbio, and many miracles, it is asserted, were performed at his tomb.

November 22.

SS. PHILEMON AND APPIA, *MM. at Colossæ;* 1st cent.
S. CÆCILIA, *V.M. at Rome;* 3rd cent.
S. MAURUS, *M. at Rome;* A.D. 283.[1]
SS. MARCUS AND STEPHEN, *MM. at Antioch in Pisidia;* A.D. 303.
S. PRAGMATIUS, *B. of Autun; circ.* A.D. 520.

SS. PHILEMON AND APPIA, MM.

(IST CENT.)

[Modern Roman Martyrology. Greek Menæas and Menologies, together with Archippus, who receives commemoration in the Roman Kalendar on March 30. Authority:—The traditional account in the Menology, of little authority.]

HILEMON was probably a native of Colossæ; at all events, he lived there when S. Paul wrote to him during his first captivity at Rome, A.D. 63, or early in A.D. 62.

S. Paul associates Archippus, who was a Colossian, with Philemon at the beginning of his letter. It is evident from this letter that Philemon was a man of property and influence, since he is represented as the head of a numerous household, and as exercising an expensive liberality towards his friends and the poor in general. He was indebted to the Apostle Paul for his conversion. His slave Onesimus having run away, S. Paul wrote the letter to Philemon to effect a reconciliation after he had converted and baptized Onesimus. The pseudo Dorothæus makes Philemon bishop of Gaza. Hippolytus confirms this assertion—that is, one worthless

---

[1] A fabulous personage, see SS. Chrysanthus and Daria, Oct. 25, p. 624 *et seq.*

witness supports another. But the Clementine Constitutions (vii. 46) say that he was ordained bishop of Colossæ.

The Menology of Basil affirms that he suffered martyrdom at Ephesus in the reign of Nero; but the usually accepted story, drafted into the Roman Martyrology, is that he and his wife Appia were arrested by the pagans of Colossæ during the celebration of a festival of Diana, were scourged by order of the governor, Artoclus, and then buried up to their waists in the soil, and stoned to death.

S. CÆCILIA, V.M.

(3RD CENT.)

[Roman Martyrology. Greek Menæas and Menologies. Usuardus, Ado, Notker, &c. Anglican Reformed Kalendar, and all Western Kalendars after 9th cent. Not in the Roman 4th cent. Kalendar, published by Bucherius, nor in the 5th cent. Carthaginian Kalendar. Authority :—The Greek Acts in Metaphrastes.]

In the 4th century appeared a Greek religious romance on the Loves of Cæcilia and Valerian, written, like those of Chrysanthus and Daria, Julian and Basilissa, in glorification of the virginal life, and with the purpose of taking the place of the sensual romances of Daphnis and Chloe, Chereas and Callirhoe, &c., which were then popular. There may have been a foundation of fact on which the story was built up; but the Roman Kalendar of the 4th century, and the Carthaginian Kalendar of the 5th, make no mention of Cæcilia. It is said, however, that there was a church dedicated to S. Cæcilia in Rome in the 5th century, in which Pope Symmachus held a council in 500. But Symmachus held no council in that year. That held at Easter, 501, was in the "basilica Julii;" that on September 1, 501, was held in the "basilica Sessoriana;" that on October 23, 501, was in "porticu

S. CÆCILIA. Nov. 22.

beati Petri apostoli quæ appellatur Palmaria." The next synod, November 6, 502, met in the church of S. Peter; that in 533, "ante confessionem beati Petri;" and that in 504 also in the basilica of S. Peter. Consequently, till better evidence is produced, we must conclude that S. Cæcilia was not known or venerated in Rome till about the time when Pope Gelasius (496) introduced her name into his Sacramentary. In 821, however, there was an old church fallen into decay with the dedication to S. Cæcilia; but Pope Paschal I. dreamed that the body of the saint lay in the cemetery of S. Calixtus, along with that of her husband Valerian. He accordingly looked for them and found them, or, at all events, some bodies, as was probable, in the catacombs, which he was pleased to regard as those of Cæcilia and Valerian. And he translated these relics to the church of S. Cæcilia, and founded a monastery in their honour.

The story of S. Cæcilia is not without beauty and merit. There was in the city of Rome a virgin named Cæcilia, who was given in marriage to a youth named Valerian. She wore sackcloth next her skin, and fasted, and invoked the saints and angels and virgins, beseeching them to guard her virginity. And she said to her husband, "I will tell you a secret if you will swear not to reveal it to any one." And when he swore, she added, "There is an angel who watches me, and wards off from me any who would touch me." He said, "Dearest, if this be true, show me the angel." "That can only be if you will believe in one God, and be baptized."

She sent him to Pope S. Urban (223-230), who baptized him; and when he returned, he saw Cæcilia praying in her chamber, and an angel by her with flaming wings, holding two crowns of roses and lilies, which he placed on their heads, and then vanished. Shortly after, Tibertius, the brother of Valerian, entered, and wondered at the fragrance and beauty of the flowers at that season of the year.

When he heard the story of how they had obtained these crowns, he also consented to be baptized. After their baptism the two brothers devoted themselves to burying the martyrs slain daily by the prefect of the city, Turcius Almachius.[1] They were arrested and brought before the prefect, and when they refused to sacrifice to the gods were executed with the sword.

In the meantime, S. Cæcilia, by preaching, had converted four hundred persons, whom Pope Urban forthwith baptized. Then Cæcilia was arrested, and condemned to be suffocated in the baths. She was shut in for a night and a day, and the fires were heaped up, and made to glow and roar their utmost, but Cæcilia did not even break out into perspiration through the heat.[2] When Almachius heard this he sent an executioner to cut off her head in the bath. The man struck thrice without being able to sever the head from the trunk. He left her bleeding, and she lived three days. Crowds came to her, and collected her blood with napkins and sponges, whilst she preached to them or prayed. At the end of that period she died, and was buried by Pope Urban and his deacons.

Alexander Severus, who was emperor when Urban was Pope, did not persecute the Church, though it is possible some Christians may have suffered in his reign. Herodian says that no person was condemned during the reign of Alexander, except according to the usual course of the law, and by judges of the strictest integrity. A few Christians may have suffered, but there can have been no furious persecutions, such as is described in the Acts as waged by the apocryphal prefect, Turcius Almachius.

Urbanus was the prefect of the city, and Ulpian, who had much influence at the beginning of Alexander's reign as

---

[1] There was no prefect of that name.
[2] "Nulla pars omnino ex ejus membris vel minimo sudoris signo fuit humectata."

The Marriage Feast.   S. CÆCILIA.   "I will tell you a secret."

Nov. 22.

principal secretary of the emperor and commander of the Prætorian Guards, is thought to have encouraged persecution. Usuardus makes Cæcilia suffer under Commodus. Molanus transfers the martyrdom to the reign of Marcus Aurelius. But it is idle to expect to extract history from romance.

In 1599 Cardinal Paul Emilius Sfondrati, nephew of Pope Gregory XIV., rebuilt the church of S. Cæcilia.

S. Cæcilia is regarded as the patroness of music, and is represented in art with an organ or organ-pipes in her hand.

November 23.

S. Clement, *B.M. of Rome*; circ. A.D. 100.
S. Felicitas, *M. at Rome*; A.D. 164.[1]
S. Lucretia, *V.M. at Merida in Spain*; circ. A.D. 303.
S. Sisinius, *M. at Cyzicus in Helespont*; circ. A.D. 304.
S. Amphilochius, *B. of Iconium*; circ. A.D. 394.
S. Trudo, *or* Trond, *P.C. in Belgium*; A.D. 698.
S. Rachildis, *V.R. at S. Gall in Switzerland*; circ. A.D. 930.
S. Alexander Nevski, *C. at Vladimir in Russia*; A.D. 1263
S. John the Good, *C. at Mantua*; 13th cent.

S. CLEMENT, B.M.

(ABOUT A.D. 100.)

[Roman Martyrology. Bede, Ado, Usuardus, Notker, &c. The 4th cent. Kalendar, published by Bucherius, the 5th cent. Carthaginian Kalendar. By the Greeks on Jan. 30, April 22, Sept. 30, Nov. 24 and 25. Authorities:—Irenæus, Adv. hær. lib. iii. c. 3; Euseb. H. E. iii. 16; Hieron, Catal. Scr. Eccl. 15, &c.]

LITTLE is known of this apostolic father beyond a few facts. He was a disciple of S. Peter, and perhaps of S. Paul. It is thought that the Clement whom S. Paul praises as a faithful fellow-worker, whose name is written in the Book of Life, was Clement, afterwards bishop of Rome. But there is great difficulty in admitting this supposition. It is certain that Clement, the idol of the Petrine party in the Primitive Church, about whom their myths and traditions circled lovingly, was quite removed in feeling from the Pauline party.

According to Tertullian, Clement succeeded S. Peter im-

---

[1] See July 10.

S. CÆCILIA. The Angel's Visit. The Brother's Conversion.

Nov. 22.

mediately in the episcopal government of the Church at Rome. But in the list of bishops given us by Irenæus and Eusebius he occupies the third place after the apostle, that is, after Linus and Cletus (Anacletus). It is, however, probable that the Church at Rome had at first two successions, one Petrine, the other Pauline, but that they speedily merged into one; and this will account for the confusion in the lists of the first bishops of Rome. Clement probably was Petrine, and Cletus Pauline bishop, the former ruling the converted Jews, the latter the Gentile converts. We know nothing of the events of his pontificate, except that there was a schism at Corinth, which drew forth a letter from him which is preserved. S. Jerome and S. Irenæus do not say that he died a martyr's death, but Rufinus and Zosimus give him the title of martyr; but this title by no means implies that he had died for the faith; it had anciently a more extended signification than at present, and included all who had witnessed a good confession, and suffered in any way for their faith.

This is all that we know of S. Clement. But imagination has spun a web of romance about his person.

The Clementine Recognitions and Homilies are an early romance representing the disputation of S. Peter and Simon Magus; they have a story running through them to hold the long disquisitions together, of which S. Clement is the hero. It is, however, pure romance, with, perhaps, only this basis of truth in it, that Clement is represented as the devoted adherent and disciple of S. Peter. The Clementines are thoroughly anti-Pauline, as are also the Apostolic Constitutions, in which again S. Clement appears prominently.

The legend of the martyrdom of S. Clement relates that, in the reign of Trajan, when Mamertinus was prefect of the city, and Toractianus count of the offices, a sedition arose among the rabble of Rome against the Christians, and especially against Clement, bishop of Rome. Mamertinus interfered to put down the riot, and, having arrested Clement, sent him to the emperor, who ordered his banishment to Pontus, where he was condemned to work in the marble quarries. He found many Christians among his fellow-convicts, and comforted and encouraged them. The only spring of drinking-water was six miles off, and it was a great hardship to the convicts to have to fetch it all from such a distance. One day Clement saw a lamb scraping at the soil with one of its forefeet. He took it as a sign that water was there; dug, and found a spring.

As Clement succeeded in converting many pagans, he was sent to Aufidianus, the prefect, who ordered him to be drowned in the sea with an old anchor attached to his neck. His body was recovered by his disciple Phœbus. The relics of S. Clement were translated to Constantinople (860) by S. Cyril on his return from his mission to the Chazars, whilst engaged in the Chersonese on his Sclavonic translation of the Gospels.[1] Some of the relics found their way to Rome, and were deposited in the church of San Clemente, where they are still reverently preserved. These consist of bones, some reddened earth, a broken vase containing some red matter, a little bottle similarly filled, and an inscription stating that these are the relics of the Holy Forty Martyrs of Scillita, and also of Flavius Clement.

In art S. Clement of Rome is represented as a Pope with an anchor at his side.

[1] See March 9, p. 177.

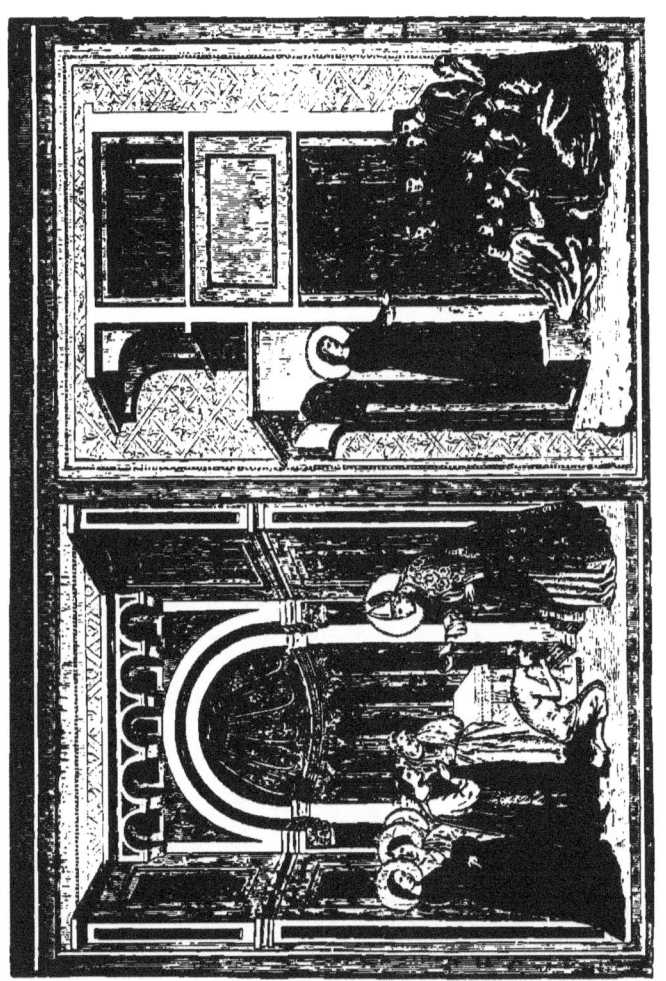

Nov. 22.

Her Husband is Baptized. S. CÆCILIA. She converts Four Hundred.

S. AMPHILOCHIUS, B.

(ABOUT A.D. 394.)

[Roman Martyrology, from Greek Menæa and Menologies. But the Menology of Basil on Oct. 19, and the 10th cent. Gallipolitan Synaxarium, and the Greek Synaxaria in the Florentine Library, on Dec. 10. Authorities :—His own letters and those of S. Basil ; Sozomen, Theodoret, Socrates, &c.]

ON the death of Faustinus, bishop of Iconium, in 374, Amphilochius, a friend of S. Basil, and most probably first cousin of S. Gregory Nazianzen, was elected to fill the vacant see. He was a native of Cappadocia, of noble family, and much younger than his two illustrious friends. He had studied elocution, and had exercised his talents as a lawyer, acquiring fame for his eloquence and for his integrity. After awhile he retired into a solitude in Cappadocia. He was elected and consecrated bishop against his will, and to the extreme annoyance of his father, who had other prospects for him. S. Basil wrote to Amphilochius on his ordination, to encourage and console him, to advise him, and express his desire to confer by word of mouth with him. Being himself too aged to visit him, he begged Amphilochius to seek him at Cæsarea. Amphilochius did so, and preached there. At the request of his guest, S. Basil wrote his work on the Holy Spirit. The occasion of this was that Basil had in public exclaimed, "Glory to the Father, with the Son, and with the Holy Ghost," and at another time, " Glory to the Father by the Son, in the Holy Ghost." Some were scandalized, thinking this latter exclamation unsound. S. Basil wrote to Amphilochius three canonical epistles on penitential discipline.

On the death of S. Basil, Amphilochius pronounced his funeral panegyric. He attended the council of Constantinople in 381. Amphilochius was desirous of obtaining a law restraining the Arians and other heretics, and forbidding them the right to assemble for worship. Theodosius, the emperor, had the good sense at first to refuse to commit such an act of intolerance and injustice. Amphilochius gained his end by a curious expedient.

Theodosius had declared Arcadius his son Augustus, in the January of 383. Arcadius was then only six years old. S. Amphilochius having come to the palace with other bishops to pay their respects to the emperor, disregarded Arcadius, who was seated near his father. Theodosius thought the bishop acted by inadvertence, and reminded him of his neglect. Then the bishop of Iconium stroked the cheek of the little Augustus with his finger, and said, "Good day, my child." The emperor, highly incensed, ordered the old man to be driven from his presence. As he reached the door, Amphilochius turned and cried, "Thou, sire, canst not endure that thy son should not receive the honour due to him; how, then, can God the Father bear that His Son should be disregarded?" Theodosius was struck with the words of the prelate, and passed in September, 383, the law forbidding the heretics to worship God in public or in private.

In the same year Amphilochius held a council at Sida against the Messalians; he attended the council of Constantinople in 394, and died apparently shortly after. He left several writings which were greatly esteemed, but only scanty portions of them have remained.

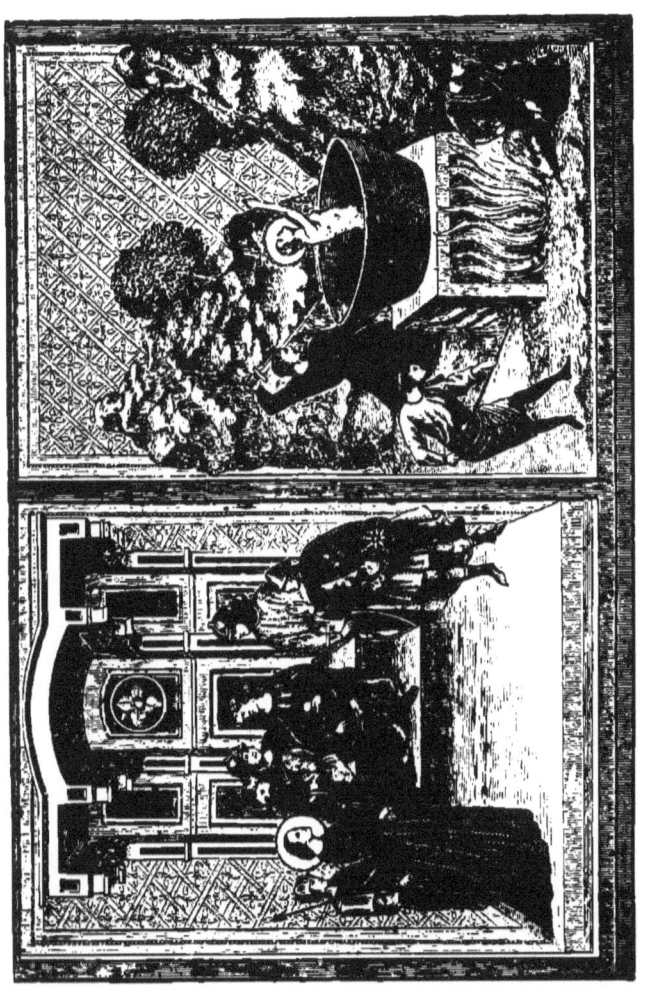

Brought before the Roman Prefect. S. CÆCILIA. Suffers Martyrdom.

Nov. 22.

S. TRUDO, P.C.

(ABOUT A.D. 698.)

[Roman and Belgian Martyrologies. Usuardus, Ado, Florus, Wandelbert, &c. Authority :—A Life by Donatus, deacon (of Metz?), written in the 8th cent., in Mabillon, Acta SS. O.S.B. sec. ii. p. 1069-1086. There is another Life, by Theodoric, abbot of S. Trond (d. 1107), but it is a mere rewriting of the earlier Life. Also a notice of the saint in the "Gesta abbatum Trudonensium," written in 1108 by the Abbot Rudolf. This is of no value compared to the Life by Donatus.]

S. TRUDO, commonly called S. Trond, was born of noble and wealthy Frank parents in Hesbain. From childhood he devoted himself to the service of God. It is said that even as a little boy he amused himself with constructing an oratory of stones on a bit of waste ground, in which he might pray. A woman thinking him a little fool, one day kicked his walls down. When Trudo's father died, and he succeeded to his estates and fortune, he went, at the advice of S. Remacle, to Chlodulf, bishop of Metz, and was by him ordained priest. He made over all his fortune and lands to the church of S. Stephen at Metz, and then returned to S. Remacle, and built a church at the place which now bears his name, S. Trond, in honour of S. Quentin. He died in the odour of sanctity at the age of sixty-five, and his relics are preserved at S. Trond.

S. ALEXANDER NEVSKI, C.

(A.D. 1263.)

[Russian Kalendar. He died on Nov. 14, but was buried on Nov. 23 at Vladimir; his translation to S. Petersburg on Aug. 30 (1724). Authorities :—Chron. Sophrense ; Karasmen, " Hist. Imp. Russ. ;" Mouravieff, " Hist. Eastern Church," &c.]

ALEXANDER I., son of Yaroslaff II., prince of Novgorod, was born on May 30, 1221. His country was in a condition of affliction after the ravages of the Great Horde. The towns were reduced to ruins, the inhabitants were hiding in the forests, the churches were in ashes and the priests slain. Yaroslaff could only exercise his office under the consent of the Mongol invaders, who had settled in the neighbourhood of Novgorod. Yaroslaff II. died in 1246, and was succeeded by his son Isyaslaff (Michael), who was killed in an engagement with the Lithuanians in 1248. His brother, Andrew II., then ascended the throne, but the khan of the Mongols expelled him the country in 1252, and then Alexander, his younger brother, became prince. Alexander had fought a battle in 1241 against the Swedes, on the banks of the Neva, and this victory procured for him the cognomen of Nevski. Pope Innocent IV. wrote to him in the hopes of drawing him into communion with Rome, but his letter produced no results. The papal legates visited his court, and urged the advantage that might accrue to him from union with the West, but in vain.

He died in 1263, on his return from an expedition to the Golden Horde. He invested himself with the monastic habit on his death-bed.

November 24.

S. FIRMINA, *V.M. at Ameria in Italy*; A.D. 303.
S. CHRYSOGONUS, *M. at Aquileja*; A.D. 304.
S. CRESCENTIANUS, *M. at Rome*; A.D. 310.[1]
S. PROTASIUS, *B. of Milan*; A.D. 352.
S. ALEXANDER, *M. at Corinth*; circ. A.D. 362.
S. ROMANUS, *P.C. at Blaye on the Garonne*; A.D. 385.
SS. ARETHAS AND COMP. *MM. in Arabia Felix*; A.D. 523.
S. PORTIANUS, *Ab. in Auvergne*; circ. A.D. 527.
S. MARINUS, *H. at S. Jean-de-Maurienne*; A.D. 731.
SS. FLORA AND MARY, *VV. MM. at Cordova*; A.D. 851.
S. JOHN OF THE CROSS, *C. at Ubeda in Spain*; A.D. 1591.

S. CHRYSOGONUS, M.

(A.D. 304.)

[Roman Martyrology. Usuardus, Ado, &c. The Carthaginian Kalendar of the 5th cent. Authority:—The not trustworthy Acts of S. Anastasia.]

CHRYSOGONUS was arrested at Rome in the persecution of Diocletian, and put in prison. S. Anastasia, a holy Roman lady, corresponded with him by letter, as to her conduct towards an unbelieving husband. He was conducted to Aquileja, where Diocletian then was, and was there executed. His head is shown enshrined in the church of his dedication at Rome, but his body is preserved at Venice.

[1] Apocryphal, known only from the fabulous Acts of S. Marcellus.

SS. ARETHAS AND COMP. MM.

(A.D. 523.)

[Ethiopic Kalendar on Nov. 24 and 26. But the Senkessar or Abyssinian Synaxarium, edited by Sapetus, on Nov. 22 and 24. In the 8th cent. S. Arethas occurs in the Constantinopolitan Menology on Oct. 24. So also Metaphrastes, and the Russian Kalendar. Menology of Basil; Ruthenian Kalendar. The Coptic Kalendar and the Sacred Kalendar of the monastery of S. Sabas near Jerusalem, drawn up by S. Sabas in 532. The Marble Kalendar of Naples of the 9th cent. The modern Roman Martyrology, however, on July 27: "Among the Hemeritæ the commemoration of the holy martyrs who were cast into the flames for the faith of Christ under the tyrant Dunaan." Authorities:—The Arabic historians Nuweir, Abulfeda, Hamza, Tabeir. Also Simeon Betharsamensis, who wrote in 524, while the persecution was still raging, and who was in Arabia at the time. His account is in Syriac. Johan. Asiæ Episcop. (op. Asseman, t. i.), John Malala, Nicephorus, Callistus, Cedrenus, Arabian accounts in d'Herbelot, "Bibliothèque Orientale," under the head of Abu-Nanàs, and the Greek Acts of the Martyrs, written certainly before 597, and probably before 565. An Armenian version exists in the book Djarrentir. The Greek Acts, and Armenian Acts, are both apparently translations from a Syriac or Arabic original. They are trustworthy.[1] The part concerning S. Arethas was certainly written shortly after 523, but the conclusion was added later, but before 597.]

THE peninsula of Arabia was divided by the old geographers into three parts: the desert plains of the north-east, which bordered on the Euphrates and the Syrian frontier, the province of Petræa, at the northern extremity of the Red Sea; and the richer and more extensive tracts of Arabia Felix. This latter division is chiefly included by native writers under the comprehensive term of Yemen, which in signification coincides with its Roman epithet. On the north the territories of Yemen extended into the mountain ranges of the interior, and were bounded perhaps by the exten-

---

[1] Some use has been made, in compiling this sketch, of Wright's "Early Christianity in Arabia," London, 1855.

sive deserts that spread out towards the Persian Gulf; on the west and south it was separated from Africa by the Red Sea; and the eastern coasts were washed by the waves of the Southern Ocean. The inhabitants of this fertile district differed widely in their character from the wandering Arabs of the desert. They were subject to kings, governed by laws, and enjoyed all the advantages of social life.

Arabia Felix contained several petty States, governed by their own princes, but all were subject to the king of Hamyar, who was called the Great King, and whose influence extended from the Red Sea to the Persian Gulf.

At what period Christianity was first introduced into Arabia Felix it is now impossible to determine, but probably it was not till long after it had spread over the neighbouring nations. From the little connection which existed between the inhabitants of Yemen and the rest of the world, the old Sabæan religion would probably remain long unexposed to invasion of hostile faiths. At the time of the introduction of Christianity, the Jews appear to have penetrated into the peninsula in great numbers, and to have formed also a great impediment to its progress. The first rudiments of the Christian faith are believed traditionally to have been planted among the Hamyarites, who were known, in common with the people of Hindustan and Ethiopia, under the general name of Indians, by the apostle Bartholomew.[1] Frumentius and Edesius (see Oct. 27) greatly advanced the faith in Hamyar in the 4th century. The troubles which affected Arabia Felix in the 5th century, were favourable to the extension of Christianity in the peninsula, and the tolerant spirit of Arabian idolatry afforded equally a safe asylum to the persecuted disciples of Zoroaster, numbers of whom settled in Bahhrein, to the Jew, and to the fugitive Christian.

As long as the kings of Hamyar adhered to their ancient

[1] Euseb. H. E. iii. 1; Assemani, Biblioth. Orient. t. iii. p. dxcii

superstitions, each of these sects was allowed the free exercise of its religious ceremonies, and the public profession of its faith. But no sooner did the followers of Judaism gain power, than the disciples of Jesus, whom they considered as their bitterest enemies, began to experience their resentment. The causes which drew upon the Christians of Arabia Felix the enmity of the king, Dzu Nowass,[1] are variously reported by the Arabian historians, but the most credible are agreed that he was excited to the persecution of them by his Jewish advisers and subjects.

The Nadjash, or king of Abyssinia, who was contemporary with Dzu Nowass, is called in the Ethiopian histories Caleb, by the Greek historians Elesbaan, or Hellesthæus. Although we discover few traces of it in any historian, yet it is probable that the Hamyarites and their Ethiopian neighbours were often at war. The king of Auxuma appears, from an inscription recently discovered at Axum, to have laid claim to the kingdom of Hamyar as early as this period, and the war which ended in the conquest of Yemen was perhaps only a renewal of the national quarrel.

On the breaking out of the persecution of the Christians of Hamyar, by Dzu Nowass, the Roman merchants engaged in the Ethiopian trade were among the first who experienced its effects. The rich merchandize contained in their caravans naturally excited the cupidity of the persecutors; the injuries which the Jews were represented to have suffered under the dominion of Rome, were eagerly embraced as a pretext by a king who had embraced Judaism, and under the pretence of retaliation, the caravans were stopped and plundered on their passage over the mountains, and the merchants put to death. The Abyssinian king was not slow in resenting the injury which his kingdom sustained by the interruption of the Roman trade. Messengers were de-

---

[1] In the Roman Martyrology called Dunaamus.

spatched to the Tobbaa, or chief king of Hamyar, to expostulate, but without effect, and they were immediately followed by a powerful army. After a long and obstinate war, the king of Hamyar was reduced to the humiliating terms of paying tribute to the Abyssinian conqueror.

Although the Abyssinians had long embraced Christianity, it does not appear to have been openly avowed by the royal family, at least all the old historians are agreed that Elesbaan was not a Christian. Theophanes calls him a Jew. Influenced, however, by his commercial alliance with the emperor, and his profitable trade with the Christians, he appears to have been always favourably inclined towards them, and when he undertook the invasion of Hamyar, he had made a vow that, should he succeed in his enterprise, he would openly receive the religion of Christ, for it was, he said, in the cause of the Christians that he had taken up arms.[1] Soon after the Abyssinian forces had been withdrawn from Arabia, Dzu Nowass suddenly raised an army, and defeated those who had been left to secure the conquests of the Nadjash. No sooner had he thus regained possession of his hereditary kingdom, than the Tobbaa prepared to wreak his vengeance on the now defenceless Christians, and all who refused to renounce their faith and embrace Judaism were put to death, without respect to age or sex.

The town of Nadjran, on the north of Yemen, was inhabited by the Benni Hâleb, who had embraced the religion of Jesus, according to Arabian historians, at the preaching of a Syrian missionary. It was under the jurisdiction of a bishop, and had a church which was frequented by many Christians from the various Arabian tribes. Against this place Dzu Nowass is said to have been instigated by the Jews of Yatreb. On his arrival before it, he found it surrounded by a wall and ditch, and the whole town in arms,

[1] For his Life see Oct. 27.

prepared to oppose him. He sent a herald into the city, bearing a cross on a pole, with the message, "Whosoever will not show insult to this sign, shall be destroyed by fire and sword. Whosoever remains Christian, whosoever has been left by the Ethiopian king in this land, and every monk, shall perish by fire and sword. The churches shall be burnt and reduced to powder. Therefore, citizens of Nadjran, choose my favour, or your religion of the Crucified." The citizens sternly refused to abandon their religion, and the Tobbaa laid siege to the place with a large army, ravaging the surrounding country. Finding, however, from the firmness and bravery of the Christians of Nadjran, that he was not very likely to succeed by force, he had recourse to treachery; and on his taking a solemn oath that he would not injure one of the inhabitants, but would allow them the peaceful exercise of their religion, if they would open the gate, and pay him an annual tribute, the town of Nadjran was surrendered.

The king of Hamyar disguised his treachery no longer than was necessary to gain the object which he had in view by it. Nadjran was plundered by his troops. The chief men of the town, with their prince, who is called in the Greek Acts Arethas, son of Chreph, but who is named by the Arabian writers, Abdallah Ibn Althamir, a man distinguished for his wisdom and piety, were thrown into chains. The Tobbaa next sought the bishop, whose name was Paul, and when informed that he had died two years previous, he ordered his bones to be disinterred and burnt, and the ashes to be scattered to the winds. On the following day the soldiers were occupied in digging large pits and filling them with fuel; fire was set to the wood, and all the priests, deacons, and other ministers of the church in Nadjran were cast into the flames, together with those who led an eremitical life in the neighbourhood, and the consecrated virgins, and "the female singers, who sang day and night in the houses of God." All these, to the number of 427, were burned alive without trial,[1] the king hoping thereby to strike terror into the minds of the Christians.

Finding them still firm, the Tobbaa collected men, women, and children, to the number of 4,252, if we may trust the author of the Acts, and his account is confirmed by Arab historians, who say that there were many thousands.[2] These were given over to indiscriminate slaughter by the soldiery. The wives and children of the chief citizens he brought before their husbands and fathers, in hopes that compassion for their weakness might move the latter to apostacy. But the heroic women implored their husbands to remain constant to Christ, and protested their readiness to die for their faith. And the children, weeping, echoed their mothers' words.

Along with these matrons were ten religious women, consecrated to God. The tyrant bade his soldiers drag the women away by their hair to the place of execution. On reaching it, the nuns stood forward and claimed their right, as dedicated virgins, to lead the way through the Red Sea of Blood to the heavenly mansions.

"Nay," said the others, "rather let us die first, that we may stand as a great company of witnesses about our husbands and sons as they die for Christ."

The soldiers fell on them indiscriminately and smote off their heads.

Ruma, a widow, the woman of highest rank in the city, was taken along with her two daughters, and brought before Dzu Nowass. She was a woman of singular beauty, and her daughters had inherited her loveliness. John of Asia has preserved a letter of the king's to the mondar of Hirah,

---

[1] In his letter to the mondar of Hirah, King Dzu Nowass says, "I killed as many as 180 priests."

[2] Tabari, a Mussulman writer of the 9th cent., in his Chronicle, says that 20,000 Christians were martyred.

giving an account of this butchery; in it he writes: "I swear by Adonai, that I am exceedingly grieved when I think of her beauty, and of that of her daughters." The king hoped to obtain her recantation of Christianity. But she, finding that she was spared when the other women were massacred, requested that she might be brought before the Tobbaa. "Then," says the Acts, "she was led by the servants of the king, under an umbrella; for she had never been exposed to the sun, except when it shone through a window." And she stood before the king, and he said to her: "Madam, you are a woman of great rank and wealth, of high family, and very beautiful. Since your husband's death you have remained unmarried, though you have a large fortune, and as many as three hundred serving-men in your house. Obey now my advice: abandon your trust in the Crucified, come to my palace, and become my queen."

"I cannot have any portion with a man who does not share my faith," she answered, firmly.

The king then ordered her and her daughters to be unveiled before every one. The command was executed, their faces were exposed, and their long hair unbound. Many Jewesses and other women present wailed and commiserated them. The younger daughter, a girl aged twelve, turned and spat at the king. Then the tyrant gave a signal, and first the heads of the daughters, then that of their mother were struck off.

Arethas and his companions were next urged to apostacy. But the sight of the heroic constancy of the women nerved them to play the man. The king condescended to argue with them. God, he said, was incorporeal, and could not therefore be crucified and slain. Christ could not therefore be regarded as God, but as a human being. Dzu Nowass then assured them he had no desire to make them worship the sun and the moon, or any created thing, but the One God who

had produced all things, and was the Father of all generation.
But his insidious arguments were treated with contempt, and
Arethas declared that he and his companions were all ready
to die in the cause of their Saviour. The Tobbaa accordingly
ordered them to be conducted to the side of a small brook
or wady, in the neighbourhood, where they were beheaded,
to the number of 340. When he had thus perpetrated the
tragedy of Nadjran, the Tobbaa returned with his army to
Sanaa.

At the time when this event occurred, an embassy had
been sent by the Emperor Justin to the mondar, or king of
the Arabs of Hirah, under the direction of the bishop of
Persia, a priest named Abraham, and Simeon Betharsamensis,
who has left us a narrative of the persecution, to conciliate
their friendship, and endeavour to detach them from their
alliance with, or rather dependence on, Persia. When he
reached the camp of the Arab chief, a messenger had just
arrived from the king of Hamyar, informing the mondar of
the success and particulars of his expedition against Nadjran,
and exhorting him to take similar measures against the
Christians who lived under him. The bishop of Persia immediately wrote a circumstantial account of the sufferings of
the Christians of Nadjran to his Roman brethren, in which
he urged them speedily to take up the cause of the believers
in Arabia, and this epistle we possess.

Amongst the few Christians who had escaped the persecution of Dzu Nowass, was Dous Ibn Dzi Thaleban, who fled
to the court of Constantinople, and implored the emperor
to advocate the cause of his persecuted countrymen. To
him we are probably indebted for the Acts of the Martyrs of
Nadjran. The emperor gave him a favourable hearing, excused himself on account of the state of public affairs and
the distance of Arabia, from personally assisting him, but
gave him letters to the Nadjash of Ethiopia. Timothy also,

patriarch of Alexandria, wrote pressing exhortations to Elesbaan, to revenge the blood of the martyrs and release the surviving Christians from the despotism of so bloodthirsty a tyrant. He sent him the Holy Eucharist in a silver pyx to enforce his appeal.

In the meantime fresh massacres had taken place. Dzu Nowass seems to have appointed as prince of Nadjran one named Sarabahal, who was quite prepared to carry on the persecution. A priest, Azquir, was arrested by him. On the Feast of the Epiphany, some fifty men came to the prison to celebrate the festival with the priest. They were taken and, along with Azquir, brought bound before the king. On their road a Christian named Cyriacus saluted the priest. The guards at once arrested him. Azquir was hung head downwards over a fire, and afterwards decapitated, and thirty-eight with him.

The Abyssinian king, who was now himself a Christian, had a double incentive to engage vigorously in his war with Hamyar—vengeance for the slaughter of the Christians, and the recovery of his own supremacy over Arabia Felix. Dzu Nowass, in pursuing his plans of vengeance, had seized the opportunity when the season of the year was unfavourable to navigation between Abyssinia and Arabia. As soon, however, as the season permitted, and the preparations were completed, an army, amounting, according to Arabian writers, to 70,000 men, set sail for the coast of Hamyar, under the command of Aryat, the nephew of Elesbaan. The Abyssinian forces were divided into two parts. One division was landed on that coast of Arabia which lies on the Red Sea, and, after having crossed the Tehama, was to co-operate with the other division as soon as the latter had effected a landing on the southern coast. The first division, however, perished, or was dispersed in crossing the desert. The Arabian king, therefore, who had been making preparations to defend his kingdom against this double attack, when he heard of the disaster which had befallen the first detachment of the Abyssinian army, and was consequently delivered from all apprehensions of danger on that side, turned his attention to the defence of the coast.

The coasts of Arabia and Abyssinia approach each other by degrees, until at the southern extremity of the Red Sea they form a narrow passage, the entrance to the ocean, which from its perilous navigation gained from the Arabian sailors the name of Bab el Mandoub, the Gate of Tears. The black, and often fatal shores of the African side were looked on with terror, and formed a bay which was called the Harbour of Death; and from its rocky extremity, Cape Garafui, or the Cape of Burials, the Spirit of the Storm was believed to listen to the shrieks of the sinking mariners.

The straits are at present scarcely three miles broad; but according to the Arabian geographers, at that time, the sea was there so narrow, that from one side a person might be recognized on the opposite shore;[1] and at the period of the expedition under Aryat, it is reported to have been no more than two stadia, or a quarter of a Roman mile, and to have been difficult to pass on account of the rocks that lay concealed beneath the waves. Through this narrow passage the Abyssinian fleet had to sail, before it could reach the coast of Hamyar, and it was the plan of Dzu Nowass to render it impassable. For this purpose, he is said to have thrown across the least dangerous part a heavy chain of iron, held firm by fragments of rock to which it was fixed, and which were sunk in the sea, and raised to the surface by masses of timber. After having taken these precautions, Dzu Nowass encamped with his army on the coast where he expected that the Abyssinians, when they found the passage of the straits impossible, would attempt to disembark.

[1] Georg. Arabi, Clim. i. p. 6, ap. Bochart.

When the Abyssinian fleet approached the straits, ten ships were sent before to reconnoitre the passage, these, ignorant of the stratagem of the king of Hamyar, and assisted by a favourable wind, entered unexpectedly the narrowest part, and almost by a miracle passed in safety. The rest were obliged, as Dzu Nowass had expected, to return. The ten ships which had passed the straits approached the shore, and would have landed at a place about two hundred stadia, or twenty-five miles, from that in which the army of Hamyar was posted, but they were prevented by the missiles of the few Arabians who had been sent to defend the southern coast.

In another attempt, seven of the remaining ships, in one of which was the Abyssinian commander, succeeded in passing the straits and joining them. The rest of the fleet, which was the more numerous portion, afterwards followed them, and proceeding farther along the coast, cast anchor at a different place, a considerable distance from the former. Dzu Nowass, who naturally concluded that the chief commander was with the larger division, proceeded with his army to hinder their landing, leaving a small force to oppose those ships which had first passed through Bab el Mandoub. Aryat, constrained by want of provisions, was not long before he attempted to effect a landing. According to Arabian accounts, the Abyssinians disembarked near the port of Aden. Their commander wished them to consider their safety as entirely depending on their bravery, and, having ordered the ships to be set on fire, he addressed them in a few words: "O Men of Abyssinia, before you are your enemies, behind you the sea; your choice is death or victory." The contest was short but obstinate: the Hamyarites were entirely defeated, and Aryat hastened towards the metropolis, the city of Taphas or Dhaphas, which being unprepared for a siege, immediately surrendered to him.

When the king of Hamyar heard of the fall of his capital, astonished at the unexpected success of his enemies, and now threatened by them on every side, his resolution entirely failed him; so that, when the Abyssinians landed from the other ships, they soon defeated the Arabians, who wanted spirit and concert to make an effective resistance, and Dzu Nowass himself was amongst the number of the slain. The native historians give a different account of the death of the Tobbaa. According to them, he fled from the field of battle, after he had witnessed the defeat of his army, but being closely pursued, and at last hemmed in between his enemies and the sea, he precipitated himself from a rock, and perished in the waves. By this action the fate of Arabia was decided. In Dzu Dyiadan, who was the successor of Dzu Nowass, and who fell in opposing the conquerors, ended the race of Hamyar. Yemen became a province dependent on the Abyssinian Nadjash, and Aryat, known to the Greeks under the name of Esimiphæus, ascended the throne as his tributary.

SS. FLORA AND MARY, VV. MM.

(A.D. 851.)

[Roman and Spanish Martyrologies. Authority:—Saint Eulogius, Memor. lib. ii. c. 8. Eulogius was a sufferer in the same persecution.]

IN the reign of Abderrammen II., Moorish king of Cordova, Flora, the daughter of a Mahometan Moor by a Christian mother, was denounced before the Cadi by her brother. She was scourged, and beaten on the head till her skull was exposed. She was then given to the care of her brother. She managed to escape over a wall, and took refuge with her sister at Ossaria. After having remained there in concealment for some time, she ventured back to Cordova, and with Mary, sister of the deacon Valabonsus, presented herself boldly before the Cadi, denounced Mahomet, and protested that they were ready to die for Christ. The Cadi sent them to prison. S. Eulogius, who was at that time also in prison, wrote to encourage them, and they were executed on the same day, November 24th.

S. JOHN OF THE CROSS, C.

(A.D. 1591.)

[Roman Martyrology. Canonized by Benedict XIII. in 1726, when his office was appointed for Nov. 24, though he died on Dec. 14. Authorities:—A Life by F. Honoratus a Santa Maria; another by F. Dositheus a S. Alexis, Paris, 1727.]

S. JOHN OF THE CROSS was born at Fontibere, near Avila, in Old Castile, in the year 1542. His family name was Yepez, and he was the son of Gonzales di Yepez and of Catharine Alvarez. His father died whilst he was still young, and he was left to the care of a mother, who instructed him from earliest infancy to turn to Mary as the fountain of solace and salvation. Consequently throughout life he manifested the most tender, unquestioning devotion to the Blessed Virgin, and was constantly in the humour to believe himself the object of her special favour.

His mother lived with him at Medina, and sent him to the Jesuit College, there to be instructed in letters, probably intending him for the Church. The administrator of the hospital associated the young man with him in the care of the sick, and John spent all his leisure in nursing the patients in the hospital with the utmost zeal, patience, and gentleness.

When he had attained the age of twenty-one, he assumed

the Carmelite habit at Medina, fully believing the Blessed Virgin to be the special patroness of this Order.

The Carmelite Order was founded by B. Albert, Latin patriarch of Jerusalem, in 1209, who founded a community of hermits on Mount Carmel, and pretended that he had seen Elijah in vision, who urged him to continue and develop his old school of the prophets formerly established there. The Carmelites endeavoured to convince themselves and the world that their Order had never ceased since the time of Elijah, and adopted a mantle striped black and white, asserting that this was fashioned after the cloak of Elijah which he cast from him as he ascended into heaven, and gave to Elisha as the habit of his Order, and that the mantle, originally white, had been scorched by the flaming chariot wheels, and thus originated these bars. Either the Order was laughed out of this pretence, or had come to the conclusion that the whole mantle was scorched, but certain it is, that it abandoned its striped habit for one entirely dark.

John Yepez having entered this Order, was sent to Salamanca to go through a course of theology. He gave himself up to singular and distressing mortifications. He made for himself a trough of boards like a coffin, and slept in it in a cell at the end of the dormitory. He fasted, and wore a rough sackcloth next his skin, which rubbed sores in it.

He affected unworthiness to become a regular member of the society, and entreated to be allowed to be only a lay brother; but his superiors would not listen to his appeal, and he was ordained priest when he had attained the age of twenty-five. He prepared himself for his first Mass by subjecting himself to fresh mortifications, regarding every torture to which he subjected his body as a savoury oblation in the nostrils of the God of love and compassion.

The Carmelite rule no longer satisfied the hunger after excessive self-immolation in this advanced ascetic of five-

and-twenty, and after a brief sojourn in the Order, he meditated transferring his valuable allegiance to another, that of the Carthusians.

But at that time he met S. Theresa, who was engaged on a reform of the Carmelite Order. The meeting took place at Medina del Campo. She set herself to work to dissuade him from entering the Carthusian Order, and to persuade him to work with her at the reform of the Order of Our Lady of Mount Carmel. She told him that she was authorized by the general to found two houses for men, and that he was undoubtedly chosen by God to assist her in this holy work. Not long after, in 1568, when he was aged twenty-six, he took up his residence in the little house S. Theresa had obtained at Durvello. But before taking this decided step, S. Theresa carried off S. John of the Cross with her, from his monastery to Valladolid, that he might see the foundation of one of her convents there; and while engaged with the workmen directing the alterations and additions that had to be made before the house could be adapted to the purposes of a nunnery, she described to John of the Cross the life led by the nuns, their mortifications, amusements, and their style of conversation.[1]

Immediately after the convent was completed and taken possession of, " we arranged," says S. Theresa, " that Father John de la Cruz should go to the house (at Durvello), and prepare it in such a way that he might be able to enter it as he desired, for I made all haste to have a beginning, because I was greatly afraid some obstacle might come in the way, and so the business was done. Father Antonio (of Jesus, late Prior of S. Anne's, Medina), had already collected a few things that were necessary, and we helped as well as we could, which was but little. He came to speak to me at Valladolid, and was full of joy, telling me what he had pro-

[1] S. Theresa, " Book of the Foundations," c. 12.

vided, which was scanty, but how he had got together five hour-glasses, which made me laugh heartily. He told me that as he wished to keep the exact hours, he did not wish to go unprovided. I think they had, as yet, no place to sleep in. There was little delay in fitting up the house, for though they wished to make several alterations, they had no money. After this, Father Antonio renounced his priorship with great willingness, and took the vows of the First Rule; and though I told him to try it at first, yet he would not, but went to the little house with the greatest content in the world. Father John (of the Cross) was there already. To neither of them did the house appear inconvenient, but rather they imagined that they lived amidst great delights. O my God! how little do such buildings and exterior delights contribute to interior joy! On the first or second Sunday in Advent (I do not remember which), in the year 1568, the first mass was said in that little portal of Bethlehem, for no better name did it appear to me to merit. The following Lent, as I was going to the foundation of a convent at Toledo, I passed by it, and came there one morning while Father Antonio de Jesus was sweeping the door of the church, with a cheerful countenance, such as he always has. I said to him, 'What is this, father? what has become of your dignity?' He replied, 'I consider that time badly spent when I was in the enjoyment of honour.' When I went into the church I was astonished to see the spirit our Lord had produced there; and not only I myself but two merchants also, friends of mine, who had come with me from Medina, did nothing but weep, so many crosses and skulls were there. Never shall I forget one little wooden cross, which was placed over the holy-water stoup, to which was fastened a paper Christ, and which produced more devotion than if it had been a crucifix very elaborately carved. The garret formed the choir, which was high towards the middle, so that they could recite the Hours;

but to enter it in order to hear mass, they were obliged
to stoop very low. They made two little hermitages on
each side of the church, where they could only sit or lie
down, and filled inside with hay, because the place was cold;
their heads almost touched the roof. Towards the altar were
two little windows, and two stones served for pillows: here
also were crosses and skulls. I understood that after the
singing of Matins, they returned to their cells, not to sleep,
but to continue in prayer, an exercise which they enjoy to a
high degree. It happened many times that when they went
to say Prime, they found their habits covered with snow, and
they had not perceived it falling on them, so absorbed were
they in prayer. They recited the Hours with another father
of the relaxed rule, who came to live with them, though he
did not change his habit, being of a weak constitution.
Another religious young man lived with them also, not in
holy orders. They went about preaching in many neighbouring places, where the people were very ignorant, so that I am
glad in this respect that the house was erected in a spot so far
from any monastery, whence the people could get instruction.
In a short time the two fathers gained so great a reputation,
that, when I heard of it, it gave me the greatest consolation.
They went to preach six or eight miles off, bare foot, for they
wore no sandals then, though afterwards they were commanded to wear them. They went in the midst of cold and
snow, and when they had finished preaching and confessing,
they returned very late to their meal, but with such joy, that
all their sufferings seemed but little to them. As for food,
they had sufficient, for the people in all the neighbourhood
provided them with a superfluity. Some gentlemen who
came to the church to confession, offered them better houses
and better situations. Among them was one Don Luis, lord
of five villas; this gentleman had built a church for a picture
of Our Lady, worthy indeed of veneration. His father had
sent it from Flanders to his grandmother or mother (I forget

which), in the care of a merchant, who became so fond of it that he kept it for many years, but on his deathbed commanded it to be restored to the rightful owner. It is a large picture, and in my whole life I have not seen a better; and others say the same. Father Antonio de Jesus having gone there at the gentleman's request, was so taken with the picture that he consented to found a monastery there. The place is called Mancera. The gentleman built a small house for them, suitable to their profession, and gave them furniture and many other things. When I saw this little house, which a short time before could not be inhabited, endowed with such a spirit that wherever I turned I found something to edify me; and when I understood the manner of living of the fathers, and the good example they set, I could not sufficiently thank the Lord, so excessive was my interior joy, for I thought I already saw a foundation laid for the great increase of our Order and the service of the Lord. The merchants who passed along with me told me that they would not for all the world have neglected going there. What power there is in virtue! they were more pleased with that poverty than with all the riches they possessed, and their minds were thereby greatly edified.

"After these fathers and myself had spoken about certain matters, I earnestly requested them not to mortify themselves with such excessive rigour, for since it had cost me so much prayer and desire to obtain such persons to begin the work, I was afraid lest the devil should find means of bringing them to their graves before the work was fully completed; and being so imperfect, I did not consider their proceedings to be the work of God, and that His Majesty could strengthen them to go through with them. But they being endowed with those virtues which I lacked, took no notice of my words, and continued their self-mortifications."[1]

Father Antonio, and Father John of the Cross, remained

---

[1] S. Theresa, "Book of the Foundations," c. 13.

together at Durvello the following year, 1569, when the Princess of Eboli, mistress of Philip II., and her husband Ruy Gomez, founded a nunnery and a monastery of Discalced Carmelites at Pastrana, and Father Antonio was removed from Durvello to become the head of the friars there. Father John of the Cross remained at Durvello. He met with much external and internal trouble. The reform was assailed by enemies, and its members regarded as runaways from their Order, and perhaps as infected with heresy. His soul was also troubled with fits of deep depression, in which he thought the face of God was withdrawn from him, a state of spiritual misery to which he has given touching expression in his book entitled "Noche obscura del Alma" (the dark night of the Soul).

The inconvenience of Durvello, and the offer of the house and Flemish picture at Mancera, led to the transfer of the monastery thither in 1570. Since then there has existed considerable rivalry between the houses of Pastrana and Mancera, as to which should be regarded as the mother house; Pastrana was founded before Mancera, but Mancera was the community of the monastery of Durvello moving to a more congenial spot. Durvello, having been deserted, returned to the estates of the donor; but in 1612, the Discalced Carmelites, having regretted their abandonment of the house in which their reform took its rise, bought it back again.

In 1570 John of the Cross was sent to Pastrana to take charge of the new house. He found there fourteen members collected by S. Theresa and Father Antonio, of these ten were novices, and four professed friars.

In 1571 he was moved from Pastrana to take charge of a new house founded at Alcala. But his successor at Pastrana, by his over-strictness, brought the novices to insubordination, and S. John was speedily recalled, to bring back order to the disturbed community.

In the same year, however, or the beginning of the next, he was hastily called by S. Theresa to assist her at Avila, where the Apostolic Visitor of the Carmelites in Castile had appointed her prioress of her old Convent of the Incarnation, from which she had escaped nine years before with a party of nuns to found her reform.

This appointment met with great opposition from the nuns, from the people of Avila, and from the magistrates of the town. The Convent of the Incarnation had been a great resort of ladies and gentlemen disposed for an afternoon gossip, and the nuns had been always ready to visit and stay with friends and relatives, when they were tired of the routine of cloister life; and, as the memoirs of S. Theresa reveal to us, were not altogether repugnant to a little flirtation, if carried on quietly. "All this must be altered," was the decision of the Visitor, and S. Theresa was the right person to reform the relaxed house. No wonder that she met with opposition. She was obliged to send for S. John of the Cross to assist her in her struggle against overt and covert hostility.

The wrath and envy of the Carmelite Order against the innovators, or rather reformers, could find no vent so long as S. Theresa and her disciples were supported by a papal nuncio and by the king, the latter of whom, if a man of unbounded licentiousness in morals, was a man also of unbounded devotion to the professors of asceticism.

But in 1575 the Grand Chapter of the Order in Spain passed decrees against the Discalced Carmelites, and the General of the Order sent Father Geronimo Tostado into Spain as his Visitor, to press on the king the necessity for suppressing the reform, or schism as he, not unreasonably, regarded it. At this time also the papal nuncio who had favoured S. Theresa, most inopportunely died, and was succeeded by another who disapproved of her work. In 1577 the Carmelite Visitor, F. Tostado, obtained a band of soldiers, and bursting open the doors of the house where

S. John of the Cross lived, seized and carried him off to Toledo, where he was brutally cudgelled, and thrown into a dark dungeon, into which light only penetrated through a little hole of three fingers' breadth, and where he was kept in filth, rags, and starvation by the Carmelite superior, for nine months, till his health was so shattered that the religious were in very shame obliged to release him, lest he should die under their ill-treatment. He was sent to a wretched convent of Calvary, in the country. But though the Discalced were under a cloud, they were not exterminated. Philip II. took them under his favour, and in 1579 John was able to found a monastery at Baëza, and in 1581 he became prior of a reformed Carmelite house at Granada. In 1585 he was made Vicar-provincial of Andalusia, and in 1588 first definitor of the Order.

His austerities exceeded the bounds of moderation and reason. He slept for only two or three hours in the night, and spent the rest of the night in prayer or dozing; and in the semi-devotional, semi-somnolent condition in which he knelt, he—as might have been expected—was visited by all sorts of visions, waking dreams, conjured up by a brain deprived of its natural rest. These were generally of an edifying nature—or at least those which he communicated to his brethren were such. In one of these dreams he thought he heard Christ say to him, "John, what recompense dost thou ask for thy labours?" He answered, "None, Lord, save that I may suffer and be condemned for Thy love." He was wont to say, "To suffer for the sake of God is the true characteristic of His love, as we see in Christ, and in the martyrs. And persecutions are the means whereby we may enter into the depth, or attain to the knowledge, of the mystery of the cross, a necessary condition for comprehending the depth of the wisdom of God and of His love." His great ambition was to be miserable. He often prayed that three things might happen to him. 1st. That he might not pass one day of his life without suffering something. 2ndly. That he might not die Superior. 3rdly. That he might end his life in humiliations, disgrace, and contempt. He was frequently found by those who came to consult him in a dazed, half-conscious condition, consequent on want of sleep, but believed to be the bewilderment of a soul recovering itself from ecstasy. Many persons with lively imaginations asserted that they had seen his face shine with a supernatural light. One lady, it is pretended, was so struck with this illumination as she came to him for confession, that she laid aside her jewels, and dedicated herself to the religious life. The whole furniture of his cell consisted of a rush cross with a paper Christ attached to it.

His acquaintance with his own condition when praying when he ought to have been asleep, enabled him to judge of the value of visions appearing to other persons in the same condition, and he was able to assure them that what they regarded as Divine manifestations were very often only waking dreams. His unhesitating judgment on visions is, that they are to be rejected. "These imaginary visions and other supernatural impressions to which the senses are subject without the assent of the will, I maintain should be avoided and not dwelt on by the soul, upon all occasions and at all times, whether in the perfect or in beginners."[1] Directors, he says, have done great mischief by encouraging their penitents in a visionary habit. "There are some spiritual directors who fall into error because their instructions to those who are liable to visions are such as to lead them astray or perplex them. They suffer their penitents to make much of their visions, and attaching so much importance to these visions they fail to build them up and stablish them in faith. This sort of direction shows that they themselves consider visions

[1] "Ascent of Mount Carmel," b. ii. c. 17.

to be matters of importance, and their penitents, observing this, follow their example and dwell on these dreams, instead of bracing up their faith. This is the necessary result of the language and conduct of spiritual directors; for, somehow, a certain sense of satisfaction springs up at these things, and that draws away the eye from the depth of faith into which it should gaze. The penitent, finding the confessor very appreciative of them, is induced also to magnify them, indulge in them, give way to them, and hold them in mighty esteem. This sort of direction is the source of many imperfections, to say the least, to the soul. It makes the soul lose humility and get self-satisfied; and the devil is not slow to foster this."[1] With strong good sense he argues that visions, even though presumably coming from God, are very likely to deceive, and that, therefore, the less attention paid to them the better.

S. John of the Cross was a vernacular poet of no low order. The poem which he composed as the text to his "Dark Night," formed on the model of the Aubades of the Troubadours, is not undeserving of ranking with the amatory compositions of Bertrand de Born and Giraud de Borneil. It has its counterpart in the aubade "En un vergier" by an unknown troubadour. It does not fall behind the graceful little piece in its poetic power, or in the sensuality of the picture it paints. The religious who reads the "Dark Night" is likely to be distracted from the cold regions of ascetic theology to the ardour of sensual imaginings conjured up by this unseemly though very beautiful poem. S. John takes the first two verses and explains them mystically, line by line. They represent a maiden eloping at night down a ladder from her house, when all within are asleep, to meet her lover, who is hiding in a grove for her. The six last verses, descriptive of the meeting, S. John abstained

[1] "Ascent of Mount Carmel," b. ii. c. 18.

from explaining; he would have done better to have abstained from writing them. The poem entitled the "Spiritual Canticle between the Soul and Christ," is based on the Song of Solomon. The "Living Flame of Love" is descriptive of the human passion of a mistress for her lover, whom she has admitted to her chamber, which may be compared with one of Herrick's warmest compositions. It has, however, quite another signification in the mouth of a mystic to whom earthly passion is unknown.

It is to be regretted that S. John of the Cross, who was possessed of such good sense in his estimate of visions, should have encouraged instead of checking that sentimental love of Christ in the breast of nuns, which has run in hysterical persons to such dangerous lengths.[1]

S. John held in dislike the dressing up of images of the saints with artificial hair and jewels, and with laces and velvet and satin gowns. "There are people," he says, "who squander that inward devotion which ought to be spiritually directed to the invisible saint, in demonstrations of endearment and curiosity towards the image, and all love and joy end there. This is an effectual hindrance to real spirituality. And this is clearly visible in that hateful custom observed

[1] As the following, from the Diary of the B. Marie de l'Incarnation:—"Allant à l'oraison, je tressaillois en moi-même, et disois : Allons dans la solitude, mon cher amour, afin que je vous embrasse à mon aise, et que, respirant mon âme en vous, elle ne soit plus que vous-même par union d'amour. . . . . Puis, mon corps étant brisé de fatigues, j'étois contrainte de dire : Mon divin amour, je vous prie de me laisser prendre un peu de repos, enfin que je puisse mieux vous servir, puisque vous voulez que je vive. . . . . Je le priois de me laisser agir : lui promettant de me laisser après cela consumer dans ses chastes et divins embrassements. . . . . O amour ! quand vous embrasserai-je ? N'avez-vous point pitié de moi dans le tourment que je souffre ? hélas ! hélas ! mon amour, ma beauté, ma vie ! au lieu de me guérir, vous vous plaisez à mes maux. Venez donc que je vous embrasse, et que je meure entre vos bras sacréz !" Some pupils of Marie de l'Incarnation also had mystical marriages with Christ; and the impassioned rhapsodies of one of them being overheard, she nearly lost her character, as it was thought that she was apostrophizing an earthly lover. Is it to be wondered at that S. Christina and S. Rose of Lima, in these unwholesome conditions of combined sexual and religious exaltation, should have supposed that they had received favours which no longer left them virgins?

now-a-days by certain persons who, instead of holding in abhorrence the vanities of the world, adorn the sacred images with the garments fashionable at the time, invented for the satisfaction of wanton recreation. They dress up the images in those garments which are objectionable when worn by themselves, and which the saints would certainly have held in detestation. The result is, that all modest and sound devotion in such people disappears, to make way for a superfluous decoration of images, and to them they cling, and on them base all their joys. You see people who are never tired of adding image to image; and they hold to their images as Micah did to his idols, who when he lost them ran out of his house crying because they had been taken away."

"When many people go on a pilgrimage," he says elsewhere, "I should advise staying at home, for in general, men return from pilgrimages more dissipated than they were before. And many become pilgrims for recreation more than for devotion."

In 1591 the Reformed Carmelite Order broke into factions. John of the Cross was dismissed his offices, and sent to the lonely monastery of Penguela, on the mountains of the Sierra Morena. Some members of the society whom he had forbidden to preach, when he was provincial of Andalusia, now became his principal accusers and enemies. One of them, F. Diego Evangelista, spread everywhere ugly reports of his conduct, which he probably regarded as insane, and he was accused of heresy. He found himself forsaken of all. Those who received his letters burned them, lest they should be involved in his disgrace.

John of the Cross was ordered to leave Penguela and go to Baëza or Ubeda. He chose the latter. He had been for some time suffering from ulcers. The fatigue of his journey caused these ulcers to burst, and discharge.

The prior behaved towards him with great inhumanity, forbade any one visiting him, locked him up in a tiny cell, denied him necessary food, and dismissed the infirmarer for treating him with compassion. Sectarian envy and spite seemed to have extinguished the common instincts of humanity in the breast of the holy prior Francis Chrysostom of Ubeda.

Fortunately the provincial came that way, and when he found how barbarously the sick and dying man had been treated by his religious brethren, he rated the prior soundly. Two hours before S. John died he repeated the *Miserere mei* with his brethren; then he desired one to read to him part of the book of Canticles, and during the lection appeared in transports of joy. He at length cried out, " Glory be to God !" pressed the crucifix to his breast, and after some time said, " Lord, into Thy hands I commend my spirit," with which words he calmly breathed forth his soul on the 14th of December, in 1591, at the age of forty-nine years, of which he had spent twenty-eight in a religious profession. S. Theresa in her epistles styles him a saint even before he had embraced her reformed Order, and says that he was one of the most pure souls in the Church, to whom God had communicated great treasures of light, and whose understanding He had filled with the science of the saints.

November 25.

S. Moses, *P.M. at Rome*; A.D. 249.
S. Mercurius, *M. at Cæsarea in Cappadocia; circ.* A.D. 250.
S. Erasmus, *M. at Antioch.*
S. Catharine, *V.M. at Alexandria;* A.D. 307.
S. Reolus, *B. of Rheims;* A.D. 693.
S. Jucunda, *V. in Emilia in Italy.*
S. Hermeland, *Ab. of Aindre in Brittany;* 8th cent.
S. Catherine Audley, *R., Ledbury; circ.* A.D. 1400.

S. MERCURIUS, M.

(ABOUT A.D. 250.)

[Modern Roman Martyrology. Greek Menæas and Menologies on Nov. 24 and 25. Authority:—The purely apocryphal Greek Acts.]

HE story of S. Mercurius is a mere Greek romance, probably wholly destitute of foundation. Although he is represented as having suffered at Rome, his name was utterly unknown to the Roman Church, till the Greek Acts came to the notice of Baronius. The Acts are the usual tissue of tortures and miraculous cures, and then the execution of the martyr with the sword.

S. CATHARINE, V.M.

(A.D. 307.)

[Roman Martyrology. By the Greeks on Nov. 24, 25, and 26. Authority:—Eusebius, H. E. lib. viii. c. 14. The Greek Acts are worthless.]

Eusebius says that when Maxentius was at Alexandria he committed shameful abominations by carrying off the wives

S. CATHARINE.
From the Vienna Missal.

Nov. 25.

and daughters of the citizens. " His unbridled passion was defeated by the heroic firmness of one female only, who was one of the most distinguished and illustrious at Alexandria, and she was a Christian. She was in other respects distinguished both for her wealth, family, and condition, but esteemed all inferior to modesty. Having frequently made attempts to bring her over to his purposes, though she was prepared to die, he could not destroy her, as his passion was stronger than his anger; but punishing her with exile, he took away all her wealth."

On this slender foundation a marvellous romance has been founded which passes as the Acts of the Martyrdom of S. Catharine. According to this, she was the daughter of a king, and of wondrous beauty and learning. Maxentius invites fifty philosophers to contend with Catharine in public argument. She of course convinces them all, and all fifty are burned to death by the enraged emperor. Then the tyrant makes amorous advances towards the saint, and although he has got a legitimate wife, Faustina, he offers to share his throne with her. As she declines the honour, he has her whipped with ox-hide lashes, and cast into prison, and then goes off to examine a castle near the mouth of the Nile.

During his absence Faustina visits Catharine along with a faithful attendant, Porphyrius, and both are converted. Porphyrius, in the ardour of his new faith, converts two hundred soldiers, and the emperor on his return kills them all along with Porphyrius and his wife. S. Faustina, the apocryphal empress, is commemorated on November 23, and the fabulous Porphyrius and his converts on November 24. A wheel set with razors was constructed for the execution of S. Catharine, but when she was placed on it, the wheel broke, and the razors flew about, hacking and cutting the throats of the bystanders. Then Catharine prayed that she might suffer death, and asked only two things—that after her death her body might be preserved from being touched by profane fingers, and that the world might be converted. Then her head was struck off with a sword, and angels came and carried off her body to Mount Sinai. Maxentius was defeated by Constantine, and the world became Christian. Such, condensed, is the wonderful rigmarole which serves as the acts of S. Catharine, who, if we may regard the account of Eusebius as referring to her, did not suffer death for her faith, but transportation, and this perhaps has been converted into the fable of the translation by angels to Sinai. Her head is shown at Rome, her body in the monastery of Mount Sinai. Various relics of her are exhibited in churches throughout Europe.

She is represented in art with her wheel, and crowned.

S. REOLUS, B. OF RHEIMS.

(ABOUT A.D. 693.)

[Gallican Martyrologies. Authority :—A Life by William, abbot of Orbais (1180), in Martene, Ampl. Coll. vi. pp. 1216-1218 ; Fredegar, Contin. &c.]

S. REOLUS, Bishop of Rheims, succeeded S. Nivard about the year 673 ; he was the husband of his predecessor's niece. He embraced the religious state in the abbey of Rebais, which had been founded by S. Philibert, and he was the disciple of this saint. His daughter took the veil in the monastery of Notre-Dame at Soissons, and Reolus endowed this monastery with some of his estates. Some time after he became bishop, he assisted at the dedication of the church of Elnon, erected by S. Amandus of Herbauges. He founded along with Ebroin the monastery of Orbais. He assisted Ebroin in beguiling Martin, one of the sons of Pepin the

S. CATHARINE CONTENDING WITH THE DOCTORS.
After a Fresco by Masaccio in the Church of S. Clemente at Rome.

Nov. 25.

Great, to his ruin. The Bishop of Rheims and Agilbert, Bishop of Paris, swore upon certain relics that Martin's life should be secure if he would deliver himself up to Ebroin. The trustful prince did so, little knowing that the crafty prelates had withdrawn the relics from the shrines, and had sworn on the empty cases. Ebroin, unrebuked by the bishops, put Martin to death.[1]

His relics are at Orbais, of which place he is the patron.

[1] "Nuntios dirigit, Ægelbertum et Reolum Remensis urbis episcopum, ut fide promissâ in incertum super vacuas capsas sacramenta falsa dederint. Quâ in re ille credens *eos* ac Lugduno-Ciavato cum sodalibus ac sociis ad Erchrechum veniens, illic cum suis omnibus interfectus est."—Fredegar, Coutin., ap. Bouquet, ii. p. 451.

November 26.

SS. FAUSTUS, PHILIAS, HESYCHIUS, AND OTHERS, *MM. at Alexandria*; A.D. 306.
S. PETER, *B.M. of Alexandria*; A.D. 312.
S. MARCELLUS, *P.M. at Nicomedia*; A.D. 349.
S. SIRICIUS, *Pope of Rome*; A.D. 398.
S. ALYPIUS THE CHIONITE, *H. at Adrianople*; *circ.* A.D. 635.
S. CONRAD, *B. of Constance*; A.D. 976.
S. BELLINUS, *B.M. at Padua*; A.D. 1149.
S. SYLVESTER, *Ab. of Fabiano in the Marches of Ancona*; A.D. 1267.
S. INNOCENT, *B. of Irkutsk in Siberia*; A.D. 1731.
S. LEONARD OF PORTO MAURIZIO, *C. at Rome*; A.D. 1751.

S. PETER, B. M. OF ALEXANDRIA.

(A.D. 312.)

[Roman Martyrology, Usuardus, Ado, Notker, &c., instead of Nov. 25, the proper day of martyrdom; displaced so as not to interfere with S. Catharine. Surius on Nov. 25. The Greeks on Nov. 25. Authorities :—Eusebius, H. E. lib. vii. c. 34, viii. 13, ix. 6; S. Gregory Nazianzen, Orat. 23, 24. Anastasius the Librarian, in his preface to the Passion of the Ten Thousand, says he had translated the Acts of this great doctor and martyr of the Alexandrian Church. These are probably the Acts given by Surius, t. vi. p. 184.]

N the death of Thomas, Bishop of Alexandria, in 300, Peter, who had previously been master in the catechetical school,[1] succeeded to the see of Alexandria. He had been a sufferer with Dionysius fifty years before in the Decian persecution, so that he must have been very aged when elevated to the episcopal throne.

In his time the question of the treatment of the lapsed,

---

[1] Philip. Sideta, ap. Dodwell, Diss. ad Iren. p. 880.

MARTYRDOM OF S. CATHERINE.   Nov. 25.

which had been agitated so warmly in the time of S. Cyprian, was revived once more. The whole Christian world, with the exception of the Novatians, had agreed now to act on the same general principles, but no definite rules had been laid down for particular cases. Before the Easter of 306 Peter undertook to do this for his own diocese. The fourteen canons which he drew up are still extant; and it is pleasing to see the venerable prelate, who had himself played the man for Christ, exhibiting lenity and indulgence towards those who had shown less courage.

About this time the persecution of Maximinus broke out in Egypt, and Peter was obliged to seek for safety by flight. The refinement of cruelty which was practised upon the Christians of both sexes in the diocese of Alexandria would exceed our belief, if it had not been related by one of the bishops who was himself a sufferer, as well as by Eusebius, who happened to be on the spot. The number of victims varied from ten to a hundred a day; and the heads of the churches were singled out for attack. Faustus, a priest of Alexandria, who was old enough to have been a companion of Dionysius in the Decian persecutions, was beheaded. Phileas, bishop of Thmuis, was imprisoned, and wrote an account of the persecution from his dungeon to his flock. With him was Philoromus, who had been a magistrate in Alexandria. They were beheaded. Three other bishops, Hesychius, Pachynius, and Theodore, were in prison. Meletius, bishop of Lycopolis, took advantage of the absence of Peter and of the other bishops to make regulations for the conduct of their dioceses. Provision had been made for the spiritual wants of the Christians, but Meletius was determined to interfere. An account of his proceedings reached Phileas, Hesychius, Pachynius, and Theodore in their prison, and they wrote a joint epistle to Meletius, expostulating with him upon the irregularity of his conduct. The letter is still extant, and it shows that these bishops looked up to Peter as their metropolitan. Meletius paid no regard to this remonstrance, and when the authors of it had closed their career by martyrdom, he went to Alexandria, and continued there the same irregular proceedings. Two persons supported him in his ambitious views: one was Isidorus, and the other Arius, who afterwards became so celebrated as a heresiarch. With their assistance Meletius was able to draw after him some of the priests who had been left in charge of the Alexandrian Church. Being now at the head of a party, he visited the confessors, who were in prison or at the mines, and two of them received ordination at his hands. When Peter heard of this open infringement of his rights, he wrote from his place of concealment to his flock at Alexandria, telling them not to hold communion with Meletius, but to wait till he could return and investigate the affair. The time of his revisiting Alexandria is uncertain, but it was probably not before 311, when Galerius died and the persecution was relaxed. Immediately on his return, Peter summoned a synod of bishops to try Meletius on the charge of having encroached on the prerogatives of the bishop of Alexandria, and of having sacrificed to save his life during the late persecutions. A sentence of deposition was passed against him; but so far from submitting, Meletius organized a schism, and treated Peter with insolence. Arius did not join the seceders. He ceased to give his support to Meletius, and Peter not only forgave him, but ordained him deacon. The reconciliation, however, did not last long. The bishop found himself obliged to issue a sentence of excommunication against all the Meletians, and he took the decided measure of not recognizing their baptisms. Arius now detached himself from Peter, and was involved in the excommunication launched against Meletius. But the persecution, which had abated, broke out again

Peter was seized by the express order of Maximinus, and was beheaded. As soon as Arius heard the sentence of Maximinus, he is said to have hasted to the church and entreated the clergy and people to intercede with Peter for him, to raise the ban from off him, hoping to be elected his successor. Peter answered with a sigh that Arius was cast forth from the face of God. Then, taking two priests to him from the throng, he said to them, "Although I am a sinner, yet I know that I am called by heaven to die as a martyr. You are elected to succeed me in order on the Alexandrian throne, first Achilles and then Alexander. In the night, when I was completing my sacrifice of prayer, I saw suddenly Christ my Lord appear in a white mantle, rent from top to bottom. And He held the portions together with His hand over His breast. And when I saw this I said, 'My Lord, why dost Thou so appear?' And he answered me, 'Arius hath done this.' Therefore I warn and exhort you not to receive Arius again into communion, for he is destined to rend the unity of the Church with a most grievous schism."

This story was probably composed after Arius had become a noted heresiarch.

S. CONRAD, B. OF CONSTANCE.

(A.D. 976.)

[Roman and German Martyrologies. Canonized by Pope Calixtus II. Authorities :—A Life by Oudalschalk, abbot of SS. Ulric and Afra in Augsburg, d. 1150; written with the purpose of inducing Calixtus to grant the canonization of Conrad. In Pertz, Mon. Scr. Germ. iv. pp. 430-436. Another Life, by an anonymous writer of the 12th century, containing no new matter, in Pertz, iv. pp. 436-445. A third Life, by an anonymous writer, in Mone, "Quellensammlung," i. pp. 79-80.]

THE Lives we have of S. Conrad come to us from so late a date that they contain little that can give a lively portraiture of the saint. They are shadowy creations of the biographers, based on a few historical facts and on more or less untrustworthy traditions.

Henry, count of Altdorf, of the Guelf family, had two sons, Conrad, and Rudolf, the fourth count of Altdorf. Conrad was brought up for the Church, and on being ordained priest was at once invested with the provostship of the cathedral of Constance. His rank and piety pointed him out to the electors in 934 as a suitable person to fill the vacant see of Constance on the death of Bishop Nothing. He was a friend of S. Ulric of Augsburg. Conrad exchanged lands with his brother, so as to obtain estates near Constance, and he endowed the see with these. He made three pilgrimages to Jerusalem. One Easter Day a great spider fell into the consecrated chalice. In those times spiders were supposed to be poisonous. Conrad deemed it most reverent to swallow the spider, after which he sat in an agony of mind, expecting death. An hour or two after he threw up the spider, and now in art he is represented with a chalice and spider. He died in 976.

S. BELLINUS, B.M.

(A.D. 1149.)

[Roman Martyrology, Ferrarius, &c. Canonized by Eugenius IV. in 1151.]

BELLINUS BERTALDUS succeeded Sinibald in the see of Padua, in the year 1128, Sinibald having been removed from it in 1124. A nobleman named Thomas Capiuaci who had lands in his diocese did not pay his tithes. The bishop proceeded against him, and forced him to refund arrears. This so exasperated the noble, that he obtained the assassination of Bellinus.

S. LEONARD OF PORTO-MAURIZIO, C.

(A.D. 1751.)

[Roman and Franciscan Martyrologies. Beatified by Pius VI. in 1796, canonized in 1867 by Pius IX. Authority :—A Life by R. P. Salvator d'Ormea, O.M., published with his works.]

PORTO-MAURIZIO, a village on the Corniche road neai Oneglia, was the birthplace of S. Leonard. He was born on December 20, 1676, of well-to-do parents, and was named at the font Paul Jerome.[1] His mother died when the youthful saint was two years old, and his father married again, and became the father of four more children. Paul Jerome instructed his half-brothers and sisters in making little altars, and dressing up and marching in procession from one to another, singing hymns, after the manner of the Corpus Christi solemnity. He was sent to study at Rome whilst living with his uncle. This worthy man treated him as one of his own children, and endured, without reproach, many of his eccentricities. But when Paul Jerome, after hearing a sermon, or reading the life of a saint, began to talk of it at supper-time, and continue an unflagging stream of pious but somewhat commonplace sentiments on the same, forgetting all the while to empty his plate, his uncle Agostino was obliged to interfere and say, " Pray hold your tongue and eat your supper."

One day, his biographer informs us, a companion—a specially "precious companion"—was walking with him, when they passed a gallows from which hung a dead and decaying criminal. "That will be the end of you, if you are a bad man," was the brilliant observation of his "pre-

[1] " Because," says a biographer, "in him were observed all the indications of a privileged soul born for heaven"—in a baby at the breast ! It is clear, of course, that the names Paul Jerome are specially calculated to designate a privileged soul.

cious" companion. The remark struck the saintly youth profoundly, and from that moment he conceived a great terror of crime, or at all events of its punishment.

He joined several pious societies of persons living in the world, and, though still young, occupied himself on festivals and Sundays in beating up loungers and laggers in the streets, and speeding them to church to hear the sermon.

He fortunately got hold of a very wholesome and altogether admirable book, the "Introduction to a Devout Life" of S. Francis of Sales, and this served him as a guide in youth. He could hardly have found a better. He learned the greater part of it by heart, and was fond of repeating it aloud at meal times to his uncle and relations at home. In after years, when preaching, he exhorted all young people to join religious confraternities, assuring them that, in his belief, his having belonged to the oratory of Father Caravita and the congregation of the Chiesa Nuova saved him from falling into laxity of life, and quickened the sparks of devotion in him into a glowing fire.

He used various mortifications. The maids pointed out to his aunt and to each other that he had not slept in his bed, but lain on a board, and they rolled a stone from under his bed, which the women in consultation together over it decided must have served him as a pillow. With feminine inquisitiveness they turned out his drawers and box, and exposed hair shirts and scourges. A minute inspection of the latter revealed clots of blood and little bits of skin. The aunt talked among all her relations of what she had seen, the maids among all their friends, and Paul Jerome found that his self-mortification was a matter of public notoriety.

He had as his confessor Father Grifonelli, and to him the young saint announced his intention of joining a religious Order. The confessor, to prove his obedience, bade him go to all the booksellers in Rome and ask for Æsop's fables, and those of Bertoldo and of Bertoldino, bound in one volume. Although the young man foresaw the impossibility of finding such a book, he at once set out in quest of it, and did not relax his efforts till he had visited ineffectually all the bookstalls in the city. After having been subjected to ridicule and rebuff, he returned to Grifonelli, and told him that he had not succeeded in obtaining the volume, but that he would endeavour next day to procure it in another quarter. Grifonelli scolded him, and called him a fool for not being able to get so common a work, and Paul Jerome took his scolding in good part, without answering a word. One day Paul Jerome saw passing by the Gesu, two friars, whose appearance specially delighted him. Whether it was their quaint costume, or their sanctified demeanour, which attracted him cannot be said, but he followed them to ascertain to what Order they belonged. They led him to the Minorite convent of S. Bonaventura, on the Palatine, and he entered the church as the friars began Compline with the words "Converte nos, Deus, salutaris noster" (Turn thou us, O God our Saviour). The words struck him as a call, and he said to himself, "Hæc requies mea" (This is the place of my rest), and resolved to join the Order, which wore snuff-coloured, coarse, hooded habits, were girded with a knotted rope, were sandalled, and did not shave. When he announced his intention to his uncle, he met with strong opposition. What did the lad know of the Order, and its rules, except that the friars wore an antiquated and picturesque habit? He had made no personal acquaintances among the Minorites; why should he enroll himself among them with such precipitation?

But Paul Jerome had made up his mind, and he was received as a novice by the Minorites on October 2, 1697, when he was aged twenty-one, and received at the time the name of Leonard, abandoning for ever those of Paul and Jerome, which had been given him at the font as adapted beyond all others to express the character of his soul as meet for heaven and highly privileged to receive Divine favours.

The year of his novitiate was spent in a condition of exaltation and highly wrought enthusiasm. In after years he looked back to this period and said that it was his Holy Year, and that he had done nothing but go back since his novitiate. His feelings had naturally become less excitable, but religious progress, as is too often forgotten, is not marked by tumultuous emotion, but by moral conquests.

He made his solemn profession on October 2, 1698, and at once applied himself to the study of theology. He had one rare but most precious gift, which he never squandered away—love of study. He loved books—they were his companions, his friends, his guides. He often urged, when he was a preacher much sought after, that he never could have obtained the influence he possessed, or been able to arrest attention, without constant study.

However, if he had the gift of study, he had also the gift of talking. His uncle and cousins had experienced this, and had sometimes wished he would have mortified himself a little more in this particular, but this was a gift which would be of eminent service to him as a preacher. A student unable to give forth fluently the substance of what he had read and thought over, might make a man of letters, but not a pulpit orator.

When walking with his brethren in the garden in time of recreation, he could not refrain from moral exhortation. Whenever the restraint of silence was removed, his tongue was heard going in the delivery of wholesome, edifying advice. He was so evidently cut out by nature to be a preacher, that his superiors would not allow him to turn to literature, or spend himself in mission work among heathen, but urged him to devote himself to the evangelization of the Italian people—a people which, with an episcopate almost equal in number to all the other bishoprics of Europe, literally swarming with clergy and monks, more preached to, and, no doubt, prayed for, than any other Christian people, is yet the most backward in morality, and sense of truth, and honesty, and the dignity of labour, of any nation that has embraced the Gospel.

Accordingly Leonard of Porto-Maurizio, after recovering from a long illness, which had reduced him to skin and bone, set to work to carry on missions in his native Italy. He began at Artallo, not far from Porto-Maurizio, whither he had been sent to regain his health, and where it began to be completely re-established. He walked over every morning to Artallo with bare feet, and returned late in the evening. Once, when on his way home in the dusk, a man followed him, sighing heavily. S. Leonard waited till he came up, when the man fell at his feet and said, bursting into tears, " My father, you have before you the greatest of sinners!" "And you have in me," answered the saint, "a father full of tenderness." He led the penitent to the convent at Porto-Maurizio, heard his long confession, and sent him away comforted, and strengthened to lead a better life.

But the zeal of Leonard urged him occasionally to inveigh against harmless customs which it was quite impossible for him to root out.

He was invited to preach on the feast of S. Bartholomew at Caramagna. He found that there, as everywhere else on a festa, the people danced in the afternoon. He preached vehemently against this. The people listened with interest, and then hastened home to get ready for the ball. Father Leonard, finding that his sermon had not produced the smallest effect, ordered the crucifix and candle bearers to precede him, and he went direct to the booth where the dance was to be held, and right in among the merry-makers, whilst the band was playing, and the young men and women were capering. The apparition of the vested preacher and the acolytes in scarlet and white, with burning tapers and uplifted crucifix, arrested the orchestra, and the saint at once raised his voice and exerted his greatest powers of eloquence against the ball. His excitement, vehement gestures, and evident earnestness, impressed a naturally excitable people, and when it was noticed that one of the arms of the figure on the cross was loose and waggled about, the dancers, or some of them at all events, took it as a sign of Divine concurrence in the denunciation. The cross-bearer at emphatic portions of the address gave a dexterous jerk to the crucifix, and made the arm wag threateningly, and some of the women screamed, and their screams drowned the titters of the men.

When S. Leonard ceased, the hearers dispersed, some overawed, most actuated by that graceful courtesy which distinguishes even peasants in Italy, and postponed their dance till next Sunday, to humour the excited and respected preacher.

The grand-duke Cosmo III. of Tuscany summoned S. Leonard to preach missions in his duchy, and offered to find him the means for travelling and subsistence. "I thank your highness," said the saint; "but my Master makes me independent." And, in fact, wherever he went, he was always supplied with abundant alms. However, the grand-duke sent a commissioner to attend him, and see that he wanted nothing. This officer wrote, after a mission held at Pitigliano; "I cannot refrain from announcing to you with feelings of the liveliest joy, the happiness which Pitigliano has had in possessing this great servant of God, who is just closing his mission, to proceed to Sorano and sanctify that place in turn; for, indeed, conversion is not the only word for designating the results, *sanctifying* expresses them far better. Father Leonard is an instrument of the Holy Spirit, who by his sweetness attracts all who hear him, even the most hardened. I had the honour of being charged by his royal highness to attend him and obtain for him all that was needed; but I have had scarcely any occasion for executing my office, for the little the father and his companions eat they obtain by begging. I had prepared for him a little house containing five rooms, with a bed for him, supplied with mattress and all necessary furniture; but no sooner had he arrived than he carried in some planks on which he sleeps, and turned out the bed. I think," added the courtier, accustomed to a feather-bed and plenty of nourishing food and wine, "I think that there is something miraculous in the maintenance of life in this manner, accompanied by such fatigue and such severe penances."

As a plague which had appeared in parts of Northern Italy did not enter Tuscany, a procession was organized to carry a miraculous image of the Virgin down and then up a hill on which was a pilgrimage chapel that contained it. It was said that a hundred thousand persons assisted in this ceremony. Leonard preached to the people from the chapel steps at the top of the hill before the procession dispersed, and gave his benediction. At the same moment, according to preconcerted signal, a cannon was fired and was answered by cannon a little way off, and these by other ordnance at a distance, so as to announce to all Tuscany the moment of benediction, that all might kneel and all receive the blessing. It was remarked that the banging of the cannon, the reverence of the vast crowd, the benediction of the saint, worked so powerfully on an impressionable multitude that many cried.

Father Leonard held missions at Massa, Arezzo, Volterra, Siena, &c. He was in the greatest request. The bishop of San Miniato, in a letter thanking the guardian of San Francesco del Monte for having sent him the missioner, said: "Father Leonard returns to retreat laden with merits. He has laboured during fifteen days, I might add fifteen nights, with admirable zeal for the salvation of my beloved flock. Nothing can surpass his devotion, except, let us hope, the fruits which it has produced. I should say that Divine grace triumphs in him, for it does not seem to me possible that one man could do so much, unassisted by the special help of God."

The priest of San Rocco, near Pistoia, wrote, after a mission: "Blessed be the hour when the thought came into my head to ask you, reverend father, to send me Father Leonard. God alone knows all that He has deigned to work by means of His servant. The whole town venerates Father Leonard as a saint, as a learned preacher, as a fervent missioner, and all hearts have been enchained by his words of fire. He breaks the callous hearts of those who readily lend the ear to those that flatter, and close it to the truth. None have been able to resist him but those who have not heard him. He has had immense congregations of hearers: in the second procession of penitence there must have been as many as fifteen thousand persons, and at the papal benediction about twenty thousand. All the confessors in the town have had their hands full, and extraordinary dispositions marked the penitents—a very lively anxiety about the affairs of their souls, and forgetfulness of everything else. He has carried away with him the regrets of everyone, as manifested by the tears of the faithful, who strove to retain him. And the whole town is looking forward to the chance of his revisiting it on some future occasion. The most notable inhabitants of Pistoia, men and women, came to San Rocco at hours most inconvenient to themselves, and in spite of the great heat, to hear him, and to make their confessions to him. Many persons spent the night in the church porch.

God be praised, who deigns to visit His Church by sending it such servants! One may judge of the fruit of the mission by merely observing the fervour with which the Way of the Cross is gone through. It is quite exceptional to see men and women of position in Pistoia, so opposed in general to outward demonstrations of piety, yet making the Stations of the Cross with so much recollection and fervour, that they are not ashamed to kiss the earth, and that, moreover, after the conclusion of the mission."

In 1715, whilst labouring at missions in Tuscany, he was appointed guardian of the convent of San Francesco del Monte at Florence. He established regularity of discipline in it, finding this greatly relaxed. For his own part he lived with great austerity, eating only vegetables, wearing a ragged and patched habit, and sleeping on hard boards.

The excitement and strain of mission work was so exhausting that he felt the necessity for entire rest and seclusion from the world. The mind could not bear the effort without being allowed time to recruit. He therefore obtained a grant of a hermitage called Santa Maria del Incontro, situated at some little distance from Florence on a mountain, and he determined to place there a few religious who aspired to a solitary life, and amongst whom he might rest at intervals, and in the peace of the mountains draw in fresh inspiration. He started from Florence for his hermitage, barefoot, when snow was on the ground, attended by a few friars, on the feast of the Annunciation. They ascended the mountain singing psalms. Everywhere the spring flowers were bursting forth: among the coppice the ground was pink with cyclamen, and here and there shone the scarlet anemone.

The hermitage was small. Each cell was so diminutive that the occupant could touch the walls by stretching out both hands—cells containing too few cubic feet of air to be healthy habitations, had not windows and doors been badly fitted, and allowed ventilation.

No member of the community was allowed to administer the sacraments, to write, or receive letters—except from very exalted personages—without leave. The fasting was severe, and almost perpetual: nine Lents were observed in the year, and on only fifteen or sixteen days were eggs and cheese and milk permitted. On all others, these, together with fish, and, of course, meat, were strictly forbidden. Vegetables and fruit formed their diet.

S. Leonard retired twice in the year to this solitude: he would gladly have remained there all the rest of his life, and made there, as he called it, his novitiate for Paradise; but this was impossible—his line of life was already marked out for him by Providence, and he must follow it.

Cosmo III., grand-duke of Tuscany, invited the saint to examine the case of a young girl condemned to death by the magistrates, but whose sentence he was reluctant to sign, as he hesitated about her being really guilty. S. Leonard went carefully through the evidence, was satisfied that the girl was innocent, and Cosmo pronounced her discharge. In a town in the diocese of Pisa he preached against giving occasion of scandal, and, as his manner was, during the sermon, bared his back and lashed himself till the blood flowed, before all the congregation in the church. This offensive spectacle no doubt produced effect on coarse and ignorant minds. It so wrought on the priest of the place, who was notorious for his immorality, that he got up into the pulpit, plucked the scourge from the hands of the preacher, bared his own back, and to the great edification of his parishioners, to whom he had been a scandal for many years, whacked vigorously till the blood began to spurt out and drop from the scourge on the upturned faces nearest the pulpit.

At Livorno, during a mission, forty women on the streets having entered the church, were so touched that they went to him for confession. He gave them a special sad-coloured habit, and during the rest of the mission they were marched in file to the church from a house which he had secured as a home and refuge for them, and created the liveliest emotion and satisfaction in the breasts of the audience by their contrition.

In 1730 S. Leonard went to Rome to conduct a mission there. To create a more startling effect, he provided himself with an iron bar, or thick piece of wire, and having stripped for his sermon to the waist, whacked himself at appropriate intervals, and showed his bloody back to the delighted people. The vulgar are always greedy of horrors. The blood smears and groans and whacks gave zest to the discourse.

From Rome he went to Velletri, where one fruit of his mission was that all the people were induced to write the name of Jesus over their doors. From Velletri he went to Lucca. Whilst there he made happy use of an accident. Whilst preaching, he saw through a window that a thundercloud was gathering. He waited his opportunity, and at a flash cried, "If my voice cannot shake your hearts, then may God speak from heaven." A tremendous crash of thunder followed, and scared the people nearly into fits.

One day, a woman with a little child was very curious to hear him. She did not like to leave the child alone, and she could get no one to supply her place. However, as the mission was drawing to an end, her female curiosity got the mastery over her maternal love. She put the child to bed, and ran off to the church to hear the famous preacher, and see him beat his back till it spurted blood.

She gratified at once her devotional instincts and taste for excitement, and when the sermon and scourging were over, returned much edified and delighted to her lodging. But what was her horror, on entering the bedroom, to see no trace of the infant! She set up a piteous cry, and ran about the house. On reaching the foot of the back stairs she saw a bundle like a blue bag with two very pink legs depending from it. Her child had scrambled out of bed, got to the stairs, crept between the banisters, and fallen, but had been caught by a projection, which gathered the clothes over its head and held the child suspended, kicking its exposed nether limbs in space. The report of this miracle spread through the town, and greatly enhanced the popular opinion of the saint.

When the scourge and the iron bar had ceased to draw congregations, Leonard adopted a crown of thorns, which he pressed on to his temples so that the blood trickled over his face when he preached, and he hung an iron chain round his neck and made it clank loudly whilst he beat his naked body. And this proved very attractive to coarse natures requiring startling sights to awaken them. Genoa and Corsica were indulged with this spectacle, and it drew as many as a hundred thousand persons at Genoa to witness it. After the mission at Genoa the names of Jesus and Mary were inscribed in letters of gold on the gate of Monte-Reale, to the firing of cannons and the pealing of all the bells in the town.

The Pope called him to Rome in 1751; he was then ill. He left Tolentino, where he had been staying, when the mountains were covered with snow. He felt the cold severely, and looked like a corpse. His fellow traveller, seeing that he was ghastly pale, asked him anxiously how he felt. "I am ill," he answered. No suffering had drawn a word of complaint from him for five-and-twenty years.

On reaching Foligno he attempted to say Mass; his comrade remonstrated with him; but Leonard said, "My brother, one Mass is worth more than all the wealth of the world." The reverse of Henry IV.'s "Paris vaut bien une messe."

When they passed through the gates of Rome, he said

to his fellow traveller, "Begin the Te Deum; I will respond." Thus chanting together the hymn of praise, they arrived at the convent of S. Bonaventura on November 26, after sunset.

He was removed from the conveyance in which he was seated, but he could not walk; he was therefore carried at once to the infirmary. His pulse was failing. He asked to be confessed, and to receive the viaticum. Having received the Holy Sacrament, he implored the doctor not to order him meat, as he desired to keep his rule to the end.

The sacrament of extreme unction was then administered, and he sank into a state of coma, which passed imperceptibly into death. He died at the age of seventy-four, wanting only a few days of being seventy-five.

His relics are in the church of S. Bonaventura at Rome.

November 27.

SS. BARLAAM AND JOSAPHAT, *CC. in India; circ.* B.C. 543.
SS. IRENARCHUS, ACACIUS, AND OTHERS, *MM. at Sebaste in Armenia;* A.D. 303.
SS. FACUNDUS AND PRIMITIVUS, *MM. in Galicia;* A.D. 304.
S. JUSTUS, *P.C. at Limoges; circ.* A.D. 370.
S. VALERIAN, *B. of Aquileja; circ.* A.D. 388.
S. JAMES INTERCISUS, *M. in Persia;* A.D. 421.
S. MAXIMUS, *B. of Riez;* A.D. 460.
S. ACHARIUS, *B. of Noyon;* A.D. 639.
S. GULSTAN, *H. at Houadec in Brittany; beginning of 7th cent.*
S. VIRGILIUS, *B. of Salzburg;* A.D. 780.
S. BILHILD, *W. at Mainz;* 8th cent.
S. SIMEON METAPHRASTES, *C. at Constantinople;* 10th cent.
B. MARGARET OF SAVOY, *W. at Turin;* A.D. 1464.

SS. BARLAAM AND JOSAPHAT, CC.

(ABOUT B.C. 543.)

[Modern Roman Martyrology. The Russian Kalendars and Menæas on Nov. 19. Authority :—The Narrative by S. John Damascene.]

HE story of Barlaam and Josaphat is a Buddhist legend of the youth of Gotama Buddha, or Sidhartta, as he was called before he was arrayed with the Bodishat.

Sudhodana, king of Kapilawastu, became the father, by his wife, Maka Maya, of a prince, Sidhartta. The Brahmins prophesied at his birth that he would become an ascetic, if he were allowed to see decrepitude, sickness, a recluse, and a dead body. His father therefore built him a palace and surrounded it with guards who should keep off poor and sick people, and not suffer an ascetic to approach, and remove every sign of death. The prince grew to the age of sixteen, enjoying life, and ignorant of the miseries to which man is heir, till one day when he was out riding he passed beyond the circuit of the guards, and lighted on an old man, decrepit, without teeth, and with grey hair. When he heard that this was the condition to which all men who live long must attain, his spirit failed within him. Four months after, Sidhartta saw a leper covered with sores, and learned that man is liable to disease. Four months after that again he came upon a dead body lying in a wood, devoured by worms. And then, full of horror, he resolved on renouncing the world. He fled from his palace, was invested in the habit of an ascetic by the Brahmin Ghatikara, and became Buddha.[1] The story came to S. John Damascene probably not as told of Buddha himself, but of his disciple Asasat, whom he calls Josaphat. The Brahmin hermit, his tutor, is called Barlaam, and made a Christian ascetic. S. John Damascene was no doubt thoroughly deceived himself in the matter. He lived amidst Mussulmans, and not Buddhists, and the Mohammedans probably mistook Indian Buddhists for Christians. The date of the death of Buddha is thought to be B.C. 543.[2]

Numerous relics of the great founder of Buddhism remain in India, the most famous being the tooth in Ceylon. We are not aware of any receiving veneration at Rome. It is not necessary here to enter into further particulars of the life of Buddha, as Baronius was probably unaware that he was introducing him into the Roman Martyrology when he

[1] The legend may be seen in R. Spence Hardy's "Manual of Buddhism," 1860, p. 140 *et seq.*
[2] It may perhaps amuse the reader to hear what MM. Guerin and Giry say about these saints. "Si nous avions l'histoire des deux glorieux confesseurs d'une plume moins fidèle et moins sûre que celle de Saint Jean Damascène, nous aurions sujet de craindre qu'elle ne passât pour fabuleuse ; mais l'autorité d'un si grand homme, qui la propose comme véritable et qui proteste l'avoir apprise de personnes dignes de croyance, ce qui fait que l'Eglise romaine l'a reçue comme authentique, et a mis ces deux saints en son Martyrologe, ne nous permet pas d'en douter."

adopted his legend from S. John Damascene.[1] The story of Barlaam and Josaphat found its way into the Golden Legend of Jacques de Voragine and into the Gesta Romanorum, and was translated into most European languages. There is even an Icelandic version of it.

SS. FACUNDUS AND PRIMITIVUS, MM.

(A.D. 304.)

[Roman Martyrology. Authority :—The fabulous Acts.]

FACUNDUS and Primitivus were the sons of the martyr Marcellus. They were tried by the prætor Atticus in Galicia. After having undergone many tortures, two angels appeared, bearing crowns. "Cut off the heads of the criminals," said the prætor, "that there may be no place on which the crowns can be set." This was done on the banks of the river Ceia.

S. JUSTUS, P.C.

(ABOUT A.D. 370.)

[Gallican Breviaries of Limoges, Perigueux, Poitiers, &c., on Nov. 27. Saussaye in his Martyrology on Nov. 26. Castellani on Oct. 27. The Bollandists on Oct. 27. Authority :—The Life of S. Justus by an unknown writer of unknown date, existing in two MSS., one of the 10th, the other of the 11th cent.]

S. JUSTUS was born in the neighbourhood of Limoges, of heathen parents, and was set as a boy to keep sheep. As he and some others took refuge under a large tree during a thunderstorm, they were all precipitated to the earth by a

---

[1] The identity of the story of Barlaam and Josaphat with that of Buddha has been remarked by Professor Max Müller in his "Essay on the Migration of Fables," "Contemporary Review," 1870, pp. 588-594.

lightning stroke, and Justus was so frightened that he vowed he would become a Christian. Against his parents' wishes he became a catechumen in the church of Limoges, and embraced the ecclesiastical state. He was baptized by S. Hilary of Poitiers, and received also from him the grace of Orders; and he accompanied the saintly bishop on an expedition he made to Perigueux.

On the death of S. Hilary, the people of Poitiers wished to elect him to the vacant see, but Justus fled and hid himself, so that he could be nowhere found, and then went to Rome with his brother Benedict. On his way back from Rome he was attacked with fever, and died at Limoges.

As the church of Limoges pretended in the Middle Ages to possess some notable relics, viz., a particle of the crimson robe with which Christ was vested when brought forth on Good Friday and shown to the people, also a portion of the dress of the B. Virgin Mary, also a thumb of S. Peter, and a head of S. Laurence, and a piece of the bread which our Lord broke at Emmaus—and found some difficulty in substantiating their genuineness, a narrative of a journey to Rome undertaken by S. Hilary and S. Justus, and pretending to be written by Justus himself, was forged, and an account given in it of the obtaining of these precious relics. As usual with forgeries, it betrays its origin by anachronisms. Constantine is emperor when S. Leo is Pope. Constantine died in 337, S. Leo between 440 and 461, and S. Hilary of Poitiers died in 367, having been elected bishop about 355. Two bodies of the same saint were preserved simultaneously at Limoges, one in the cathedral, the other in the abbey of S. Martin, and there was a great contest between the regulars and seculars as to which possessed the genuine body. Some relics of the saint are shown at the present day at Couseiz, others in the church of S. Just.

S. JAMES INTERCISUS, M.

(A.D. 421.)

[Roman Martyrology. By Greeks, Copts, Maronites, &c. on same day. Authority :—The genuine Chaldee Acts in Assemani, Acta Mart. Orient. i. p. 237. A Greek version in Metaphrastes, simplified.]

S. JAMES was a native of Beth-Lapetha, a royal city in Persia, of high rank, and much in favour with the king, Isdegerdes. When Abdias, the bishop, had burned down a fine temple in a fit of intemperate zeal, the king persecuted the Christians, and James shrank from disgrace and death, giving up outward conformity to Christianity.

His wife and mother were grieved at his fall, and withdrew from his society. Upon the death of King Isdegerdes they wrote to him the following letter: "We were informed long ago, that, for the sake of the king's favour and for worldly riches, you forfeited the love of the immortal God. Think where that king now lies, on whose favour you set such store. Unhappy man! behold he is crumbled to dust—the fate of all mortals: nor can you any longer hope to receive honour or gifts from him, much less be protected by him from eternal torments. And know that if you persevere in your estrangement from God, you yourself, by Divine justice, will suffer damnation along with the king your friend. We, for our parts, will have no more commerce with you." James was strongly affected on reading this letter, and began to reflect what just reproaches his apostacy would deserve at the last day from the mouth of the Judge of quick and dead. He appeared no more at court, shunned the company of those who would have endeavoured to seduce him, and renounced honours, pomp, and pleasure. He bitterly bewailed his fall, and his words of self-condemnation were speedily carried to Vararanes, the new king.

He was sent for, and boldly confessed he was a Christian. The king asked him where was his gratitude for the favours which had been showered on him by Isdegerdes. "And where is that prince now? What has become of him?" asked James. Vararanes threatened him with a lingering death. "Let me die the death of the righteous," said the saint. "Death is but sleep."

"Death," said the king, "is not sleep; it is a terror to kings."

"The hope of the wicked shall perish," said James.

"Do you call us wicked, you who worship not sun, moon, fire nor water?"

"Sire," answered James, "I give not the incommunicable name to creatures."

The king, greatly incensed, after discussing the case with some of his counsellors, came to the decision that if James would not renounce Christianity and conform to the established religion, he should be hung on the rack, and his limbs be cut off one after another, joint by joint. The sentence was no sooner made public than the whole city flocked together to see this uncommon execution, and the Christians, falling prostrate on the ground, poured forth their prayers to God for the martyr, who had been carried from the court without delay to the place of execution. When he arrived there, he begged a moment's respite, and, turning his face towards the east, he fell on his knees, and, lifting up his eyes to heaven, prayed with great fervour. After having allowed him time for his devotions, the executioners approached, and displayed their weapons; then they took hold of his hand, and violently stretched out his arm; and in that posture explained to him the cruel death he was to suffer, and pressed him to avert so terrible a punishment by obeying the king. His birth, and the high rank which he had held in the empire, the flower of his age, and the comeliness and majesty of his person, moved the whole multitude of spec-

tators to tears. The heathens conjured him to dissemble
his religion only for the present, saying he might return to
it again after the wrath of the king was overpassed. The
martyr answered them: "This death, which appears to you
so dreadful, is very little for the purchase of eternal life."
Then, turning to the executioners, he said: "Why stand ye
idly looking on? Why begin ye not your work?" They
therefore cut off his right thumb. Upon which he prayed
thus aloud: "O Saviour of Christians, receive a branch of
the tree. It will decay, but will bud again, and will be
clothed with glory." The judge who had been appointed
by the king to oversee the execution, burst into tears, and
many cried out to the martyr: "It is enough that you have
lost thus much for the sake of religion. Suffer not your
body to be cut up piecemeal, and destroyed. You have
riches: bestow part of them on the poor for the good of
your soul, but die not in this manner." S. James answered:
"The vine dies in winter, yet revives in spring: and shall
not the body when cut down sprout up again?" When his
first finger was cut off, he cried out: "My heart was glad,
my glory rejoiced: my flesh also shall rest in hope. Receive, O Lord, another branch." The joy of his heart
seemed visible in his countenance. At the lopping off each
finger he thanked God afresh. After the loss of the fingers
of his right hand, and again after those of his left, he was
conjured by the judges to conform and save himself. To
whom he meekly answered: "He is not worthy of God, who,
after putting his hand to the plough, shall look back." The
great toe of his right foot was next cut off, and followed
by the rest; then the little toe of the left foot, and all the
others after it. At the loss of each part, the martyr repeated
the praises of God, exulting as at a triumph. When his
fingers and toes were gone, he cheerfully said to the executioner: "Now the boughs are smitten off, cut down the

trunk. Do not pity me; for my heart hath rejoiced in the Lord, and my soul is lifted up to Him who loveth the humble and the feeble." Then his right foot, after that his left foot: next the right, then the left hand were cut off. The right arm, and next the left: then the right leg, and after that the left felt the knife. While he lay weltering in his blood, his thighs were torn from the hips. Lying a naked trunk, and having already lost half his body, he still continued to mutter prayers, till a guard, by severing his head from his body, completed his martyrdom. This took place on the 27th of November, in the year of our Lord 421, the second of King Vararanes. The Christians offered a considerable sum of money for the martyr's relics, but were not allowed to redeem them. They afterwards seized an opportunity that presented itself, and carried off the body. It was sunset, and the last rays falling on the mangled body and its fragments, bathed them in a ruddy glory.

S. MAXIMUS, B. OF RIEZ.

(A.D. 460.)

[Roman and Gallican Martyrologies. Usuardus, Ado, Notker, Wandelbert, &c. Authorities:—A Life by Dinamius the Patrician, a disciple, addressed to Urbicus, B. of Riez (584—585). A Homily on S. Maximus by Faustus, his disciple, who succeeded him in the see. This homily is falsely attributed to Eusebius of Emesa. Both Life and Homily in Surius. Also Gregory of Tours, De Glor. Conf. c. 33.]

MAXIMUS was born of Christian parents at Decomerus, in Provence, now Château-Redon, near Digne. He entered the monastic isle of Lerins, and placed himself under S. Honoratus, and when that saint was raised, in 426, to the episcopal throne of Arles, Maximus succeeded him as abbot of Lerins. Thinking he was likely to be made bishop of

Frejus, he fled and hid in a forest till the see was filled. But he was elected to that of Riez in 433. He assisted at the council of Riez in 439, at that of Orange in 441, and that of Arles in 454. He built a church in his city to S. Albinus, and was one of the Gallican bishops who received the letter of S. Leo to Flavian of Constantinople, against the errors of Eutyches, and joined in the synodal letter condemning them. He died in 460, and his body is preserved in the cathedral at Riez.

S. VIRGILIUS, B. OF SALZBURG.

(A.D. 780.)

[Roman and Benedictine Martyrology. Canonized by Pope Gregory IX. Authority :—A Life written after 1181, derived from the "Libellus de conversione Bagoariorum et Carantanorum," by an anonymous writer in 871. This Libellus in Pertz, xi. pp. 4-15. The Life in Mabillon, Acta SS. O.S.B. sæc. iii. 2, and Pertz, xi. pp. 86-95. Fragmenta ex Libro donationum Eccl. Saltzburgensis, in Mabillon, after the Life. Also S. Boniface, Ep. 140.]

VIRGILIUS, an Irishman, came to France in the beginning of the 8th century, and was well received by Pepin, then Mayor of the Palace, at Cressy, and remained at court nearly two years. After that he was made abbot of S. Peter's at Salzburg. It was then that he had a difference with S. Boniface. Virgilius and his companion Sidonius found a priest in Bavaria who was so ignorant of Latin, that when baptizing he used the formula, "Baptizo te in nomine Patria, et Filia, et Spiritua sancta." They corrected his error, but did not judge that his baptism had been invalidated by his bad Latin. S. Boniface heard of this decision of theirs, was indignant, and pronounced that these baptisms were not valid, and that the sacrament must be reiterated over those who had received it from the ignorant priest. Virgilius and

Sidonius wrote to Pope Zacharias, and he at once sent a letter to Boniface expressing his surprise at his decision, and confirming the opinion of Virgilius. "We cannot," said he, "consent to the rebaptism of those whom this priest baptized thus in ignorance of the language, and without any error of doctrine; for those who have been baptized by heretics are admitted to have received the valid sacrament, if they have received it in the name of the Trinity."

Apparently S. Boniface was mortified at not getting the better of Virgilius, and he lay in wait to find some accusations against him, and effect his humiliation, if not his ruin. Such an opportunity shortly occurred. Virgilius seems to have believed the popular legends of elves or gnomes prevalent among the people, of little folks who lived in the depths of the mountains, in a marvellous world illuminated by a mysterious sun and moon of brilliants and other precious stones, and whose little hammers, clinking as they worked the ore, were heard by the miners in their shafts.

S. Boniface wrote to the Pope denouncing his error. Zacharias answered that the doctrine of a world of men underground, with another sun and moon, was "a perverse and unjust doctrine, uttered against God and his own soul," and that Virgilius, if he taught it, should be tried by a council, and deposed from his priesthood.[1] It has been often asserted, erroneously, that Zacharias condemned the doctrine of the world being round and of there being antipodes.[2]

It is impossible to say exactly what Virgilius taught; we only know about his doctrine from the letter of Zacharias, as that of S. Boniface is lost. But it would seem from the

---

[1] "De perversa et iniqua doctrina, quam contra Deum et animam suam locutus est, si clarificatum fuerit ita eum confiteri, quod alius mundus et alii homines sub terras sint, hunc accito Concilio ab Ecclesia pelle sacerdotii honore privatum."—Zach. Ep. 140.

[2] See also "L'évêque Virgile et les Antipodes," in Barthélemy, "Erreurs et mensonges historiques," Paris, 1866.

wording of the letter, that his teaching was not that of the world being round, but rather that of there being an underground world with a sun and moon of its own, different from those which illuminate our skies. And as this is precisely the popular superstition among mountaineers and miners with whom Virgilius lived, it is quite as probable that he believed their tales, as that he had adopted the theory of Thales of Miletus and of Pythagoras.

Zacharias wrote to Odilo, Duke of Bavaria, to send Virgilius to Rome to justify himself. What the result was is not known. It does not seem that he went to Rome, or that a council sat on his heresy. Probably he wrote an explanation of his views to the Pope, and the matter was allowed to drop.

After the death of S. John, bishop of Salzburg, Virgilius was appointed to the see, at the request of Pepin, by Odilo, Duke of Bavaria. Virgilius most reluctantly received the appointment. He would not, however, at once be consecrated, but made an Irish bishop, Dobda, who had accompanied him from Ireland, his coadjutor, to ordain and confirm, and it was not till two years after, in 767, that Virgilius was consecrated.

In the reign of Dagobert, Samo, duke of the Sclaves in Carinthia, killed the ambassadors of the Frank king sent to him. Dagobert revenged the outrage by subduing the Carinthian Sclaves. Whilst Virgilius was bishop of Salzburg the Huns attacked Carinthia, and Boruth, the duke, appealed to the Bavarians for help, and the united forces of the Carinthians and Bavarians repelled the invaders; but in return for their assistance, the latter required the duke to give up his son Charast as a hostage of submission to the empire, and to be educated as a Christian. On the death of Boruth, Charast was sent back to Carinthia as duke. He died three years after, and by order of Pepin the Carinthians received

Chetimar, the nephew of Boruth, as their duke, who had also been baptized and taught Christian truth. Chetimar invited S. Virgilius to visit Carinthia and preach to the Sclaves, but the bishop was unable to do so. He, however, sent Modestus, a bishop, and four priests to Carinthia. Modestus remained there till his death. Then Chetimar again urged Virgilius to visit his people, but Virgilius again refused, not apparently being endowed with much missionary enthusiasm or energy of disposition. There was some disturbance, moreover, in the duchy, and he considered it wiser to send Latinus, a priest, to Carinthia, than to risk his own person. Latinus found the place too hot for him, and refused to remain. As soon as tranquillity was restored, Virgilius sent thither the priest, Madelhohus, and after him the priest Wargmann.

On the death of Chetimar, a contest for the succession distracted the duchy and impeded missionary enterprise. But when Watung became duke, a third appeal was made to Virgilius to come in person and organize the infant Church in Carinthia. He sent two priests, Heumann and Reginbald, and a deacon, Majoran; and afterwards another batch of ecclesiastics. When Carinthia was brought under the Gospel, at least unto outward uniformity, Virgilius went himself throughout the duchy arranging and ordering all as seemed best fitting. On his return from this visitation, which cost him great labour, he fell sick and died at Salzburg, at an advanced age, in 780. His relics are preserved at Salzburg.

S. BILHILD, W.

(8TH CENTURY.)

[German, Gallican, and Benedictine Martyrologies. Authority :—A short Life in the Mainz Breviary.]

BILHILD was born at Hochheim, on the Main, not far above where that river enters the Rhine, in the reign of Clovis. Her father's name was Eberim, and her mother's Mechtrude. The family was noble. She was married to a man of birth and position, who fell in battle, leaving her with one child, which died soon after its father. Then, having nothing to live for, she went to her uncle Sigebert, bishop of Mainz, who gave her the veil, and she built and endowed a large monastery for women in that city.

This memoir is not happy in its chronology.

The date of Clovis is 482—510. Sigebert, bishop of Mainz, appears on the register in the Mainz cathedral library immediately before Gerold, who was killed in 743, the predecessor of Gewilieb, whom S. Boniface deposed in 745. Consequently the date of Sigebert will be about 716, and this must fix the date of S. Bilhild.

S. SIMEON METAPHRASTES, C.

(10TH CENTURY.)

[Modern Roman Martyrology. By the Greeks on Nov. 28. Authority :—An encomium on Simeon Metaphrastes by Michael Psellus (flor. 1100), published by Leo Allatius, Paris, 1664. See also Bolland. Acta SS. Præf. gen. t. i. c. 1, 3, 6 ; and Surius, Nov. 27.]

SIMEON METAPHRASTES was born at Constantinople of an illustrious family, and was educated with great care. He advanced to offices of trust in the court, and was logothete, or high treasurer. While still young he went to the island of Crete with Hermerius, grand captain of Leo the Philosopher, about A.D. 900. On this voyage he heard the particulars of the life of S. Theoctiste of Lesbos, a counterpart of S. Mary of Egypt,[1] which he heard from a monk named Simon, who enjoined him to write the Life. And this was the beginning of his great hagiographical collection. After this he undertook to collect as many as he could, at the request of the emperor himself, apparently Constantine Porphyrogenitus. As Simeon was wealthy, he was able to procure the manuscripts he required, and all the libraries of the monasteries in Constantinople were open to him. Unfortunately, Metaphrastes, instead of compiling the ancient acts of the martyrs and lives of the eremites in their original form, re-wrote and polished them up, and, apparently, added marvels and horrors either out of his own imagination, or from idle traditions, to suit a depraved popular taste for the horrible and the marvellous. The difference may be seen between the version of Metaphrastes and the original in the acts of the martyrs Tharacus, Probus, Andronicus, which have been preserved. If we compare the life of S. Demetrius of Thessalonica as written by Metaphrastes, with that by Anastasius the librarian, and that by Photius, written in the preceding century, we see what strides that imagination had made in playing with facts; if we compare the simple narrative of the passion of S. Procopius in Eusebius, with the romance of Procopius the duke, in Metaphrastes, we see facts distorted beyond recognition by the same faculty. S. Simeon was given the name Metaphrastes, or Translator, on account of this work. He is also thought to have written a chronographia or history compiled out of ten earlier historians. But great uncertainty reigns as to whether the

[1] See Surius, Nov. 10.

author of this chronographia was the same as the author of the Lives of the Saints. And it is also doubted whether Simeon Logotheta be the same as Simeon Metaphrastes. Michael Psellus gives us little detail and much pompous declamation.

S. Catherine. See p. 60.

ALTAR OF GOLD, IN THE CLUNY MUSEUM.
Presented to the ancient Cathedral of Basle by the Emperor Henry II.

November 28.

S. Sosthenes, *C. at Corinth;* 1st cent.
S. Rufus, *M. at Rome; circ.* A.D. 304.
SS. Papinian and Mansuetus, *BB. MM.*, and Valerian, Urbanus, and Others, *BB. CC. in Africa;* A.D. 430.
S. Secundinus, *B. of Dunshaglin in Meath;* A.D. 448.
S. Patrician, *B. in Sutherland;* 5th cent.
S. Philip, *B. of Vienne; circ.* A.D. 580.
SS. Hilary and Quieta, *CC. at Dijon;* 6th cent.
S. Gregory III., *Pope of Rome;* A.D. 741.
S. Stephen the Younger, *M. at Constantinople;* A.D. 764.
S. James de la Marca, *O.M. at Naples;* A.D. 1476.

S. SOSTHENES, C.

(1ST CENT.)

[Roman Martyrology, Usuardus, &c. By the Greeks with Apollo, Cephas, Tychicus, Epaphroditus, Cæsarius, and Onesiphorus on March 29 and 30 and Dec. 8. The Menology of Sirletus on Dec. 7, the Menology of the Emperor Basil on Dec. 9. Authority:—Acts xviii. 12-17; 1 Cor. I.]

OSTHENES, a Jew of Corinth, was seized and beaten in the presence of Gallio, in the insurrection made by the Jews against S. Paul. He was ruler of the synagogue, and apparently succeeded Crispus, who "believed on the Lord with all his house." Sosthenes was probably a bigoted Jew, and a crowd of Greeks, taking advantage of the indifference of Gallio, and ever ready to show contempt for the Jews, no doubt also irritated at the disturbance made by them in the matter of Paul, turned their indignation against the ruler of the synagogue as the representative Jew.

S. Paul wrote the first epistle to the Corinthians jointly in his own name and that of a certain Sosthenes, whom he terms "the brother." The Roman Martyrology identifies him with the ruler of the synagogue, and supposes that this ruler suffered because of his devotion to the truths spoken by S. Paul. But it would appear from the context that Sosthenes, the chief ruler, suffered from quite another cause, and represented the anti-Christian party among the Jews. It is not therefore probable that he and "the brother" are one. The name was a very common one, and little stress can be laid on that coincidence. If the Sosthenes of the epistle be the Sosthenes of the Acts, he must have been converted at a later period, and have been at Ephesus and not at Corinth when S. Paul wrote to the Corinthians. The pseudo Dorotheus and pseudo Hippolytus make him bishop of Colophon.

S. SECUNDINUS, B. IN MEATH.

(A.D. 448.)

[Irish Kalendars. Authority :—The Lives of S. Patrick.]

SECUNDINUS, a bishop, arrived in Ireland in 439, along with Auxilius and Iserninus, to assist S. Patrick in his great apostolic work. Secundinus and Auxilius were brothers, and nephews of S. Patrick by his sister Darerca, according to some authorities, but no reliance can be placed on stories told about the relationship of S. Patrick and the early saints of Ireland. They were probably disciples of his whom he sent into Gaul or Britain to receive episcopal consecration, and returned to him in 439. Secundinus planted himself in Meath, and made Dunshaglin his see, about 443; he died in 448. He appears erroneously in some lists as bishop of Armagh.

S. GREGORY III., POPE.

(A. D. 741.)

[Roman Martyrology. Authorities :—Anastasius the Librarian, and his own Letters.]

GREGORY III., who succeeded Gregory II. in the see of Rome, was a Syrian by birth, skilled in the Greek and Latin tongues, and noted for his knowledge of the Scriptures and his eloquent preaching. He was liberal and charitable, and spent large funds in redeeming captives and relieving widows and orphans. Gregory II. died in 731, in the heat of contest with the Emperor Leo III. in the matter of images. Gregory III. was elected by acclamation of the people, whilst he was following the coffin of Gregory II. to its tomb. His nomination was at once forwarded to the exarch of Ravenna, for his approbation and confirmation. But no sooner had he obtained this, than he sent a deputation to Constantinople to announce to the emperor his inflexible adhesion to the sacredness of images. The mission was confided to George the priest, but the language of the message was so sternly condemnatory of the emperor's proceedings, that the trembling ambassador had hardly begun his journey when he fled back to Rome, and confessed that the enthusiasm and faith to carry him to martyrdom were wanting in his breast. The Pope indignantly threatened to degrade him from his priestly office, and was hardly persuaded to content himself with forcing the timorous George to resume his dangerous mission. George was arrested in Sicily and not allowed to proceed. Gregory thereupon summoned a council, November 1, 732. It was attended by the archbishops of Grado and Ravenna and ninety-three Western bishops, together with the consuls and people of Rome, and many laics of distinction. The council decreed that " In future whoever shall carry off

destroy, dishonour, or insult the images of the Saviour or of
'the immaculate and glorious Virgin,' or of the apostles, &c.,
should be forbidden to receive the body and blood of the
Lord, and be excluded from the Church." All signed this
decision. The Pope then sent another letter to the Emperor
Leo, and made the Defender of the Poor—an officer of the
Roman Church—bearer of the despatch. He also was
arrested in Sicily, and his papers taken from him. The same
fate attended the ambassadors of the Italian towns who
were made bearers of similar missives. A fourth attempt
was made, but we do not learn the result.

In 732, Leo the Isaurian sent a fleet to punish Rome,
the Pope, and Italy for their opposition to his enterprises
against images. But the fleet was wrecked in the Adriatic,
and the emperor was obliged to content himself with raising
the imposts in Sicily and Calabria, and in confiscating the
"patrimony" of the apostles Peter and Paul, consisting of
three and a half talents of gold, which was paid annually
to the Church of Rome. The emperor also detached
Sicily and Calabria and the provinces of Illyria from the
Roman see, and placed them under the patriarchate of
Constantinople. With the wreck of the imperial navy, the
authority of the eastern emperor over northern Italy virtually
came to an end. The exarch of Ravenna, unsupported,
could not make his power and authority felt, and some years
later he abandoned the seat of government, and took refuge
in Naples.

Now, however, that the real power of the empire in Italy
was extinguished, it might seem that nothing could resist
the Lombards. Though King Luitprand and Gregory III.,
at least for the first eight years of Gregory's pontificate,
maintained their outward amity, the Lombards, albeit now
no longer Arians, were dreaded as barbarian invaders, and
the Pope shuddered lest he should become the subject of a

sovereign of savage manners and foreign origin. At this juncture the attention of Europe, of all Christendom, was centred on the Franks. The great victory of Tours had raised Charles Martel to the position of protector of the liberties and the religion of the Western world.

When at last the Lombards and the Pope were involved in open war, Gregory was forced to appeal to Charles Martel for protection. "His tears," he wrote, "were falling day and night for the destitute state of the Church. The Lombard king and his son were ravaging by fire and sword the last remains of the property of the Church, which no longer sufficed for the sustenance of the poor, or for providing lights for the daily service. They had invaded the territory of Rome, and seized all his farms; his only hope was in the timely succour of the Frankish king." Gregory knew that the Lombards were negotiating with the Frank, and dexterously appealed to his pride. "The Lombards were perpetually speaking of him with contempt,—' Let him come, this Charles, with his army of Franks; if he can, let him rescue you out of his hands.' O unspeakable grief, that such sons so insulted should make no effort to defend their holy mother the Church! Not that S. Peter was unable to protect his successors, and to exact vengeance upon their oppressors; but the apostle was putting the faith of his followers to trial." Gregory sent Charles the keys of the tomb of S. Peter, and the offer of the titles of Patrician and Consul of Rome. Charles Martel received the first mission of Gregory III. with munificence, yet not without hesitation. He owed a debt of gratitude to the Lombard king for services rendered, perhaps all Western Christendom was also indebted to him, for according to the Lombard's epitaph, he had fought in person by the side of Charles against the Saracens. Accordingly Charles returned a courteous but evasive answer, and sent presents to Rome.

It is curious to note that while the Pope was appealing to Charles as the champion of Christendom, the clergy of France were denouncing him to damnation as a sacrilegious person, a robber of churches. He had, in fact, in the hour of need, when the fate of Christendom trembled in the balance, laid his hand on the wealth of the rich bishops and abbots, to pay his mercenaries and soldiers who were to fight and repel the wave of invading Mohammedanism. A second letter of Gregory met with no better result.

Charles Martel died almost immediately after, in 741, at Quercy on the Oise, and Gregory followed him in the same year. Although the patrimony of the Church was so plundered that there was not money for the support of the poor, he was able to adorn sumptuously several of the churches in Rome. Six silver columns given him by the exarch Eutychius he placed round the Confession of S. Peter, and set on them silver architraves and statues of the Saviour and the apostles, and on six other columns the images of the B. Virgin and female saints. He hung silver lilies and candelabra above the sacred spot. He built an oratory in honour of all the saints, which he adorned with a gold chalice encrusted with jewels, an image of the Virgin, and a crown with a cross dependent from it, all of gold. He gave a gold statue of the Virgin Mother holding her Divine Child, enriched with jewels, to the church of S. Maria Maggiore. He gave a similar costly statue of S. Andrew to the church of that apostle. The amount of gold he used for these ornaments weighed 73 lbs.; of silver, 376 lbs.: a considerable amount considering the circumstances of destitution in which the Papacy, the poor, and the lamps then found themselves. He also gave lands and slaves to the monks of S. Chrysogonus. He paid for rebuilding the walls of Rome, and he purchased of Thrasimund, duke of Spoleto, a castle, which threatened the estates of the Church.

S. STEPHEN THE YOUNGER, M.

(A.D. 764.)

[Roman Martyrology. Greek Menæas and Menologies on Oct. 20, 21, 28, and Nov. 28. Authority:—The Acts compiled forty-two years after his death by Stephen of Constantinople. Also Cedrenus and Theophanes.]

S. STEPHEN, surnamed the Younger, was born at Constantinople in 714, and dedicated to the religious life even before he was born. His parents were wealthy, but as they desired to concentrate their fortune in the hands of their elder children, so soon as Stephen's mother gave promise of bearing another child, it was resolved to dispose of him in the most economical way possible, by obliging him to become a monk. He was delivered over in early youth to monastic teachers, and educated within the walls of a convent. At the age of sixteen he took the irrevocable vows in the monastery of S. Auxentius, near Chalcedon. The great advantage of this monastery in the eyes of his parents was its absolute poverty, and that it required no payment with those who entered or were put into it. The monastery consisted of little cells about the mountain, in which the religious lived like hermits.

After the death of his father, Stephen put his mother and sister into a convent in Bithynia; he had another sister, a nun, in Constantinople.

Stephen wore only a sheepskin girded round his loins by an iron belt. A young widow, named Anne, placed herself under his direction, and took the veil in a nunnery at the foot of his mountain. He became abbot when aged thirty, but resigned the office in his forty-second year, and built himself a low cell, so cramped that he could neither lie nor stand in it, and into this he shut himself.

In the iconoclastic persecution of Constantine Copronymus a council was held at Constantinople (A.D. 754) against images. Three hundred and thirty-eight bishops assembled, and knowing the objection entertained by the emperor against the veneration of images, obsequiously condemned it. As Stephen was greatly respected for his austerities, and the nakedness, dirt, and starvation in which he lived attracted a swarm of devotees, it was thought advisable to secure, if possible, his adhesion to the decree of the Council. Constantine sent a patrician named Callistus to sound him, but Stephen had made up his mind on the matter, and answered the overtures of the officers with such disdain, that Callistus returned baffled to the emperor. Constantine sent a body of soldiers to bring him from his cell. He lay down and refused to move, and they were obliged to enter the odorous and disgusting den and remove him by force. He was brought to the foot of Mount S. Auxentius, and was placed under a guard there till he could be tried. Various charges were raked up against him, as absurd as they were false—one, that he had criminally conversed with the widow Anne, was ridiculous. A hermit covered with vermin and plastered with filth was not likely to attract the affection of a passionate young woman. As she refused to confess what the emperor wished, she was scourged, imprisoned, and died shortly after of ill-usage.

The emperor, seeking a new occasion to put Stephen to death, persuaded one of his courtiers called George Syncletus to draw him into a snare. Constantine had forbidden the monasteries to receive a novice. George went to Mount S. Auxentius, fell on his knees before S. Stephen, and begged to receive the monastic habit. The saint knew him to belong to the court, because he was shaved: the emperor having forbidden any at his court to wear beards. But the more S. Stephen urged the emperor's prohibition, the more earnestly the impostor pressed him to admit him to the habit, pretending that both his temporal safety from the persecutors, and his eternal salvation depended upon it. Soon after he had received the habit he ran with it to the court, and the next day the emperor produced him in that garb in the amphitheatre before the people. Constantine inflamed them by a violent invective against the saint and the monks; then publicly tore the habit off his back, and the populace trampled upon it. The emperor immediately sent a body of armed men to Mount S. Auxentius. They dispersed the monks, and burnt down the monastery and church. They took S. Stephen from the place of his confinement, and carried him to the sea-side, striking him with clubs, taking him by the throat, tearing his legs in the thorns, and insulting him with opprobrious language. In the port of Chalcedon they put him on board of a small vessel, and carried him to a monastery at Chrysopolis, a small town not far from Constantinople, where Callistus and several iconoclast bishops, with a Secretary of State, and another officer, came to visit and examine him. They treated him at first with civility, and afterwards with harshness. He asked them how they could call that a General Council which was not accepted either by the Pope of Rome or the patriarchs of Alexandria, Antioch, and Jerusalem. The emperor, on learning the determination of the hermit, condemned him to be carried into banishment in the island of Proconnesus, in the Propontis. In that place he was joined by many of his monks, and his miracles increased the reputation of his sanctity. The tyrant, two years after, ordered him to be removed to a prison in Constantinople and loaded with irons. Some days after, the saint was carried before the emperor, and asked whether he believed that men trampled on Christ by trampling on his image. "God forbid," said the martyr. Then taking a piece of money in his hand, he asked what treatment he should meet with, were he to stamp insultingly on the image of the emperor? There was but one answer to this question.

"Is it then," said the saint, "so great a crime to outrage the representation of the earthly emperor, and none to cast into the fire the image of the King of Heaven?"

The emperor ordered him to execution, and Stephen was led forth to death, but Constantine recalled the sentence at the last moment, and ordered him back to prison, and that he should be scourged. He was cruelly beaten and left half dead on the dungeon floor, bleeding and bruised. When the tyrant heard that he was still alive, he said, "Will no one rid me of this monk?" Thereupon two monks, with some soldiers, entered the prison, carried off the wretched sufferer, and dragged him by the feet through the streets over the rough pavement, whilst some beat at him with sticks, or pelted him with stones. At last his brains were dashed out with a club. His body was torn to pieces by the ferocious mob.

S. JAMES DE LA MARCA, O.M.

(A.D. 1476.)

[Roman and Franciscan Martyrologies. Beatified by Urban VIII., canonized by Benedict XIII. in 1726. Authorities :—A Life by Mark de Lisboa, B. of Porto.]

S. JAMES was born at Montebrandone in the Marches of Ancona, of poor parents. He was sent to Perugia to be educated, and he was there appointed tutor to a Florentine young man of rank. He joined the Franciscan Order in the Portiuncula at Assisi. For forty years he never passed a day without lashing his back with a knotted scourge; he wore a hair shirt, which was, no doubt, conducive to his health, which otherwise might have suffered from want of ablutions. Sometimes he varied his mortifications by putting on a mail coat set with spikes, in place of the hair shirt. He never touched meat, and slept only three hours. Had his mind been active, more sleep would indubitably have been necessary, but as his brain was apparently little exercised, a very slight amount of repose refreshed it after its slight labours. He was so scrupulous in the matter of obedience, that having once received an order to go on a certain mission, when he had raised a cup to his mouth full of water, for the purpose of drinking, he started on his errand without tasting the water.

He accompanied S. John Capistran in some of the inquisitorial missions of that saint in Germany, Bohemia, and Hungary; and the two holy men were well matched in their zeal for the advance of the reform of their Order, instituted by S. Bernardin of Siena, their hatred of heresy, and indifference to human suffering.

The enthusiasm and relentless severity with which James de la Marca proceeded against the heretics drove them to desperation.

The Fraticelli, an offshoot of his own Order, which had fallen into error, incurred his liveliest hostility. Many, trembling for their lives, made an enforced and dissembled submission. His conduct even excited the indignation of Catholic bishops and clergy, and they preached against him, and his manner of dealing with the refractory sheep of the fold of Christ, which they thought resembled rather that of the wolf than of the shepherd. He was even denounced to the Pope as tainted with heresy himself, but as he was arguing his case before the Inquisition, an image of the Blessed Virgin was seen to nod its head at him, and either the miracle, or the conviction that he was too useful a servant to be lost, moved the Inquisition to acquit him.

He died of colic, at the age of ninety, in Naples. His body was buried in the church of S. Maria Nuova, but was dug up and exposed to the veneration of the faithful by permission of Pope Sixtus IV. He is regarded as one of the patrons of the city of Naples. In 1631, when Vesuvius was in eruption, some imaginative persons believed they saw him thrusting back the flames into the crater and arresting the streams of lava. His association with pyres in which heretics were burnt may have suggested this apparition.

S. Andrew, Ap. See p. 63.

November 29.

S. SATURNINUS, B.M. *of Toulouse; middle of 3rd cent.*
SS. PARAMON AND CCCLXX. *MM.; 3rd cent.*
S. PHILOMENUS, *M. at Ancyra; circ.* A.D. 274.
SS. BLASIUS AND DEMETRIUS, *MM. at Veroli.*
SS. SATURNINUS AND SISINIUS, *MM at Rome; circ.* A.D. 309.[1]
S. RADBOD, *B. of Utrecht;* A.D. 918.

S. SATURNINUS, B.M.

(MIDDLE OF 3RD CENT.)

[Roman and Gallican Martyrologies. Usuardus, Ado, Notker, Wandelbert. Authority:—The Acts written about 420, as they mention the building of the church of S. Saturninus by Exuperius, B. of Toulouse, 405-415, and Exuperius is spoken of as a "saint," so that he must have been dead.]

 SATURNINUS is said to have gone to Gaul at the command of Pope Fabian in 245. In 250, when Decius and Gratus were consuls, S. Saturninus fixed his episcopal see at Toulouse. Fortunatus says that he converted many by his preaching and miracles. We know nothing more of him till his martyrdom. The author of the Acts, who wrote about sixty years after his death, says that he assembled his flock in a small church, and that the Capitol, in which was the chief temple of the city, lay in the road between his house and the church. As he was one day passing, the priests drew him into the temple, and declared that if he would not do sacrifice they would have him put to death. Saturninus refused to give worship to stocks and stones. A bull had been

---

[1] Only known from the fabulous Acts of Pope S. Marcellus (Jan. 16).

brought to the temple for sacrifice, and they tied his feet to the tail of the beast, which plunged about with him and then ran down the hill from the Capitol, dragging Saturninus with it and dashing his head against the stones. The cord broke eventually, but not before Saturninus was dead. Two Christian women hastily buried the body in a wooden coffin, in a moat, and there it lay till Constantine gave peace to the Church, when it was exhumed, and Hilary, bishop of Toulouse, built a chapel over it. The martyrdom perhaps took place in the reign of Valerian, in 257, but it is difficult to fix its date from want of sufficient information in the Acts. The imagination of legend writers has added greatly to this simple and authentic narrative. A Life much more calculated to gratify the popular taste was forged, and the forger audaciously and unscrupulously asserted that he drew his facts from the lips of Honestus and Gratian, the disciples of Saturninus. According to this impudent fabrication, which receives general credence at Toulouse, Saturninus was the son of Ægeus, king of Achaia, and Cassandra, daughter of Ptolemy, king of Nineveh. He became a disciple of S. John the Baptist, followed Christ, was one of His most devoted disciples, and after the Ascension attached himself to S. Peter, who sent him into Spain and Aquitain. He preached at Pampeluna and Toulouse. In Spain he converted two girls, the daughters of the king of Huesca, and when their father was indignant at their deserting the established religion, they eloped from Huesca with Saturninus, who left his disciple Honestus to rule the Church of Toledo.

As he was about to be tied to the tail of the bull, Saturninus besought two priests who attended him to remain with him to the last. They, however, were so frightened that they ran away, and Saturninus thereupon cursed Toulouse, that no priest, a native of that city, should ever mount its episcopal throne: an imprecation which, we are assured, has been ratified.[1] An angel appeared to the martyr, to console him for this base desertion, and prepare him for a succession of hideous tortures, of which the early writer of the Acts knew nothing. At the prayer of the saint all the idols fell and were broken to fragments, and the idolaters pelted the martyr with the bits. As the bull dragged him down the stairs of the Capitol, his brains were dashed out. The two princesses of Huesca diligently collected them into a vessel, and then ran after the bull to mop up the scattered blood of the martyr, and finally bury his body. These maidens—whom Fortunatus merely calls a woman and her servant—receive veneration in the church of Toulouse as "Les deux Pucelles," two holy virgins. For their attention to the remains of the saint they were soundly scourged, and they then fled Toulouse, and took refuge in a village near Castelnaudary, now called after them Mas des Saintes-Pucelles, where they died and were buried. Their relics were afterwards translated to Toulouse. The relics of S. Saturninus are shown at Toulouse in the cathedral.

In art he is represented with a bull.

S. RADBOD, B. OF UTRECHT.

(A.D. 918.)

[Benedictine Martyrology. Commemorated at Utrecht. Authority:— A Life written by a contemporary, in Mabillon, Acta SS. O.S.B. sæc. v.]

S. RADBOD was born of noble Frank race. He spent his youth with Gunther, archbishop of Cologne, his uncle, and

---

[1] Guerin and Giry say, with their wonted imbecility: "Quelques-un rejettent ce récit comme indigne de la charité de Saint Saturnin, qui l'aurait porté à prier pour ces prêtres ——, mais ces sortes d'imprécations prophétiques sont justifiées par une infinité d'exemples des saints, et l'Esprit de Dieu leur a inspiré ces mouvements de zèle pour la terreur des pécheurs."

when educated he was sent to the courts of Charles the Bold, and Louis, his son. He composed an office and some hymns on S. Martin, an account of S. Liafwin, and a hymn on S. Swidbert. In a short chronicle which he compiled, he says, under the date 900: " I Radbod, a sinner, have been assumed, though unworthy, into the company of the ministers of the Church of Utrecht; with whom I pray that I may attain eternal life." Before the end of that year he was elected bishop of Utrecht, on the death of Egibold, who occupied the see hardly a twelvemonth.

Whilst he was bishop, the Danes threatened an incursion, and the destruction of Utrecht. He prayed, and the unwholesome marsh water produced dysentery, which carried off so many of the pirates that the rest deserted the country without having sacked Utrecht. He is reported to have been very kind to the poor, and careless about his own comforts. He died on November 29, 918, at Deventer.

November 30.

S. Andrew, *Ap. M. at Patras in Achaia;* 1st cent.
SS. Maura and Justina, *VV. MM. at Constantinople.*
S. Constantius, *C. at Rome; circ.* A.D. 418.
S. Zosimus, *C. in Palestine; beginning of 6th cent.*
S. Trojanus, *B. of Saintes in France;* A.D. 532.
S. Tugdual, *B. of Tréguier in Brittany; circ.* A.D. 564.
S. Francis Xavier, *S.J. at San-Chan;* A.D. 1552

S. ANDREW, AP. M.

(1ST CENT.)

[Roman and all Western Martyrologies, also all Greek, Russian, Koptic, Syriac Kalendars, Menæas, and Menologies. In 337 Constantine brought the relics of the Apostle Andrew to Constantinople. In some Martyrologies on May 9 is the commemoration of this translation; in others on this day, "At Milan the commemoration of S. Andrew in the basilica at the Roman Gate." In the Martyrology wrongly called that of S. Jerome, this translation on Sept. 3, and on Nov. 3, "The dedication of the basilica of S. Andrew," whilst on Nov. 30 is the "Dies natalis." S. Andrew's Day (Nov. 30) in the Gothic Missal, in the list of festivals of the Council of Rheims, 625, in that of Charlemagne, and that of S. Boniface. In the Sacramentary of Leo I., the pontifical of Egbert of York, the Sacramentary of S. Gregory. In the Ordo Gelasianus, and in the ancient Missale Gellonense this festival has an octave (Martene, De Antiq. Eccl. Discip. c. 30).]

. ANDREW was one among the first called of the apostles of our Lord.[1] He was the brother, probably the younger brother, of S. Peter, and of Bethsaida; and therefore the son of Jonas the fisherman. He became a disciple of S. John the Baptist. On hearing Jesus a second time designated by him as the Lamb of God, he left his former master, and in company with another disciple of John, attached himself to Christ

[1] John i. 40; Matt. iv. 18.

By his means his brother Simon Peter was brought to Jesus. In the catalogue of the apostles, Andrew appears in Matthew x. 2 and Luke vi. 14, second, next after his brother Peter; but in Mark iii. 16 and Acts i. 13, fourth, next after the three—Peter, James, and John—and in company with Philip. And this appears to have been his real place of dignity among the apostles, for in Mark xiii. 3, we find SS. Peter, James, John, and Andrew inquiring privately of our Lord about His coming; and in John xii. 22, when certain Greeks wished for an interview with Christ, they applied to S. Andrew, who consulted Philip, and in company with him made the request known to our Lord. The last circumstance, combined with the Greek character of their names, may point to some shade of Hellenistic connection on the part of the two apostles.

On the occasion of the five thousand in the wilderness wanting food, it was Andrew who pointed out the little lad with the five barley loaves and the two small fishes. In the scanty notices we have of Andrew, we see him represented as bringing others into notice—his brother Peter, the Greeks, this lad—and this indicates a kindly nature.

There are various traditions about him. The earliest represents him as apostle to the Scythians.[1]

According to a later account of no authority,[2] he travelled in Cappadocia, Galatia, and Bithynia, and the foundation of the Church at Byzantium was attributed to him on his return from his mission to the Scythians. Thence he travelled through Thrace, Macedonia, and Thessaly. Gregory Nazianzen (Orat. 26) says that Andrew preached in Epirus.

Pseudo Dorotheus says that he travelled in Bithynia, Pontus, Thrace, and Scythia, that then he went to Sebastopol, and to the castle of Apsarus near the river Phasis, and that

---

[1] Euseb. H. E. iii. 5.   [2] Nicephorus, H. E. ii. 39.

S. ANDREW, APOSTLE AND MARTYR.
After Wilhelm Kandler.

Nov. 30.

he was crucified and buried at Patras of Achaia. S. Jerome says (Ep. 148) that he preached in Achaia.

Pseudo Abdias gives a long account of his apostolic journeys, preaching, and death. It is generally supposed that he died on a cross shaped like an ×. The Syriac history of S. Andrew published by Dr. Wright, makes him carried whilst asleep by angels to the kingdom of the cannibals. The king had so many prisoners killed for his table every day. By the help of Andrew the prisons were opened and the captives took occasion to run away. Whereupon the king ordered the seven keepers to be killed and cooked for his victuals, "and straightway collect us all the old men of the city, and let them cast lots among themselves, and those on whom the lot falls we will go on killing every day, seven by seven, for our food, whilst the young men go on board ships, and go to the countries round and procure us men for our victuals." One of the old men on whom the lot fell, offered his little son and daughter in place of himself. These, as tenderer morsels, were of course accepted, and the old man discharged. S. Andrew, however, saved these children, and preached to the people against their cannibalism. When they would not hearken, he made a statue they worshipped spout water from its mouth over the city and submerge it so that the cattle and children were all drowned. It is satisfactory to know that Andrew also made the earth open and swallow up the old man who had in such a dastardly manner devoted his children to death to save his own life. The Syriac acts do not give an account of the death of S. Andrew.

The story by Abdias is not quite so foolish. It may be briefly condensed as follows, omitting the most grotesque and impossible incidents.

Ægeas, proconsul of Achaia, came in his circuit to Patras, where, observing that multitudes had abandoned paganism, and had embraced Christianity, he endeavoured by all arts both of favour and cruelty, to recover the people to their former idolatries; but so far was he from succeeding in this, that his wife Maximilla, and his brother Stratocles, having been cured by S. Andrew of dangerous diseases, embraced the faith which he preached. He therefore called the apostle before him, and derided him as an innovator in religion, a propagator of that superstition whose Author the Jews had infamously put to death on a cross. Upon this S. Andrew took occasion to rehearse the infinite love and kindness of our Lord, who came into the world to purchase the salvation of mankind, and for that end did not disdain to die upon the tree. Whereupon the proconsul replied that S. Andrew might persuade those who would believe him; but, for his part, unless he was obeyed by the apostle's doing sacrifice to the deities of the empire, he would cause him to suffer upon that cross which he had so much extolled and magnified. S. Andrew replied that he did sacrifice every day to God, the only true and omnipotent Being—not with incense and bloody offerings, but in the sacrifice of the Immaculate Lamb of God. Upon this the apostle was remanded to prison, at which the people were so enraged that they would have broken out into a mutiny had not he restrained them, persuading them to imitate the mildness and patience of our meek and humble Saviour, and not to hinder him from receiving the crown of martyrdom that now awaited him. The next day he was again brought before the proconsul, who urged him not to destroy himself foolishly, but live and enjoy with him the pleasures of this life. The apostle told Ægeas he should share with him eternal joys, if, renouncing his execrable idolatries, Ægeas would heartily entertain Christianity, which Andrew had hitherto so successfully preached among his people. Upon this the proconsul could hold out no longer, but passed sentence of death upon him. He was first scourged, seven lictors successively whipping his naked body ; and then the proconsul, beholding the apostle's invincible patience and constancy, commanded him to be crucified, but not to be fastened to the cross with nails, but with cords, that so his death might be more lingering and tedious. As he was being led to execution with a cheerful and composed mind, the people cried out that he was an innocent and good man, and unjustly condemned to die.

On coming within sight of the cross he saluted it, exclaiming, " Hail, precious Cross, that hast been consecrated by the body of my Lord, and adorned with His limbs as with rich jewels. I come to thee exulting and glad ; receive me with joy into thy arms. O, good Cross, that hast received beauty from our Lord's limbs : I have ardently loved thee. Long have I desired and sought thee ; now thou art found by me, and art made ready for my longing soul: receive me into thine arms, take me from among men, and present me to my Master ; that He who redeemed me on thee, may receive me by thee." Having prayed, and exhorted the people to constancy and perseverance in that religion which he had delivered to them, he was fastened to the cross. Thereon he hung two days, and refrained not all that while from teaching and instructing the people. When the excited Christians urgently besought the proconsul to spare the apostle's life, Andrew prayed our Lord to let him depart, and seal his confession of the faith with his blood.

His petition was heard, and he immediately expired, on the last day of November, but in what year is uncertain. The instrument of his martyrdom seems to have been somewhat peculiar, and is generally affirmed to have been a cross *decussate*, formed of two pieces of timber crossing one another in the form of the letter X—a form of cross which has become known by his name.

Constantine brought the relics of S. Andrew from Patras to Constantinople in 337. Tiberius II. gave an arm to S. Gregory the Great. Another body at Amalfi. A head was brought from Patras, 1462, by Thomas, brother of Constantine Palæologus. An arm-bone is at Notre Dame at Paris; other bones at Bordeaux, Agde, Avranches, in the abbey church of Saint Remi at Rheims, in the collegiate church of S. Amé, and in the Cistercian monastery at Douai. Others at S. Bertin, at S. Omer, at Liesse near Avesnes, in Belgium, others in the palace chapel at Brussels. A foot of the Saint at Aix in Provence, with skin and flesh on it, incorrupt. Other relics before the Huguenot spoliation at Orleans. The cross of S. Andrew, formerly at Beaune, near Marseilles,[1] another at S. Victor in Marseilles, made of olive wood. Portions of the cross at Tournai. S. Andrew is the patron of Russia and of Hungary, Burgundy, and Scotland. For the reason of his being regarded as patron of Scotland see the Life of S. Rule or Regulus (Oct. 17), who carried off the body of S. Andrew, or at all events considerable parts of it, to Scotland. In art S. Andrew is represented with his ✕ cross.

S. TROJANUS, B. OF SAINTES.

(A.D. 532.)

[Gallican and Roman Martyrologies. Usuardus, Ado, &c. Authority :—Gregory of Tours, De Gloria Confess. c. 59.]

TROJANUS, Bishop of Saintes, was raised to the episcopal office in 511. He rendered himself celebrated by his virtues. Eumerius, Bishop of Nantes, consulted him on the

---

[1] This was lost at the Moorish invasion in the time of Charles Martel. In 1250, Hugues, a monk of S. Victor, pretended to rediscover it, and the cross of his "invention" is now venerated at S. Victor.

subject of a child who could not remember having been baptized, but recalled having had his head wrapped up in linen, which was probably the chrisom cloth.

S. Trojanus replied, "It is ordered that whoever cannot remember having been baptized, and there is no one who can prove that he has, shall receive baptism as soon as possible, lest you should be held responsible for that soul, should it be deprived of the sacrament." He was popularly believed in an uncritical age to be endowed with the gift of miracles, both during his life and after his death, which took place in 532. He was buried beside Bibianus, one of his predecessors.

S. TUGDUAL, B.

(ABOUT A.D. 564.)

[Gallican Martyrologies. Kalendars of the dioceses of Brittany. Authorities :—The ancient Breviaries of Rennes, Léon, Nantes, Vannes, Quimperlé, in which the Life is given in nine lections. The Legendarium of the church of Tréguier; Le Grand, and Lobineau.]

ACCORDING to Breton tradition S. Tugdual (Tual, Tudal, Tugduval, Tudgual, Tuzal, Tudwal) was a native of Wales. His father's name is not given, but that of his mother was Popæa (in Breton Copaja),[1] sister of Riwal Murmaczon, who is thought to have been the same as Hoel I. of Brittany. According to Welsh genealogists, he was the son of Cadfan, son of Cynan Meiriadog. The Welsh accounts do not name the mother. He was placed early in the school of S. Iltyt with his brother Leonor, probably at Lantwit Major. The Bretons say that on the departure of S. Iltyt, Tugdual was made abbot in his room, but the Welsh, who were much more likely to know the early career of the saint,

[1] She was buried at Land-Coat, near Roche-Derien, and is the patron of that church.

assert that he married Nefydd, daughter of Brychan, and had by her a son, Ifor, who is regarded as a saint, and another, Cynfor, father of Constantine Coronog. An island off the coast of Carnarvonshire is called after S. Tugdual or Tudwal; in it are the ruins of a chapel bearing his name, and it is probable that when he left the world he passed some time in retreat in this island. The Welsh accounts say nothing more about him, except that he was a bishop and a saint, they do not even give the name of his see. Here the Breton accounts step in to complete the story. They relate that he was warned by an angel to come to Brittany, and he started with S. Ruelin, S. Guevroc,[1] S. Goneri,[2] S. Loëvan,[3] S. Brioc,[4] S. Libouban, mother of S. Goneri, and his sister S. Seva.[5] When they reached the coast of Léon, and landed at Ker-Morvan, in a little island, Plowmoguer, the ship with all its crew vanished before their eyes, and thus they were made aware that they had been supernaturally wafted across to Brittany.

Tugdual obtained a grant of land from the lord of Léon, and built a little monastery, where now stands the church of Tre-Pabu. When this was full he obtained from Derog, prince of Domnonia, a valley then called Traoun-Trecor, now Tréguier, and went to it; he built there a monastery, and round the monastery a town grew up. He is said to have there destroyed a monstrous serpent—that is, he rooted out the great stones of one of those interesting serpentine monuments, like that of Karnac, which were used for superstitious rites. After some time he left, hearing that the inhabitants of Lexobia or Coz-Guevded were determined to elect

---

[1] Called also S. Kirecq, founder of Land-mewr, venerated on Feb. 17.
[2] S. Goneri was buried at Plougrescant; he is venerated on July 18.
[3] S. Loëvan, Loenan, Laouenan, or Lavan, is patron of Treflaouenan in Léon. His festival is on the 2nd Sunday in August.
[4] See Dec. 17.
[5] S. Seva, Seo, Seuve, Secon, patroness of S. Sève, near Morlaix.

him as their bishop on the death of Tiridran. He took refuge with S. Albinus at Angers (538-550), but Childebert interfered, and Tugdual was consecrated bishop. He moved the seat of his bishopric to his little monastery of Tréguier. There he died, about A.D. 564. But a curious mistake had led to the growth of an astonishing fable, which has forced its way into all the breviaries of Brittany. He went by the name of Pabu-Tugdual, or Father Tugdual, and sometimes, to distinguish him from other abbots, as Léon-Pabu, the Abbot in Léon. In course of time this led to his being supposed to be Leo the Pope, and as Leo V. is said to have been of unknown nationality,[1] the legend writers of the middle ages who composed the lections for the breviaries boldly identified Tugdual with Leo V., though Tugdual belonged to the 6th century, and Leo V. to the year 903. The following story was told to account for the Bishop of Tréguier becoming Pope of Rome. Tugdual was obliged to leave his diocese because of the hostility of the nobles, and his determination to maintain his rights over the land given to the see. He went to Rome when the Pope was just dead, and arrived whilst the people were praying in the basilica of S. Peter for guidance in the election of a new pontiff. When Tugdual entered, a dove settled on his head. The people accepted the omen, and he was elected unanimously. After sitting in the throne of S. Peter for part of a year, an angel appeared to him and advised his return to Tréguier, from which he had absented himself two years, that he might restore joy to his disconsolate diocese, where all the women had become barren since his departure. A snow-white horse was brought him by the angel; he mounted, and the steed bore him through the air and lodged him on a hillock near Tréguier, and then in a blaze of light the horse went up into heaven. Babies at once appeared

[1] "Leo V. cujus patriam historici non ponunt," &c.-- Platina, De Vit. Pont.

throughout the diocese, as plentiful as blackberries. S. Tugdual, after this, built a chapel on the mount dedicated to the archangel. The hill still bears the name of Crech-Mikel. In the office for the collegiate church of S. Tugdual at Laval, this preposterous story occurs. In the hymn for vespers,

"Item, mutato nomine, Dictus Leo Britigene,
Sedit in Petri culmine, Clarus et charus advena,"

the antiphon for the Magnificat is :—

"O quem Tugalum Trecoria, Roma Leonem
Invocat, in Christi virtute repelle draconem."

The seventh response at Matins is :—

"In Papam eligitur, nutu Deitatis,
Tugalus, et efficitur Rector Petri ratis,
Claves coeli bajulat, portis reseratis,
Hic facit ut pateant coelestia regna beatis."

In art he is represented as a Pope, with a dragon at his feet. The only relics that remain after the havoc of the Revolution are, some bits of tibias and femurs at Laval, and a few fragments of an arm-bone in the cathedral of Tréguier.

S. FRANCIS XAVIER, S.J.

(A.D. 1552.)

[Roman Martyrology on December 3 ; but inserted in this volume for convenience. Beatified by Paul V. in 1554, and canonized by Gregory XV. in 1662. By brief of Benedict XIV., in 1747, S. Francis Xavier was honoured with the title of Patron of the East Indies. Authorities : —(1) His own Letters. (2) A Life by Tursclini, published in Rome 1594. (3) A Life by P. Bouheurs, S.J., 1687. (4) Faria y Sousa, Asia Portugesa, Lisb. 1655. (5) The acts of canonization of S. Francis; and the biographies by Lucena, Orlandino, Garci, Maffei, &c. In compiling this biography much use has been made of "The Life and Letters of S. Francis Xavier," by F. Henry J. Coleridge, S.J., London, 1872.]

S. FRANCIS XAVIER was born at the castle of Xavier, near Pampeluna, in 1506. His father's name was Don Juan

S. FRANCIS XAVIER. After Cahier. Nov. 30

de Jasso, and he was one of the privy council of John III. of Navarre. After a common Spanish custom, Francis received the surname of his mother, who was the heiress of the family of Xavier as well as of that of Azpilcueta.[1]

Francis was sent to the university of Paris, to be educated for the Church, and took his degree of Master of Arts in 1530. There he met S. Ignatius Loyola and Pierre Lefévre, and these two holy men exerted the influence of their respective qualities of resolution of purpose and tenderness of devotion on the susceptible character of Xavier at the time when most open to impression. The father of Francis had been put to considerable expense in order to support his son at the university, and now that his education was complete, he obtained for him a canonry at Pampeluna, and desired him to return to Spain, where he could easily obtain him honourable and lucrative benefices.

But Francis was already fallen under the control of the master spirit of Ignatius, and he could not tear himself away. A servant, impatient at the spell which that remarkable man was weaving round the soul of his young master, attempted to assassinate Ignatius. His attempt failed, and served the contrary purpose, it drew Xavier closer to Loyola.

In the vacation of 1535 he yielded himself up to the direction of his friend, who put him through his course of spiritual exercises. He had already, along with Ignatius, and the five other first founders of the Jesuit Order, made a vow of poverty and chastity at Montmartre, on the feast of the Assumption, 1534. These confederates were bent on visiting the Holy Land together, and together labouring at the impracticable task of converting Mussulmans to the Gospel and the sacred obligations of humanity. On the

---

[1] Martin Azpilcueta married Joanna Xavier, heiress of the family of Xavier; and left an only child, Maria, the mother of the saint, married to Juan di Jasso.

15th of November, 1536, they started together to go to Venice, and there embark on their mad enterprise. Ignatius was not with them, he was then in Spain, but he promised to meet them at Venice.

The party of pilgrims travelled on foot through France. It was not a propitious time for travellers. Charles V. had invaded the south-eastern provinces of France, and Francis I. had ordered the devastation of the country before him. The northern frontiers of France were invaded from the Netherlands. Xavier, Rodriguez, and others of the party were Spaniards, and it was probable that they would be taken up as spies. At the outset of the pilgrimage, Francis Xavier obstructed the progress by falling ill. He had bound cords round his legs and arms as tight as they could be drawn, as a sort of penance for having formerly indulged in healthy exercise and athletic sports. Walking with whipcord bound about his thighs proved painful and impracticable, and before reaching Meaux his power of endurance failed, and he was obliged to allow his companions to remove the strings. It was found that they had buried themselves in the flesh, and that the legs and arms were swollen. In after times some of the companions loved to imagine that there was something miraculous in the removal of the cords. The party had fallen prostrate in prayer round the swelled legs, and the cords snapped of their own accord. But one can hardly suppose that there was not a member of the party with a pocket knife, or a knife procurable in the hostelry, in which case only would they probably have resorted to prayer.

On reaching the frontiers of France toward Lorraine, they went to confession and communion. Lorraine was dangerous ground to them. Whilst they travelled through France, the Frenchmen of the party spoke, and said that they were pilgrims bound for a shrine of S. Nicolas near

Metz. On crossing the border, the Spaniards became spokesmen, and the French relapsed into silence. They met with great linguistic difficulties when they crossed the Vosges and got among Germans.

At Basle they rested three days. Between Basle and Constance they passed through a village which was keeping high holiday for the marriage of its parish priest, who had probably lived previously in concubinage. The villagers were breathing free at the illicit connection being transformed nto a recognized and religious union. Near Constance they were challenged to controversy by another parish priest, who was already married and had a large family of children. He invited them to supper, but they declined to eat at the same table with him.[1] The priest argued that as S. Peter was married, and S. Paul allowed marriage to bishops, his union was allowable. We are told by Rodriguez that the party speedily reduced him to silence, by what arguments he does not say.

Constance, like Basle, was in the hands of heretics; and mass was only allowed in a church outside the walls of the town, and all who assisted at it had to pay a certain fine. A little further on the pilgrims came to a hospice, at the door of which an old woman met them, and began to genuflect, kiss their rosaries, and cry out in German that she was an old Catholic, delighted to see men who were still faithful to the Church. She ran in, and brought out a lapful of legs, and arms, and heads, and fingers of sacred statues, and the fathers prostrated themselves in veneration before the sacred fragments.

The band of companions arrived at Venice about the feast of the Epiphany, 1537. Ignatius was there, awaiting

---

[1] The Pope whose benediction they were about to seek and obtain was Paul III., who, as Cardinal Alexander Farnese, had become the father of an illegitimate son and daughter.

them. Several months must pass before they could sail for Jerusalem, and it was determined to spend part of this time among the poor in the hospitals at Venice, and the rest in a journey to Rome to obtain the blessing of the Pope.

Francis Xavier was appointed to attend the hospital of the Incurables. He was to be the servant of all there, to wait upon the sick, dress their wounds, sores, and ulcers, make their beds, prepare their food, instructing them, consoling them, preparing them for the last sacraments, and after their death carrying them forth for burial. He here indulged himself in what seems to be a preliminary process among aspirants after sanctity of modern days,—sucking ulcers. All the filthy particulars may be read in Turbellini and Rodriguez, and in English, by any one who cares to have his stomach turned, in the Life by Father Coleridge.

After nine weeks thus spent in Venice, the little party set out on foot for Rome. Ignatius did not go with them, for Cardinal Carafa, afterwards Paul IV., was jealous of the scheme of the new society. He had helped S. John Cajetan to found the Theatine Order, and he did not wish to see a new society tread on its heels and usurp the attention of the world, always attracted by novelty.

The party that started for Rome was composed of nine companions. It was determined that they should observe the strictest poverty, and keep Lent with severe fasting. The roads were bad, the rains incessant, and the country in parts flooded. They begged for their food. Simon Rodriguez gives us a picture of such a proceeding. At Ancona one of the companions, who seems to have been Francis Xavier, went about the market barefoot, his robe tucked up to his knees, begging of the market-women apples, radishes, and lettuces.

Untroubled by any suspicions about the truth of the fable attaching to the shrine of Loreto, and unobservant of the fact that the holy house was built of the red stone of Ancona, the nine companions poured forth their devotions at Loreto, and gathered a plentiful supply of indulgences.

At Rome each went to the hostel of his own nation. They were presented to the Pope, Paul III., by Pedro Ortiz, ambassador of the Emperor Charles V. at the Roman Court, and they amused the jovial pontiff during his dinner by disputing on points of theology. He gave them leave to go to Jerusalem, if they particularly desired it; and they returned with joy to Venice. The whole party received ordination on the ensuing Midsummer Day, 1537. As for the expedition to the East, that had to be postponed, as war between the Turks and Venice had broken out.

It was determined, when the hopes of going to Palestine grew fainter, that they should disperse among the cities of Italy for a twelvemonth, and do what they could for the good of souls. Xavier went with Bobadilla to Bologna. There Xavier lodged with Hieronimo Casalini, rector of Santa Lucia. His time was spent in preaching in the public piazzas, in hearing confessions, visiting the hospitals, and catechizing children. Towards the end of winter he was summoned by S. Ignatius to meet him in Rome.

The whole of the little company assembled in Rome; Ignatius submitted to them his thoughts concerning the erection of the society into a religious Order. The mission to Palestine was rendered impossible; in its place God had opened to them a work in Italy, a mighty harvest to be gathered in. To extend the faith of Christ, to root out heresy and vice, such were their objects, and they could be attained elsewhere than in Palestine. Let them bind themselves together by vow, under one head, and perpetuate, beyond the span of their own lives, the bond of charity which united them. Ignatius did not insist on an immediate answer to his proposals, he would leave his companions time to reflect and pray God to guide them in arriving at a satisfactory decision.

There were difficulties internal and external. The chief difficulty as to the formation of a body under one head seems to have consisted in the intention of the companions to offer themselves unreservedly to the Pope. If the Pope were to send them hither and thither, how were they to maintain the tie that bound them together? There were also great external difficulties to contend with, much opposition and calumnies raised against them. The religious Orders were at this time so corrupt, so luxurious, and lax, and giving such occasion of scandal, that there were thoughts in high places of either abolishing them altogether, or of reducing them to four. The idea of a new Order would hardly be tolerated—a new Order, moreover, which was to depart from the normal monastic type in many essential particulars.

The question as to the retention at all costs of the union which had proved so happy and so useful was unanimously decided upon; the question of obedience to one head cost much hesitation and dispute. The decision, however, was unanimous in favour of the addition of a third vow of obedience to the vows of poverty and chastity; and a document was drawn up, and signed by all the companions on the 15th of April, 1539, pledging them all to enter the society as soon as it received papal approval and confirmation. A fourth vow was shortly after added, binding the members to go on any mission on which the Pope should send them, whether among heathen or among Christians.

The desired papal confirmation was granted by Paul III. in 1540, but the bull was not formally promulgated till the spring of 1541.

In May of the year 1539 the brethren dispersed again on their missionary labours; but Xavier was required to remain at Rome with Ignatius, to act as secretary to the Society. But suddenly, on March 15th, 1540, Ignatius summoned Francis Xavier to his room, and told him that he was to leave Rome next day in company with the Portuguese ambassador, Pedro de Mascarenhas, to join Rodriguez on the first missionary expedition of the Society to the East Indies. It was one of those providential arrangements which seem the result of chance. Govea, privy councillor of John III. of Portugal, had written to Ignatius about the spiritual wants of the Indies, and he had recommended the king to apply for several of the companions of Ignatius as missionaries to the heathens there.

The king ordered Mascarenhas to ask for six, Ignatius could only spare two. He nominated Rodriguez and Bobadilla. Rodriguez sailed at once to Lisbon to see the king, taking with him as a companion Father Paul of Camarino, a late acquisition to the Society. Bobadilla did not arrive in Rome till just before the ambassador was about to start, and then fell too ill to be moved. Mascarenhas could not wait, and Ignatius was obliged on the spur of the moment to nominate a substitute. His choice fell on Xavier.

S. Francis had just time to seek and obtain the blessing of Paul III., then he embraced S. Ignatius for the last time, and set forth on his long wanderings, which were to end twelve and a half years later on the coast of China.

Francis went direct to Lisbon, leaving behind him his written promise to agree to any arrangements that should be made in the constitution of the Society when finally approved, and his suffrage for the election of the superior. He declared that he thought it right that Ignatius, as their old and true master, should be their head.

On reaching Lisbon, Francis was presented at court. King John was an eminently pious monarch, and all the courtiers affected enthusiastic piety; had he been the reverse, they would have accommodated themselves with equal facility to his most profane and licentious caprices. Now they rushed breathless from one religious ministration to another, vying with one another as to who could confess and communicate oftenest. And the court presented to the eye the sanctity of a convent. The king and queen were so delighted with Francis Xavier and Rodriguez, that after the first interview they ordered off all the pages to confession to them. These youths were required by their Majesties to go to confession twice a week, and this discipline, if it did not make them hypocrites, made them saints. One Miguel de Souza is reported to have survived the process of having his spiritual concerns regulated for him like an ordinary piece of court etiquette, without any deadening and deterioration of his conscience, and he became eventually a Jesuit.

Francis had two companions given him before he started, Father Paul of Camarino, and Francis Mancias, a Portuguese. The latter was a dull, homely, ignorant man, not yet in Holy Orders, and certain to be plucked if examined for Orders by a bishop in Europe. It was hoped that the bishop of Goa would be less exacting. Xavier was nominated Papal Nuncio of the Indies.

Francis was to sail for India with the new governor, Don Martin Alfonso da Sousa. The king commanded the count of Castaneras to provide Francis with everything he might need for the voyage. Francis said that he professed religious poverty, and would rely on the providence of God. He could only be induced to accept a few books of devotion, and some warmer clothing for the storms of the Cape of Good Hope. The count asked him if he did not want a servant to attend on him. It would ill become the dignity of a papal nuncio to cook his own food and wash his own linen.

Francis answered that he had his two hands, and that they alone should wait on his necessities. On April 7, 1541, his thirty-fifth birthday, S. Francis set sail from Lisbon. He found himself in the midst of society to which he was new. Hitherto he had lived either with students or with his own religious brethren; he had associated with men of position and learning, with men who felt, or affected, great respect for religion. He was now brought into contact with the boisterous licence of rude sailors and adventurers, cooped up together for a tedious and dangerous voyage of six months within the wooden walls of a galleon. The vessel contained nine hundred sailors, soldiers, and passengers. He was of a refined, delicate, even haughty nature, and those with whom he was cast were coarse, rude, and disorderly. He, however, threw himself into the life amidst these strange associates with earnest purpose of doing the best he could for them.

Many years afterwards, Don Diego di Norona, a Portuguese captain, was in the same vessel with S. Francis. He was curious to see and know him, on account of his reputation for sanctity: on asking which he was, he was shown a person standing in the midst of a group of men round a table where a game of chess was going on. He was talking with the soldiers, the crew, the merchants' clerks, who composed the crowd, at his ease with all, and all at their ease with him. The gentleman was scandalized, and declared to a friend that the Padre Santo, as he was called, was just like any other priest. At the end of the voyage, however, he sent a servant to follow and see what became of him. Francis went aside into a wood and began to pray, and the servant soon ran to call his master to see the saint in an ecstasy lifted from the ground in his prayers.

There was ample field for his zeal on board the ship in which he sailed. He mixed freely with all, especially with those who had most need of him, and he won upon them so far that the habit of swearing sensibly decreased, and many enmities were temporarily made up. He began to hear confessions regularly and frequently. Under the Line the scurvy broke out and caused great ravages, it was a sort of plague : friends neglected friends, the sick were left to themselves, the medicine ran short, there was no one but Francis and his companions to tend the sufferers. Francis washed them and their linen, dressed their food, and fed them with his own hands. He had a little cabin of his own, but he gave it up to the sick. He had refused to take his meals at the governor's table, but not to receive the daily portion of food which was sent him from it: this he divided among the sick. On Sundays he preached on deck, the governor himself attending the sermon.

Francis himself appears to have suffered greatly from sickness in the first part of the voyage, which was lengthened beyond the usual time, probably by the calm which often detains vessels near the equator. It was the custom of the Portuguese navigators to sail at a distance round the Cape, so far southwards as to reach a latitude where the cold was sensibly felt. The ship did not reach Mozambique till late in August, at a time when under ordinary circumstances it would have been approaching Goa; and the lateness of the season as well as the prevalence of sickness determined the governor to winter in the island. Francis wrote to the Society at Rome an account of his voyage, and the stay at Mozambique. In it he makes no mention of his own sufferings from a violent fever, of which we learn from the testimony of others. He would not accept the better lodging and care offered him by some of the Portuguese inhabitants, and took his chance with the rest of the sick in the hospital. Indeed, the physician found him, in the height of his fever, visiting and instructing the others. On one occasion when he was ordered to bed, he is said to have answered humbly that he was anxious about the case of one who had not made his peace with God, and that as soon as he had attended him, he would take rest himself. This was a poor sailor delirious with fever, and of whose recovery little hope could be entertained. Francis had him conveyed from the ship to his own bed; next day the man was sensible enough to make his confession; but he died at night, after having received the sacraments. Francis then consented to be nursed himself, and was soon able to resume his labours.

In the letter descriptive of his voyage, Xavier gives a curious account of an interview with the sultan of Melinda, into the port of which the vessel put after passing Zanzibar. The sultan, with oriental politeness and exaggeration, in his desire to say something pleasing to the missionary, informed him that the mosques were thinly attended, and the religion of Mohammed was losing its hold on the people. He asked, with a touch of sarcasm, whether it was so among Christians. Xavier repudiated the idea, and told the sultan that Allah held in abomination the prayers of the Mussulmans, and had so willed that their worship, which He rejected with loathing, should come to naught. The sultan "was not satisfied with what I said," observes the saint in his letter. He adds, " One sees in such cases as this in what anxiety and despair the life of unbelievers and wicked men is so often passed: and indeed this is in itself a blessing, for thereby they are warned of their state and urged to conversion." A little further acquaintance with Mohammedans later probably modified this opinion of the restlessness of their souls.

After leaving Melinda, the vessel put into Socotra, and Xavier gives a curious account of the Christian inhabitants, belonging apparently to the Abyssinian Church.

"The people," he says, " are wonderfully ignorant and rude: they cannot read or write. They have consequently no records of any kind. Still they pride themselves on being Christians. They have churches, crosses, and lamps. Each village has its caciz, who answers to the parish priest. These caciz know no more of reading or writing than the rest; they have not even any books, and only know a few prayers by heart. They go to their churches four times a day—at midnight, at daybreak, in the afternoon, and in the evening. They use no bells; but wooden rattles, such as we use during Holy Week, serve to call the people together. Not even the caciz themselves understand the prayers which they recite; which are in a foreign language (I think Chaldæan). They render special honours to the Apostle S. Thomas, claiming to be descendants of the Christians begotten to Jesus Christ by that apostle in these countries. In the prayers I have mentioned they often repeat a word which is like our Alleluia. The caciz never baptize any one, nor do they know the least what baptism is. Whilst I was there I baptized a number of children, with the utmost goodwill of their parents. Most of them showed great eagerness to bring their children to me, and made such liberal offerings out of their poverty of what they had to give, that I should have been afraid to refuse the dates which they pressed upon me with such great goodwill. They also begged me over and over again to remain with them, promising that every single person in the island would be baptized. So I begged the governor to let me remain where I found a harvest so ripe and ready to be gathered in. But as the island has no Portuguese garrison, and it is exposed to the ravages of the Mussulmans, the governor would not hear of leaving me, fearing that I might be carried off as a slave. So he told me that I should soon be among other Christians who were not less, perhaps more, in need of instruction and spiritual assistance than the Socotrians, and amongst whom my work would be better spent.

"One day I went to Vespers as recited by the caciz; they lasted an hour. There was no end to their repetitions of prayers and incensings: the churches are always full of incense. Though their caciz have wives, they are extremely strict in regard to abstinence and fasting. When they fast they abstain not only from flesh meat and milk, but from fish also, of which they have a great supply. So strict is their rule that they would rather die than taste anything of the kind. They eat nothing but vegetables and palm dates. They have two Lents, during which they fast; one of these lasts two months. If any one is profane enough to eat meat during that time, he is not allowed to enter the church."

The governor was no doubt right: the Portuguese Christians of Goa wanted an apostle quite as much, if not more, than the poor Socotrians. On reaching Goa, Xavier soon discovered what a deplorable condition the Church was in there. The population of Goa was mixed. There were Catholics, Mohammedans, and Hindoos; the Portuguese were composed of sailors, merchants, and soldiers, living in the practice of all the licence of their Mussulman neighbours, with the vice superadded, of drinking intoxicating liquors. As few Portuguese women ventured on the long voyage, the settlers lived in concubinage with native women, and their children grew up nominal Christians, but real infidels. There were several churches at Goa, a college called Santa Fé, a languid, ill-supported "Confraternity of Mercy," for doing works of charity. An active Inquisition for burning heretics was not yet instituted, it was transplanted from Portugal later, at the request of S. Francis.

Turselini gives a lively picture of the manner in which Xavier went about doing all the good he was able to the souls and bodies of men.

"Xavier," says Turselini, "thinking within himself that he ought to apply some remedy to this great evil, began to cultivate the society of the Portuguese by courteous means; thus, on meeting one of them in the streets, he would request him to invite a poor priest to dinner or supper, and this was readily granted. Accordingly, sitting at table he would entreat his host to cause his children to be called ; whereupon the little children coming presently at their father's call, Francis would take them up in his arms and hug them to his bosom, thanking God who had given the father such children, and would pray to God to grant them a good and holy life. Then he would ask that their mother might be called (a thing which in another would have been temerity, but his sanctity easily excused it). When she was come, he would speak sweetly unto her, and commend her heartily to his host, thereby trying to draw him to take her to be his wife, saying that doubtless she was of a disposition as excellent as her countenance was lovely, so that she might well be accounted a Portuguese, that the children which he had by her were certainly worthy of a Portuguese as their father. Why therefore did he not marry her? What wife could he have better? And he would do well to provide with all speed for his children's credit and the woman's honesty.

"His wholesome counsel proved not unprofitable. For he succeeded in persuading many of them to marry their mistresses. But if by chance he lighted upon any one who had by some ill-favoured Indian woman children like herself, then assuming great indignation, he would cry out, 'Good God! what a monster have we here! Do you keep a devil in your house? Can you keep company with this ugly beast? Can you have children by her? Follow my counsel: drive this monster, this hideous creature, out of your house, and seek a wife more worthy of yourself.'"

In other words, Francis persuaded the Portuguese to marry such of their mistresses as were good-looking, and to repudiate the ugly ones, and take to their arms women better featured in legitimate marriage.

We may add, to complete the picture, what the same writer adds of another practice of Francis Xavier: "He, thirsting more after the salvation of souls than his own praise, was always thinking of some new ways how to help them. And he had one invention which showed his Christian simplicity, and was also more profitable in effect, than fair to show. He, a man of grave years and authority, went up and down the highways and streets with a little bell in his hand, calling the children and servants together to Christian doctrine, at the corners of the streets and crossways, sometimes stirring up the inhabitants to piety with these or such like words: 'Faithful Christians, for the love which you bear to Christ, send your children and servants to the Christian doctrine.' This new invention made infinite numbers of children, slaves, and others, flock to him from all quarters; and marching before them, he would lead them into our Blessed Lady's church, singing the catechism aloud, set to music, and teaching them the same, thereby to cause them the more willingly to come and hear him, and the more easily to remember what was taught them in a song."

As the metrical versions of the catechism set to popular melodies proved very successful, the bishop of Goa introduced them throughout his diocese, till "in the schools, the highways, the streets, the houses, fields, and ships, the verities of the Christian faith supplanted idle and loose songs."

From Goa Xavier started for the Fishery coast, where some of the Indians had embraced Christianity. Either before leaving Goa for this mission, or on his return from it, he wrote to S. Ignatius to request him to obtain permission from the Pope that the priests might be permitted in the Indian missions, to administer confirmation with oil consecrated by the bishop, as is customary in the Eastern Church, and occasionally permitted in the Roman Church. He was anxious also that Lent might be moved in India to June and July, as the time of Lent was that most busy, and one in which it was impossible to engage the Portuguese and native Christians in devout exercises.

He also entreated that the Pope would grant several indulgences, "a list of which I send in a separate letter. . . . Of all nations that I have seen," he says, " the Portuguese is that which goes farthest in prizing indulgences from Rome." He asks for an indulgence for an altar that it may be privileged, so that whenever mass is said at it, a soul may be set free from purgatory. He begs for indulgenced rosaries as a present to the governor and his wife; and as the native Christians have a great opinion of S. Thomas, whom they regard as their apostle, he asks that there may be a plenary indulgence attached to his festival and octave.

The pearl-fishery coast to which S. Francis went extended from Cape Comorin to Paumbun Pass, a narrow strait between the mainland and some islands and reefs which bridge across to Ceylon. The warm waters of the Gulf of Manaar abound in pearl oysters. The natives had lately been engaged in war with the Mussulmans of Madura, and had been assisted by the Portuguese on condition that they should embrace Christianity.

The Indians occupying this district were called the Paravas. Xavier found them docile and amenable to instruction, as, indeed, they have since proved. The Anglican mission of Tinnevelly, which is the most flourishing in all India, is seated amidst this race, and embraces among its disciples the descendants of the converts of S. Francis. The account he gives of his work amongst these Paravas is too interesting not to be given in his own words.

He says, in a letter to the Society at Rome, dated December 31, 1543:—

"It is now the third year since I left Portugal. I am writing to you for the third time, having as yet received only one letter from you, dated February, 1542. God is my witness what joy it caused me. I only received it two months ago—later than is usual for letters to reach India, because the vessel which brought it had passed the winter at Mozambique.

"I and Francis Mancias are now living amongst the Christians of Comorin. They are very numerous, and increase largely every day. When I first came, I asked them if they knew anything about our Lord Jesus Christ? but when I came to the points of faith in detail, and asked them what they thought of them, and what more they believed now than when they were infidels, they only replied that they were Christians, but that as they are ignorant of Portuguese, they know nothing of the precepts and mysteries of our holy religion. We could not understand one another, as I spoke Castilian and they Malabar; so I picked out the most intelligent and well-read of them, and then sought out with the greatest diligence men who knew both languages. We held meetings for several days, and by our joint efforts and with infinite difficulty we translated the catechism into the Malabar tongue. This I learnt by heart, and then I began to go through all the villages of the coast, calling around me by the sound of a bell as many as I could, children and men. I assembled them twice a day, and taught them the Christian doctrine; and thus, in the space of a month, the children had it well by heart. And all the time I kept telling them to go on teaching in their turn whatever they had learnt to their parents, family, and neighbours.

"Every Sunday I collected them all, men and women, boys and girls, in the church. They came with great readiness and with a great desire for instruction. Then, in the hearing of all, I began by calling on the Name of the most Holy Trinity, Father, Son, and Holy Ghost, and I recited aloud the Lord's Prayer, the Hail Mary, and the Creed in the language of the country: they all followed me in the same words, and delighted in it wonderfully. Then I repeated the Creed by myself, dwelling on each article singly. Then I asked them as to each article, whether they believed it unhesitatingly; and all, with a loud voice and their hands crossed over their breasts, professed aloud that they truly believed it. I take care to make them repeat the Creed oftener than the other prayers; and I tell them that those who believe all that is contained therein are called Christians. After explaining the Creed I go on to the Commandments, teaching them that the Christian law is contained in those ten precepts, and that every one who observes them all faithfully is a good and true Christian, and is certain of eternal salvation, and that, on the other hand, whoever neglects a single one of them is a bad Christian, and will be cast into hell unless he is truly penitent for his sin. Converts and heathen alike are astonished at all this, which shows them the holiness of the Christian law, its perfect consistency with itself, and its agreement with reason. After this I recite our principal prayers, as the Our Father and the Hail Mary, and they say them after me. Then we go back to the Creed, adding the Our Father and the Hail Mary after each article, with a short hymn; for, as soon as I have recited the first article, I sing in their language, 'Jesus, Son of the living God, grant us the grace to believe firmly this first article of your faith: and that we may obtain this from you, we offer you this prayer taught us by yourself.' Then we add this second invocation: 'Holy Mary, Mother of our Lord Jesus Christ, obtain for us from your most sweet Son that we may believe without hesitation this article of the Christian faith.' We do the same after all the other eleven articles.

"We teach them the Commandments in the following way: After we have sung the first, which enjoins the love of God, we pray thus: 'Jesus Christ, Son of the living God, grant us the grace to love Thee above all things;' and then we say for this intention the Lord's Prayer. Then we all sing together, 'Holy Mary, Mother of Jesus Christ, obtain for us from your Son the grace to observe perfectly the first of His Commandments;' and then we say the Hail Mary. So we go on through the other nine, changing the words of our little invocation as occasion requires. Thus I accustom them to ask for these graces with the ordinary prayers of the Church, and I tell them at the same time that if they obtain them, they will have all other things that they can wish for more abundantly than they would be able to ask for them. I make them all, and particularly those who are to be baptized, repeat the form of general confession. These last I question after each article of the Creed as it is recited, whether they believe it firmly; and after they have answered Yes, I give them an instruction in their own language, explaining the chief heads of the Christian religion, and the duties necessary to salvation. Last of all, I admit them thus prepared to baptism. The instruction is ended by the Salve Regina, begging the aid and help of our Blessed Lady.

"As to the number who become Christians, you may understand them from this, that it often happens to me to be hardly able to use my hands from the fatigue of baptizing often in a single day I have baptized whole villages. Sometimes I have lost my voice and strength altogether with repeating again and again the Credo and the other forms.

"The fruit that is reaped by the baptism of infants, as well as by the instruction of children and others, is quite incredible. These children, I trust heartily, by the grace of God, will be much better than their fathers. They show an ardent love for the Divine law, and an extraordinary zeal for learning our holy religion and imparting it to others. Their hatred for idolatry is marvellous. They get into feuds with the heathen about it, and whenever their own parents practise it, they reproach them and come off to tell me at once. Whenever I hear of any act of idolatrous worship, I go to the place with a large band of these children, who very soon load the devil with a greater amount of insult and abuse than he has lately received of honour and worship from their parents, relations, and acquaintance. The children run at the idols, upset them, dash them down, break them to pieces, spit on them, trample them under foot, kick them about, and, in short, heap on them every conceivable sort of indignity."

A judicious introduction of images of the Blessed Virgin, S. Joseph, S. Thomas, and other saints, on which the children were directed to lavish their devotion and towards which to offer their incense and worship, filled the void in their routine of religious exercises which would otherwise have been caused by the havoc wrought among the idols.

Xavier proceeds:—

"I have also charged these children to teach the rudiments of Christian doctrine to the ignorant in private houses, in the streets, and the crossways. As soon as I see that this has been well started in one village, I go on to another and give the same instructions and the same commission to the children, and so I go through in order the whole number of their villages. When I have done this and am going away, I leave in each place a copy of the Christian doctrine, and tell all those who know how to write to copy it out, and all the others are to learn it by heart and to recite it from memory every day. Every feast day I bid them meet in one place and sing all together the elements of the faith. For this purpose I have appointed in each of the thirty Christian villages men of intelligence and character who are to preside over these meetings; and the governor, Don Martin Alfonso, who is so full of love for our Society and of zeal for religion, has been good enough at our request to allot a yearly revenue of 4,000 gold *fanons* for the salary of these catechists."

Xavier was brought by his work in opposition to the Brahmins. He did not trouble himself with their religion, otherwise than to denounce it as the worship of devils. He heard of the Vedas, which have proved of such incalculable profit to students, but he contemptuously dismissed them from notice as unworthy of translation or serious refutation. Later, the Jesuit missionaries saw the mistake, and forged the Kristni Veda, and endeavoured to pass it off on the Hindoos as one of their ancient works, which contained manifest prophecies of Christ, and exhortations to follow His disciples.

Xavier gives a curious account of a meeting with some Brahmins :—

"One day lately, I happened to enter a pagoda where there were about two hundred of them, and most of them came to meet me. We had a long conversation, after which I asked them what their gods enjoined them in order to obtain the life of the blessed. There was a long discussion amongst them as to who should answer me. At last, by common consent, the commission was given to one of them, of greater age and experience than the rest, an old man, of more than eighty years. He asked me, in return, what commands the God of the Christians laid on them. I saw the old man's perversity, and I refused to speak a word till he had first answered my question. So he was obliged to expose his ignorance, and replied that their gods required two duties of those who desired to go to them hereafter—one of which was to abstain from killing cows, because under that form the gods were adored ; the other was to show kindness to the Brahmins, who were the worshippers of the gods. This answer moved my indignation, for I could not but grieve intensely at the thought of the devils being worshipped instead of God by these blind heathen, and I asked them to listen to me in turn. Then I, in a loud voice, repeated the Apostles' Creed and the Ten Commandments. After this I gave in their own language a short explanation, and told them what Paradise is, and what Hell is, and also who they are who go to Heaven to join the company of the blessed, and who are to be sent to the eternal punishments of hell. Upon hearing these things they all rose up and vied with one another in embracing me, and in confessing that the God of the Christians is the true God, as His laws are so agreeable to reason. Then they asked me if the souls of men like those of other animals perished together with the body. God put into my mouth arguments of such a sort, and so suited to their ways of thinking, that to their great joy I was able to prove to them the immortality of the soul. I find, by the way, that the arguments which are to convince these ignorant people must by no means be subtle, such as those which are found in the books of learned schoolmen, but must be such as their minds can understand. They asked me again how the soul of a dying person goes out of the body, how it was, whether it was as happens to us in dreams, when we seem to be conversing with our friends and acquaintance? (Ah, how often this happens to me, dearest brothers, when I am dreaming of you!) Was this because the soul then leaves the body? And again, whether God was black or white? For as there is so great a variety of colour among men, and the Indians being black themselves, consider their own colour the best, they believe that their gods are black. On this account the great majority of their idols are as black as black can be, and moreover are generally so rubbed over with oil as to smell detestably, and seem to be as dirty as they are ugly and horrible to look at. To all these questions I was able to reply so as to satisfy them entirely. But when I came to the point at last, and urged them to embrace the religion which they felt to be true, they made that same objection which we hear from many Christians when urged to change their life—that they would set men talking about them if they altered their ways and their religion, and besides, they said that they should be afraid that, if they did so, they would have nothing to live on and support themselves by."

The saint had been working for fifteen months among the Paravas when, towards the close of 1543, he was obliged to return to Goa to procure assistants. A seminary had been established there, dedicated to S. Paul, for the education of young Indians, but it was as yet in its infancy, and unable to furnish him with efficient assistance. This was placed under the charge of Father Paul of Camerino. The following year he went back to the Paravas with one European missionary, Francis Mancias, and two native priests, Francis Coelho and Joam de Lizana, and with a layman named Joam d'Artiaga. Mancias was a stupid but well-intentioned man, hot-tempered and violent, wanting in energy, and readily disheartened; he gave S. Francis much trouble. This little party was dispersed among the villages of the Pearl Fishery coast, whilst the saint went into Travancore, the rajah of which was desirous of obtaining the assistance of the Portuguese against certain tributary rajahs who were ambitious of shaking off their dependence. The people of Travancore received him gladly, and he proceeded amongst them as among the Paravas, breaking down idols and substituting for them saints, baptizing the young, catechizing the children, and distributing a written abridgment of Christian doctrine. By the end of the year it is said that no less than forty-five infant churches had been founded in Travancore.

Francis had hardly learned sufficient of the language

during his labours on the Pearl coast to make himself understood. Those eager to discover miracles everywhere relate that at this time he preached in their own tongue to the people of Travancore, which he had never learned, and was perfectly understood not only by them, but by others speaking different dialects. This statement, however, is disposed of by the plain words of Francis himself, in a letter to Mancias from Punical, dated August 21, 1544: "I am almost alone here since Antonio has remained ill at Murappud, and what is very inconvenient, I am working in the midst of a people whose language I do not understand, and I have no interpreter. You know yourself how much the natives understand of our language, so you may easily imagine how I live here, what sort of instruction I can give, when the persons who ought to explain to the people what I say don't understand me, nor I them. My only eloquence at present is that of signs. However, I am not without something to do, for I require no interpreter to assist me in baptizing the little children just born, and when I see people without clothes or starving, the sight of them tells me what they want."[1]

The rajah of Jafanapatam, in Ceylon, at this period was a usurper, who had dethroned his elder brother, the rightful rajah. The latter appealed to the Portuguese for protection, and the inhabitants of Manaar took up his cause with enthusiasm. In order the more readily to induce the Portuguese to support him, the dethroned rajah invited Portuguese missionaries to Manaar. The reigning prince at once fell on the islanders and massacred them to the number of six hundred. The heirs to the throne fled to Travancore, and thence to Goa, to entreat the Portuguese to send an expedition to revenge the massacre and dethrone the usurper.

[1] Such is the fact. Fiction says: "In Travancore he spoke very well the language of those barbarians without having learned it, and had no need of an interpreter when he instructed them."—Alban Butler, and the "Process of Canonization."

Francis visited Cambai, where the governor Da Sousa then was, to urge in person the claims of the young princes. He had little difficulty in persuading him to undertake the punishment of the rajah of Jafanapatam. The subordinate officers along the coast received orders to collect their forces, and Negapatam was named as the place at which the armament was to assemble, and Francis undertook to attend the expedition.

Francis sailed for Negapatam, and a characteristic incident is related of the voyage. The pilot of the vessel was a licentious and godless sailor. Xavier got into conversation with him, and drew him on to speak of religion. He extracted from the rough sailor a promise that he would go to confession when he reached land. When the time came, however, the pilot repented of his promise, and avoided the sight of Xavier. S. Francis, however, met him by chance on the shore, and the man, rather out of shame than any better feeling, consented to make his confession on the spot. Francis told him to begin at once, and they paced up and down for a time, whilst the pilot confessed his sins in a perfunctory way, without the confessor attempting to interrupt or reprove him. After awhile they approached a little chapel, when Francis led him inside, placed a mat for the man to kneel on, and made him begin again. Grace worked on the pilot's conscience, and he made a thorough and perfect confession.

When he arrived at Negapatam, Francis found the Portuguese armament almost ready to sail, but the expedition was put an end to by a strange accident. A Portuguese vessel, richly laden with merchandize from Pegu, ran ashore on the coast of Jafanapatam, and was at once seized by the rajah. The Portuguese officers at Negapatam were either interested themselves in the cargo, or had friends whose money had been staked in it, and they thought of nothing for the moment but recovering it from the rajah by negotiation. He was probably glad enough to buy them off so easily; at all events, the expedition was abandoned.

S. Francis now started on a visit of devotion to Meliapore, the traditional place of entombment of S. Thomas the Apostle. Meliapore is on the Coromandel coast. S. Francis reached it in April, 1545, and took up his quarters in the house of the Portuguese priest, Gaspar Coelho, close to the church of S. Thomas. The presumed relics of the apostle had been discovered by order of King John of Portugal in 1521. They consisted of some bones, a staff, a lance, and a bottle of blood. Somewhat later they were removed to Goa; but at this time they were still at Meliapore, together with a wooden church which had miraculously defied the ravages of white ants for fifteen centuries, and which the Portuguese were pleased to believe, or pretend, had been erected by the apostle himself.

There S. Francis indulged in an ecstasy of devotion, spending whole nights in prayer before the tomb containing the supposed relics of S. Thomas, or in a wooden chapel presumably of his erection. After four months spent at Meliapore S. Francis sailed for Malacca. An odd story is told of this voyage. The soldiers who were being conveyed to the fort at Malacca gambled hard. One day a soldier had lost all at cards and fell into despair. S. Francis took the pack in his hands, blessed them, and gave the man money to go on and try his luck once more. He did so and won. When he had recovered what he had lost, Xavier stopped his play, and refused to allow him to proceed. Xavier reached Malacca on September 25, 1545.

No sooner had he arrived than he gave himself up to the immense spiritual needs of Malacca. He began by very great austerities and continual prayers. He is said to have passed two or three days together without eating; his nights were spent in prayer, save a few short hours which he gave to necessary sleep. Two brothers, by name Pereira, watched him by night, and afterwards related how they had seen him immovable on his knees before a crucifix, his eyes swimming with tears, and his face burning like fire. The whole of the day, after he had said mass and recited his office, he gave to the exercise of charity of various kinds which he had already practised in Goa—visiting the sick in the hospital, the criminals in the prison, waiting on them, instructing them, giving them the sacraments, or hearing confessions and teaching in the churches; gathering the children together for the Catechism, teaching them pious songs, with which, as time went on, the houses and the streets began to ring; and going with them through the city at nightfall, calling on the people, by the sound of a bell, to pray for those in mortal sin, and for the suffering souls in purgatory. He preached to the people on Sundays, but his instructions to the children were given daily, and he frequently found time for the slaves, who were in great numbers in the city.

Malacca was never thoroughly converted by Francis Xavier, though he spent more labour upon it, perhaps, than upon any other city in the East, and he left it at last, shaking off the dust of his feet against it, as a testimony that its conversion was hopeless, and ordered the priests of the Society of Jesus to withdraw from it. But this was yet future. One notable improvement he effected. Hitherto full-grown girls had been allowed to frolic about the town dressed as men and without escort. This custom Francis succeeded in putting down. It had naturally led to great licence.

S. Francis wrote to John III. on November 10, 1545, that "Jewish misbelief was daily increasing in the parts of the East Indies subject to the crown of Portugal," and he urged the king with great vehemence to establish the Inquisition there to remedy this evil. Accordingly Cardinal Henry, who was then Grand Inquisitor in Portugal, organized an Inquisition in Goa, consisting of inquisitors and their officers, clerks, torturers, and executioners, under Alexius Diaz Falcono. The Holy Office did not, however, begin its bloody work in Goa till March 15, 1560, when S. Francis had been dead some years.[1] During his labours and journeys he had been embarrassed for want of missionaries to carry the Gospel to the heathen and to confirm the converted in the faith, but there seems to have been no difficulty found in supplying inquisitors for the racking and burning of those whose faith was doubtful.

He spent only four months in Malacca, and then started for the Moluccas, January 1, 1546. His immediate destination was the island of Amboyna. He was now entering on one of the most adventurous periods of his missionary life, sailing almost beyond the reach of communication with Europe; for on his return he wrote to his friends at Rome that a letter to the Moluccas from thence could not be answered, under the most favourable circumstances, in less than three years and three-quarters. He found, however, Portuguese merchants in most of the places which he visited, and his principal stay was in islands under the Portuguese crown, where there were garrisons, churches, and priests.

At Amboyna, Xavier found seven villages of native Christians, but Christians only in name. He at once began his system of baptizing and catechizing. He went about in a native boat from one small island to another on his mission of mercy. A little north of Amboyna lies the island of Ceram, the scene of a miracle gravely recorded in the "Process of the Canonization." As Xavier was sailing to Ceram a storm came on, and to allay it Xavier, who knew nothing, and believed less, of the law of storms, their periodicity and their spiral progress, took from his neck a crucifix, "one

---

[1] Ludov. Paramus, "De Origine Inquisitionis," lib. ii. c. 15; and Limborch, "Hist. Inquisitionis," lib. i. c. 25.

finger length," and which he regarded as eminently adapted to arrest the forces of nature and restore the equilibrium of the air. He dipped this crucifix in the sea as he leaned over the side of the boat. It chanced to slip from his fingers, and Xavier was visibly distressed by his loss. On the morrow they reached the island in which is the town of Taroeno, whither the crew was bound; so the vessel was drawn ashore and Xavier got out, and with one companion walked along the shore to Taroeno. And when they had walked half a mile, and far from where the crucifix had been lost, " behold a sea crab runs out of the sea on to the shore with the aforesaid crucifix, holding it in his claws on either side, upright and lifted up, and so ran to Xavier and stopped in his sight. And Xavier flung himself on his knees, and the crab waited until he had taken the crucifix from its claws, and then ran back again into the sea whence it had come. And Xavier kissed and embraced the crucifix, and crossing his arms on his breast, lay prostrate on the ground in prayer for half an hour, and his companion, who was by his side, did the same, thanking the Lord Jesus Christ for so strange a miracle."

Francis next visited Ternate, a little islet off Gilolo in the Moluccas, and met there also with some success. His most distinguished convert was the widow of one of the rajahs, a woman who had suffered so much from the ill-usage and injustice of the Portuguese that she had conceived a lively hatred of Christianity. From Ternate he made an expedition to Tolo, a little town probably on the large island of Gilolo, where there were some native Christians. He succeeded there in bringing the people to conversion, and to casting off their allegiance to the rajah of Gilolo; but no sooner was the back of Francis turned, than the rajah appeared at Tolo, and the people, without much difficulty, relapsed into Mohammedanism and into obedience to their prince. The Portuguese governor of Ternate, Bernardino da Sousa, organized an expedition of 5,000 men and reduced Tolo to submission to the crown of Portugal and the cross of Christ.

The lovers of marvel have here invented an incident. The town was on a height, and approach to it was difficult, as the only road to it had been blocked with iron spikes. The Portuguese hesitated; the attack seemed likely to fail ignominiously. Then S. Francis fell on his knees and prayed. Suddenly there was an earthquake, then a rending of the mountain which hung over the town, and it exploded, casting forth fire and smoke and cinders with a roar like thunder. The panic-stricken inhabitants came to make their submission, and were reconciled by S. Francis, who obliged them to rebuild the church they had destroyed, and do suitable penance for their apostacy.

Faria y Sousa gives an account of this expedition in his "Asia Portugesa," which is both circumstantial and reasonable. He was profoundly ignorant of the marvels which attended it, and which have found their way as authentic details of history into the bull of canonization.

Xavier returned to Malacca in July, 1547. He was overjoyed on his return to find there three members of the society, the first recruits whom he had seen since he left Europe more than six years before. These were Joam Beira, former canon of Corunna; Nunez Riberio, a Portuguese priest; and Nicolo Nunez, not yet a priest. S. Francis had ordered Father Mancias to come to Malacca, but this man refused to do so; he preferred remaining on the Comorin coast. This disobedience cost him his dismissal from the society. Whilst Francis was at Malacca, the sultan of Aicheen, in Sumatra, sent an expedition to Malacca, which was partially successful. The boats entered the harbour at night and burnt several vessels. The Aicheenese intercepted some fishermen, cut off their noses, ears, and heels, and sent them to the governor of Malacca, with a letter written in their own blood defying him to battle.

The governor was not, however, disposed to revenge this insult; he doubted whether he had vessels and soldiers sufficient. But S. Francis allowed him no rest. He stirred up soldiers and civilians to a passion of rage and revenge, and the governor was forced to organize an expedition for the chastisement of the Aicheenese, which proved successful. A great number of the chief officers of the Aicheenese fleet were killed, and about four thousand were put to the sword. "Francis, to whom chiefly this victory was due," says Turselini, "went first to meet the general, and embrace him and the other captains," on their return in triumph to Malacca.

At Malacca S. Francis met with Anger, a Japanese. The story of this man is curious. He was a person of some distinction in Japan. In the heat of passion he had committed homicide in his own country. He was pursued by the relatives of the man whom he had slain, and took refuge in a monastery of bonzes, expecting to find there not only protection from the avengers of blood, but also peace for his remorseful conscience. He found safety for a time, but was not secure against punishment, and his own conscience gave him no rest. His acquaintance with some Portuguese merchants led him to open his heart to one of them, Alfonso Vaz, who offered him all the help in his power, and suggested that he should secretly depart from Japan in one of the Portuguese ships. In India he would find persons who would assist him to set his soul in order and regain peace of conscience. Vaz was not about to sail immediately himself, so he gave Anger a letter to another merchant, whose ship was to start sooner than his own. This was a certain Ferdinando Alvarez, but the Japanese took the letter by mistake to another Alvarez, George by name, who received Anger with great kindness, disregarded the mistake, and carried him off to Malacca, talking to him a great deal on the voyage about Francis Xavier, who was his great friend. Anger became very desirous of seeing Francis, but when he arrived at Malacca Francis was absent in the Moluccas, and after waiting for some time, the Japanese gave up his intention of applying to him, and started on his voyage homewards. He was within sight of Japan when a tempest drove his ship back, and he was forced to land on the coast of China; and when he sailed again from China towards Japan, another storm drove him back into the port whence he had started. There he met again with Alfonso Vaz, who persuaded him to return to Malacca; and on his landing there, the first person he fell in with was Ferdinando Alvarez, who took him at once to Francis, who had arrived in the meantime from Amboyna. The rest of the history of Anger will be related presently.

Francis himself embarked in a vessel belonging to Garzia da Sousa, and which was bound for Cochin instead of Goa. He had determined to visit the Christians on the Comorin coast before proceeding further northward. This ship had to encounter much storm. When there seemed danger of the ship becoming a wreck, Francis confessed the passengers and crew, and then retired to a corner, and became rapt in prayer. A companion went to seek some comfort from his conversation, but found him immovable before his crucifix, and unwilling to speak. At last, after three days and nights, he arose, took a sounding-line from the steersman, attached a portion of his robe to it, and flung it into the sea, calling on God the Father, the Son, and the Holy Ghost to have pity on the crew and on himself. Then, or soon after, as those who were present pretended, there was a calm. The writers of his life suppose that his meaning in dropping the portion of his robe into the sea was to plead before God the merits of the society of which he was a member; but why for that purpose a rag of his cassock should have been exhibited to the fishes is not abundantly clear.

A few days later he landed safely at Cochin, January 13, 1548. From Cochin the indefatigable missionary went to the Pearl Fishery coast, and examined the churches he had founded there. He found them in a tolerably flourishing condition. After which he returned to Goa, March 20, 1548, and rested there for nearly two months. But ever since he had met Anger, his mind had been fired with ambition to carry the Gospel into Japan. With this intention he left Goa again, and revisited Cochin. He sailed from Cochin on April 25, and reached Malacca on May 31, 1549.

The voyage of Francis Xavier and his little band of companions from Cochin to Malacca was prosperous, though Lucena speaks of one storm in the course of the passage, when the captain was so alarmed at the danger which threatened his heavily-laden vessel, that he had given the order to throw some of his cargo overboard, but was prevented by the intercession of Francis, who assured him that the wind would fall, and that they would sight the land before night. All came about as he had said. But this incident probably belongs to a later voyage to the same place. This voyage, however, had its memorable conversion. A man of noble birth was one of the passengers, and he was accompanied by a woman with whom he was living. Francis made himself the friend of this sinner, and paid him so much attention, without taking the least notice of the profligacy of his life, that, as Lucena tells us, those on board the vessel were inclined to say of him as the Pharisee said of our Lord, that if he had been a prophet he would have known what sort of a person his chosen companion was. When they disembarked at Malacca the victory was won. "Sir, it is now time!"

said Francis. The man was at his feet in a moment, he made his confession, provided for the woman, and began to lead a good life.

In a letter to King John III. of Portugal, dated Malacca, Feast of Corpus Christi, 1549, he speaks highly of the kindness shown him by the governor, and of the warmth with which he was received by the inhabitants of Malacca :—

"We have now got as far as the port of Malacca on our way to Japan. There are two of our society with me, and three Japanese Christians, lately converted, but very good. After having been fully instructed in the mysteries and doctrines of the life and teaching of our Lord Jesus Christ, they were baptized at Goa in the College of Santa Fé. They have learned to read and write in our manner, they recite the prayers of the Church, and make meditation at regular hours. What moves and affects them most of all is the consideration of the labours and sufferings of Christ, and the remembrance of His cross and death. They often meditate upon these things with very deep and strong sentiments and very tender affections. They have exercised their minds with very great attentiveness in the ascetic meditations of Father Ignatius, and have carried away from them most remarkable fruits in the clearer knowledge of God. They frequent of their own accord the sacraments of confession and communion, and they feel urged to join us in this voyage to their own country by great desire of leading their own people to the religion of Christ.

"We, the six whom I have mentioned, arrived at Malacca on the last day of May of this year, 1549. The commandant of the fortress of Malacca has received us with the usual kindness. He at once offered us most readily all the favour and assistance that could be expected from him towards the carrying out and promoting this expedition of ours—undertaken, as it is, with great hopes of serving God and pleasing your Highness: and his sedulous carefulness in all good offices has gone far even beyond the courtesy of his words. He has put himself to so much pains in seeking for us a comfortable ship, and providing us with every other convenience for going whither we are bound with all safety and ease, as to fulfil most abundantly all the liberal and kind promises which he made to us on the first day of our landing here. Nothing could exceed his extreme courtesy in readily and with full goodwill offering to us whatever was in his own power to give."

Anger the Japanese was with him; he had been baptized, and was now called Paul of the Holy Faith. After a short stay in Malacca, S. Francis and his party went on board a Chinese junk bound for Japan. His account of the voyage is sufficiently interesting to be condensed. The narrative is given in a letter to the Fathers of the Society at Goa, written from Kagosima, in the kingdom of Satsuma, in the isle of Kiusiu, on November 11, 1549:—

"I wrote to you at great length from Malacca about our voyage thither after we left India, and about all that happened there as long as we remained. Now for the rest. We arrived in Japan, by the favouring help of Almighty God, on August the 15th, having set out from Malacca on the Feast of S. John Baptist at evening. We sailed on board the ship of a heathen merchant, a Chinaman, who promised the commandant at Malacca that he would carry us to Japan. By the goodness of God we had very favourable winds. However, as perfidy so often rules barbarians like him, our captain at one time changed his intention, and began to abandon his course towards Japan, and loiter about the islands that came in the way, for the sake, I suppose, of wasting time.

"There were two things in this especially hard to bear. The first was that God had given a most favourable wind, and yet we were not using it, whereas if it failed, we should not be able to hold on our course to Japan, but have to winter on the coast of China, and wait for another favourable season. The other was that the captain and sailors were always, in spite of all our efforts to prevent them, offering abominable worship to an idol which they had with them on the poop, and consulting the devil, whether it would be advantageous or not to sail to Japan. They would also ask him whether we should be able to hold on our course with favourable weather; and, as they told us, the result was at one time good, at another unfavourable.

"When we had sailed three hundred miles, we put into a certain island, and there made ready our rigging and equipment for the severe storms of the Chinese sea. Thereupon our sailors offered many sacrifices to the idol, and fell again to casting lots, asking the devil whether we should have good winds. By chance the lot so fell as to promise us a very favourable wind, so that we were not to stay any longer where we were. So without delay we heaved up our anchor and set sail in high spirits; they relying on their idol, which they worshipped with great devotion, burning candles and sticks of aloe-wood on the poop; and we trusting in the God who rules heaven and earth and sea, and in Jesus Christ His Son, for whose sake we were on our way to Japan. But while we were thus on our way, these pagans took it into their heads to ask the devil whether their ship would return safely to Malacca from Japan. The lots declared that she would reach Japan, but would not return to Malacca. Thereupon the pagans came to a standstill, and made up their minds to give up for the present the voyage to Japan, to winter in China, and to put off going to Japan till the next year. What do you imagine we thought and felt during that part of the voyage, while the devil was being consulted by his own worshippers as to our voyage, and the captain of the ship managed the whole business just as the devil willed and chose? Well, as we were sailing on slowly, off a port in Cochin China, belonging to the Chinese, two serious things happened.

"It was the Feast of S. Mary Magdalene, about vesper time, and the sea was swelling, and the water became rougher on account of the wind. The ship was anchored off a shoal, when, all at once, Emmanuel the Chinese, one of our companions, fell head foremost, as the vessel rolled, into the hold of the ship, which was open. We thought he must have been killed, for he had fallen from a great height, and the hold was full of water. However, by the goodness of God, he escaped death. He stuck some time in the pump, with his head downward, and up to his middle in water, but at last, with great difficulty, we got him out, badly wounded on the head. He lay a long time without coming to himself, but by God's great mercy he was at length restored. Just as we had begun to attend to his cure there came another roll of the ship, and the daughter of the captain fell overboard. The violence of the storm was so great that our efforts to help her were in vain, and she sank in the waves in the sight of her father and of all of us, close to the ship. There was so much wailing and groaning all that day and the night which followed, that everything seemed mournful and miserable, both on account of the grief of the barbarians and of the danger we were in. For the pagans turned to appeasing their idol with sacrifices and ceremonies: they spent the whole day and night, without rest, in killing birds and placing dishes before the idol. And when the captain asked why it was that his daughter had perished, the lots told him that if Emmanuel had been killed in the hold, his girl would not have come to harm. You see what great danger we were in, as our life depended on the answer given by the devil, and on the caprices of his servants. As soon as the tempest had relented, we raised anchor and set sail, resuming with many tears the course which had been interrupted. In a few days we reached a port of China called Canton, and the sailors and the captain made up their minds to winter there. We opposed their decision, partly by prayers, partly by threats that we should complain of their breach of faith to the commandant at Malacca. So God in His goodness put it into their minds not to stay longer in the island of Canton, but to weigh anchor and sail for Tchintcheon. God was also so good as to give us a favourable wind, and in a few days we drew near to this second port on the Chinese coast. The captain was just about to enter the port with the intention of spending the winter there, because the season for sailing to Japan was nearly past, when a boat put out to us in a great hurry, to warn us that the harbour was infested by pirates. This bit of news frightened the captain, and so, to avoid that danger, he determined to shun that port. But now the wind was adverse to a return to Canton, and favourable to sailing to Japan, and so we held our course thither against the will of the captain, the sailors, and the devil himself. So by the guidance of God we came at last to this country, which we had so much longed for, on the very feast of our Blessed Lady's Assumption, 1549. We could not make another port, and so we put into Cagoxima, which is the native place of Paul of the Holy Faith. We were most kindly received there both by Paul's relations and connections and by the rest of the people of the place.

"In the native place of Paul of the Holy Faith, in whom we have found a true and genuine friend, the governor of the city, the chief citizens, and indeed the whole place, have received us very kindly. Everybody came to visit the new priests from Portugal. They are not displeased with Paul for having become a Christian, but rather respect him for it, and all his kindred congratulate him on having gone to India, and seen things which no others of his countrymen have seen. The prince of this place was six leagues away from Cagoxima, and when Paul went to pay his respects to him, he showed him much honour, and asked a great many things about the manners, the power, and the resources of the Portuguese. When Paul told him all about them, he seemed to be highly delighted with what he heard.

"Paul had taken with him a fine picture of our Blessed Lady with the Child Jesus sitting in her lap, which we had brought from India. When the prince saw the picture, he was struck with wonder; he fell on his knees and venerated it in the most pious manner, and ordered all who were present to do the same. After this, his mother saw it and gazed upon it, and was filled with admiration. A few days after, when Paul had returned to Cagoxima, she sent a man—and a very good person he was—to get it copied. However, there were no means of doing the thing at Cagoxima, and so the matter went no further. The same lady sent us a request by the same hand, that we would give her in writing the chief points of the Christian religion. So Paul devoted some days to this work, and wrote out in his native language a great many things concerning Christian mysteries and laws.

"You may take my word for it, and also give God great thanks, that a very wide field is here opened to you for your piety to spend its energies in. If we knew the Japanese language, we should long ere this have been at work at this large uncultivated field with great fruit of souls. Paul, indeed, has diligently preached the Gospel day and night to some relations and friends, and has thus brought his wife and daughter to the faith of Christ, as well as many kinsmen and intimate friends. And, so far as things have gone as yet, those who become Christians do not find themselves blamed for what they have done. As the Japanese for the most part know how to read, they soon learn our prayers by heart.

"On S. Michael's day we had an interview with the prince of Cagoxima. He received us very honourably, and advised us to keep with diligence the precepts of our Christian law. If he come to see that it is true and good, the devil will burst with rage. A few days later he gave leave to all in his dominions to embrace the Christian religion if they like. These bits of good news I have wrapped up in the last sheet of my letter, that you may the more rejoice and give thanks to God. This winter we shall spend, I think, in explaining the articles of the Creed at length in the Japanese language, with the intention of having the explanation printed, so that as we cannot ourselves be present everywhere, the Christian religion may be spread in as many places as possible; for most of the Japanese are able to read, and our good Paul will most faithfully render into his native language all that is necessary for salvation."

The reason why the prince of Satsuma showed such favour to S. Francis and his companions was, that he was anxious to secure for his port at Kagosima (or Cagoxima, as S. Francis spells the name), the monopoly of the Portuguese trade. But the port is unsheltered, and the Portuguese trading vessels went instead to the more sheltered harbour of Firando, in an island north of Nagasaki, and established there their emporium. This filled the prince of Satsuma with rage, and he withdrew his permission to teach Christianity, and forbade his subjects embracing the new religion under pain of death. It does not appear that this edict was followed by active persecution, but the attitude of the people towards Francis was changed; and he saw it necessary to move to another place. He resolved on visiting Firando first, and then going on to Meaco. He left Paul of the Holy Faith as head of the little community at Kagosima, and started for Firando.

Francis travelled on foot, carrying himself the little bundle in which was contained all that was necessary for the celebration of mass. He took with him his European companions, Cosmo Torres and Joam Fernandez, a convert named Bernard, a native of Kagosima, and another Japanese. He had not gone many miles on his road when he was invited by one of the great lords of the country, whose name is given as Ekandono or Eshandono, to visit him in one of the great castles which are described by travellers in Japan. Ekandono had heard wonders of the "bonze" from the West who had been teaching a new religion at Kagosima, and was eager to see and hear him. Francis preached with great earnestness and power, and was able to baptize seventeen persons before he left the castle. Among these, though in secret, were the lady of the house and her eldest son. Ekandono himself was doubtfully inclined, but allowed their baptism. Francis left them a copy of the Japanese explanation of Christian doctrine, and carefully regulated the exercises of piety and manner of life of the little community.

This little Christian community was found many years afterwards, in 1562, still flourishing, when Father Luis d'Almeyda was sent to visit the Christians in Firando, Kagosima, and Bongo. On his way he was told to call at the castle of Ekandono, and his letter gives a description of it which seems to justify the wonder with which it filled him. It had, he says, ten distinct bulwarks or walls connected by drawbridges, "so high that the head swims when you look down," and a very deep ditch: all was said to have been cut out of the rock by sheer work, but Father Luis thought it could hardly be the work of man. In the centre of these outer fortifications rose the principal castle, where the visitor was received with much joy, especially by the lady of the nobleman who owned the castle, and fourteen others whom Francis had baptized himself. They came round him, he says, "asking for news of Father Francis, and of the progress of Christianity in other parts of Japan, rejoicing much in the good tidings which I gave them, for it was many years since they had seen a father or brother of the society. He that after God kept them in the faith was an honoured old man, a steward of the castle, whom all loved very much on account of his virtue." He and the lady related many miracles which God had wrought since Father Don Francis went away, for he had left them some devout prayers and litanies written by his own hand, and these they used to apply to sick persons and so heal them. One of these sick had been Ekandono himself, whose life had at one time been in danger, and who had been at once cured. Once a week the Christians met to take the discipline together with a scourge which Francis had left behind; but the old man considered it so precious that he would not let any one give himself more than three strokes with it, lest it should be worn out. Almeyda baptized some children, two of whom were lads, sons of Ekandono, whom he found perfectly prepared for baptism by the instructions of the steward. On the return of Father Luis a week or two after, he found that the old man was dead. He preached several times, and converted some of the heathen in the fortress, one of whom wrote down the instructions which Almeyda gave him. He and the eldest son were left in charge of the rest. On Sundays and feast-days they all met, and a chapter of the instructions on Christian doctrine was read. They frequently assembled for prayers. Ekandono himself told the father that he was only prevented from becoming a Christian by fear of the prince.

Firando was the scene of a triumph for Xavier. A Portuguese ship was trading there; the captain received Francis with a salvo of artillery, and conducted him with all honour to the prince, who gave him leave to preach freely. Conversions were now very numerous. In a few days more Christians were made at Firando than had been gained in Kagosima in a year. Francis, however, could not remain there. He was eager to reach Meaco. He left one of his companions in care of the converts, and pushed on. The journey was a trying one, as it was undertaken in winter, when much snow encumbered the roads. Francis arrived with three companions at Meaco in February, 1551. He was unable to obtain an audience of the Mikado; and though he preached in the streets, he made no converts. He laid the foundations of the future Church of Meaco, which was to spring into life ten years later, by his sufferings rather than by his successes. It is probable, however, that Francis learnt by this visit to the capital much as to the state of things in Japan which he had not suspected. He may have seen that even if the Mikado gave him leave to preach, his authority would not practically extend far beyond the walls of his own residence; that Japan was not a kingdom in which the sovereign was everything, and his word absolute law throughout his dominions. There was a significant contrast between the apparently secure tenure and exercise of power which he observed in the petty prince of Satsuma and the titular magnificence of the Mikado. On leaving Meaco Francis Xavier seems to have determined to adopt a somewhat different line of conduct from that which he had hitherto pursued. He resolved to make his advances at the courts of the local sovereigns, and to lay aside the appearance of poverty, which, as he learned by experience, retarded instead of advanced the cause he had at heart. The Japanese were not like the Hindoos, attracted by asceticism.

The journey to Meaco, therefore, was not entirely unfruitful even of other results than the humiliations to which it had exposed Francis Xavier. He had baptized a few dying children, whom he had found exposed by the roadside, and he had reaped a harvest of sufferings; in some cases even his life had been in danger, for he was assailed by crowds, and more than once was wounded by arrows and almost stoned to death. He seems to have returned from Meaco by sea, taking boat probably at Osaka. After a brief stay at Firando, he went to Amanguchi, capital of Nagato. He made up his mind to begin his new career of preaching there. He took with him the letters and presents from the governor of the Indies, the bishop of Goa, and the captain of Malacca, which had been originally intended for the Mikado himself. He dressed himself in a manner more becoming the envoy of Portugal, and, with his companions as attendants, demanded an audience of the prince or king of Nagato. He was very well received by the king, who was charmed with the presents—among which were a "manicordio e relox," a musical instrument of some sort, and a watch. Oxindono, as he was called, was unwilling not to show all courtesy to the representative of the secular and religious authorities of Portugal, the great trading power of the Eastern Archipelago. The next day an edict was placarded in the city of Amanguchi, allowing of the preaching of the Christian religion, and an empty "bonzery" or monastery was assigned for the residence of the new teachers.

After labouring some while at Amanguchi, Francis heard that a Portuguese vessel had arrived at Fucheo, the capital of Boungo, in the island of Kiusiu, under Captain Duarte da Gama, with letters for him, and that the king of Boungo would be glad to receive him. Francis at once went to Fucheo, and was warmly received by the Portuguese merchants and the captain. A solemn visit to the king was arranged, of which Mendez Pinto gives an amusing account. "We embarked in the shallop of the ship, and in two pinnaces (manchuas), which had their standards and their banners of silk, on board which also there were trumpets and hautboys, which sounded alternately—a novelty which seemed so great to the people of the country, and astonished them so much, that when we arrived at the quay, we had a difficulty in landing, on account of the great number of people who had crowded together there. There met us the Quamsyandono, captain of Canafama, and by the express order of the king he had a litter with him in which he wished to place the father. But he would not accept it on account of his respect for us, and walked straight to the palace, accompanied by a number of nobles and thirty of us Portuguese. There were also our servants, in number as many as ourselves, all finely dressed, and having gold chains round their necks. Father Francis had a full cassock of black camlet, a surplice over it, and a stole of green velvet brocaded with gold. In his suite walked our captain with a baton in his hand, as major-domo, and there followed him five of the most honourable and richest of the merchants, who, as if they had been the father's servants, carried with much ceremony certain things in their hands. For instance, one carried a book in a cover of white satin" (this book was the translation of the "Catechetical Instruction"), "another some slippers of black velvet which we happened to have with us, another a Bengal cane with a gold enchasing, another a picture of our Blessed Lady wrapped in a scarf of violet damask, and another a parasol to be held over a person when walking; and in this order and array we passed through the nine principal streets of the city, where there was so great a crowd that every place was full of people to the very roofs of the houses."

Mendez goes on to relate how, when they arrived at the court of the palace, they found a hundred men drawn up, armed with lances and scimitars. They next came to a long gallery, and there the merchants knelt before the father, and each presented to him the article he had been carrying, so as to impress the Japanese nobles with the dignity of the person to whom they paid homage. Then they came to a great hall, in which were a number of gentlemen clothed in satin and damask of divers colours, with short swords covered with plates of gold. Here a child of six or seven years, led by an old man, approached the father, and made him a little speech, which expressed the hope that his arrival in the palace might be as pleasant to both the king and his visitor as the rain that drops on the thirsty rice-fields. Francis returned the compliment, and then they went on through another chamber, where a number of "lords of the kingdom rose up to make their *gromenares* to the father, as they call their compliments," putting their heads thrice to the ground; then through another long gallery, bordered by orange trees, to another hall, where the king's brother received the visitors; and at last, after an almost endless series of rooms, they arrived in the presence-chamber of the king, who advanced five or six steps to meet Francis. The king was a fine young man, of stately appearance and courteous manners; his morals were not, as Francis learned to his regret, good even for a heathen.

The king received S. Francis with great respect, made him sit at his side, and eat at his table. Francis knelt to the king and kissed his sword—a sign of great respect in Japan—and prayed that God would reward the prince for his courtesy and favour. The interview ended with expressions of amity on both sides.

On another visit the king bade a famous bonze argue with the father. The name of the bonze was Fucarando. The bonze asked if he remembered him.

"How should I?" said Xavier. "I have never seen you before."

"I must correct you," said the bonze. "Fifteen hundred years ago you sold me fifty 'picos' of silk at Frenojama."
"Then how old may you be?" asked Francis.
Fucarando replied that he was fifty-two.
"How, then, is it possible that fifteen hundred years ago you were a merchant, and that I sold merchandise to you? And if it is true what you bonzes preach publicly, that Japan was only peopled six hundred years ago, how can you have traded at Frenojama fifteen hundred years ago, since you would have us believe that at that time the country was a desert?"

The bonze, rather disconcerted, proceeded to lay down the doctrine of the eternity of the world, and the number of lives through which human souls pass, and how that sometimes the recollection of what passed in a former stage of existence survives after transmigration. All this the Father, says Mendez Pinto, refuted thrice over with words so clear, reasons so evident, and comparisons so apt and natural, that the bonze was struck with confusion; "of which reasons," he adds, "I shall not speak here, in order to avoid prolixity, and much more because I avow that my wit is not capable of understanding them."

The bonze flew into a passion and began to abuse the saint; whereupon the king, who wanted his dinner, and was tired of the sport, interfered.

This led to several conferences with the bonzes before the king, lasting through five days. It was arranged by Francis that the king and nobles present should be umpires, and decide which side argued best. The conferences, however, led to nothing save the exasperation of the bonzes, who, finding themselves defeated in argument, stirred up the populace against the preacher of a strange faith.

Francis had to leave Boungo, so he resolved to return to Goa, to revisit his first foundations, and stir up the society to enthusiasm for the hopeful Japanese mission. He sailed from Japan at the close of the year 1551.

The vessel in which he embarked at the port of Figi was bound for Canton, or rather for the island of San Chan, which was the station where the Portuguese traffic with Canton was carried on. Mendez Pinto, whom we shall find more at home on nautical subjects than on the theological questions discussed between Francis Xavier and the bonzes in the presence of the king of Boungo, was, as has been said, one of the Portuguese passengers on board the ship in which Francis embarked. Mendez tells us how at first for some time they hugged the Japanese coast, and then struck across the open sea in the direction of China. After a week, however, the moon changed, and the weather changed in consequence. A violent storm fell on the vessel, and she was obliged to put about and run before the wind in a north-north-westerly direction, "through an unknown sea which no one had ever yet navigated," as Mendez says. For five days they were at the mercy of the storm, and saw neither sun nor star, and the helmsman lost all reckoning. On the second day of the five something had to be done to clear the deck of all encumbrances, and the ship's boat was secured at the stern, fastened by two strong cables, with fifteen men in her. Night came on, and they were unable to get on board the ship again. Francis Xavier was the life of the whole party during the storm, working himself in clearing the decks, encouraging and comforting the rest. "After God," says Mendez, "he alone was the captain who encouraged us, and made us take breath so as not to sink under the labours and abandon ourselves entirely to chance, as some wished to do if he had not hindered them." About midnight loud cries were heard from the boat: the ropes by which she was held to the ship had given way, and she was dropped off. The captain's nephew, a lad whom he loved most tenderly, was with the party in the boat, and his uncle endeavoured to get the ship round in order to recover the boat, thus placing the vessel herself in imminent danger; she lay across the waves, was deluged by the heavy seas, and was almost swamped. At the moment of greatest peril Francis was on his knees in the captain's cabin. The ship righted and got once more before the wind, but the boat was lost sight of. Francis Xavier, however, bade the captain be of good cheer, as within three days "the daughter would come back to the mother." He is said to have been especially anxious to save two Mussulmans, who were in the boat with the rest. When daylight came, nothing could be discerned from the ship but the sea covered with foam. The rest of the story we may give chiefly in the words of Mendez Pinto.

"It was a little more than an hour after daylight, when the blessed Father Xavier, who had retired to the captain's cabin, came on deck, where were the master, the pilot, and seven other Portuguese. After having given good-day to all with a serene countenance, he asked them if they saw the boat, to which answer was made, 'No;' and then he asked the master pilot to send one of the sailors aloft to see if he could discover it. At the same time one of those present said: 'We shall see her only when we have lost another like her.' On which the father answered him: 'O, Pedro Velho'—such was his name—' O, Pedro Velho, how little faith you have! Think you that anything is impossible to our Lord? For my part, I have such confidence in Him and in His most sacred Mother, the Blessed Virgin Mary, to whom I have promised that I will say three masses in her blessed house of the Mount at Malacca, that I hope that they will prevent the souls which are in that boat from perishing.' Pedro Velho said nothing more. However, the master pilot, to satisfy the father, went up with another sailor to the top, and after having looked round for half an hour, they made their report that nothing was in sight. On which the father answered: 'Come down then, since there is nothing to be done;' and having called me to the forecastle, where he then was, very sad as far as we all could judge, he told me that I would oblige him if I warmed a little water for him that he might drink it, as he had a weakness of stomach. But my sins hindered me from doing him this good turn, because the day before, when the hurricane came on, the stove had been flung overboard to lighten the deck. Then he complained to me that he had a great pain in his head, on account of the sickness which came on him from time to time; and I answered him: 'It cannot be otherwise than that your reverence should be indisposed, because for three nights you have not slept, and you have not eaten a morsel,' for one of the servants of Duarte da Gama had so told me. 'I assure you,' replied the father, 'I am sorry for the unhappiness of the young man; all the last night, after the boat was lost, he was in tears for the loss of his nephew, Alonzo Calvo, who is in her with the rest of his companions.' Seeing, then, that the father was yawning every moment, I said to him, 'Your reverence would do well to retire into my cabin; perhaps you might get some rest there.' He accepted my offer, saying: 'So be it, then, for the love of God.' Thereon he begged me much to send a Chinese servant to shut the door after him, and to wait and open it for him when he called; and this he said to me about six or seven o'clock. After having retired into my cabin, he remained there all day until sunset, and as I once happened to call my servant, who was at the door, to ask him for a little water, I inquired of him also whether the father was asleep. 'He has not slept at all,' he answered, 'and he is still on his knees on the couch, weeping, with his head down.' On which I told him to go back and sit at the door, and go to him as soon as he called him. In this way the father remained unceasingly engaged in prayer until sunset, and then at last left the cabin, and came to where all the Portuguese were sitting down on the deck under the bulwarks, on account of the great rolling of the ship.

"After having saluted them, the father asked of the pilot if the boat was to be seen? He answered that it was impossible to suppose otherwise than that she had been lost amid such seas; and that even supposing that it had pleased God to save her, she was more than fifty leagues off. 'So it seems naturally,' said the father; 'but I should be very glad if you would go aloft again, or send some sailor up, who might cast his eyes over the surface of the sea.' The pilot told him that he would very willingly go; and he went up with the master's mate, more to satisfy the desire of the father than from any thought of discovering what he wished. They were both up there a long time, and at last they affirmed that they had seen nothing. This grieved the father very much, as all could judge, so that he bent his head upon the bulwark, and was for some time sighing, as if he would fain shed tears. Then after he had taken a little breath, as if to try to rest under the sadness which he felt, he raised his hands to heaven, and said, with tears in his eyes, 'O Jesus Christ, my true God and Lord, by the merits of Thy sacred death and passion I pray Thee to have pity on us, and save the souls of the faithful who are gone astray in that boat!'

"Then he leant his head again upon the bulwark, and remained for the space of two or three *Credos* as if asleep; and then a little boy, who was seated up in the shrouds, began to cry, 'Miracle! miracle! here is our boat!' All in the ship came running up at these words, and at that same moment they saw the boat not more than a gunshot off, and every one was so astonished that all began in a throng to weep like children, so that they could not hear one another in the ship for the loud cries that were made. They came to the father to throw themselves at his feet; but he would not permit it, and retired into the cabin of the captain, and shut himself up, that no one might speak to him. All those who were in the boat were immediately received into the ship, with the rejoicing which was natural in such a case. And, therefore, I forbear now to relate here the particulars of this welcome, because it is a thing which can better be imagined than written. About half an hour afterwards, the father sent a little boy for the pilot, and told him to praise God who had done these marvels, and that he should at once get the ship ready, because the bad weather would soon end. So all was done to satisfy the father's desire with all possible diligence, and at the same time the devotions which he enjoined were performed. And it followed that before the great yard was hoisted and the sails set, the hurricane ceased entirely, so that we found good wind from the north, and continued our voyage amid general rejoicings."

It is evident that the ship had been carried round and round in the vortex of the cyclone, and had not been swept far from the spot where the boat had been lost. Many particulars of gross exaggeration were afterwards added to the story to make it more marvellous, and were sworn to by witnesses with more imagination than sense of truth.

The ship arrived soon after at San Chan, but she was so battered by the storm that she could not proceed, and Francis took passage in a vessel to Malacca which was then in harbour. The captain of the vessel was Diego Pereira, an adventurous merchant. But Francis had now a scheme for the conversion of China. He wished to get the Viceroy of India to send an ambassador to the coast of China, and in the train of this ambassador Francis would go, and thus find a way to preach the Gospel. Don Pereira entered heartily into these plans, and offered his ship and his fortune to carry them out, if Francis could obtain his nomination to the embassy. As ambassador, Pereira shrewdly saw means of driving a trade with China which would recoup all his outlay. His ship was the "Santa Croce." While Francis was on her, she was caught in a storm; but, so runs the tale, he raised his hands and blessed the vessel, and predicted that she should never be lost at sea, but go to pieces of old age.

Those who collected material for the canonization of S. Francis followed the history of this old ship. She never was lost.

"The ship," says the 'Relatio,' "survived Father Francis for twenty years, and old as it was, rotten and battered by the waves during so many voyages and storms, it always escaped safely. The sailors and merchants, trusting to the aforesaid prediction, used eagerly to embark their merchandise therein, and sailed from place to place without any fear of shipwreck or loss. Whenever it came into port, the ship was received with salutes and shouts of joy, and all India called it the 'ship of the holy father.' At last it was sold to a certain captain of Diu, who after many voyages, took it into the port of Cochin, and it was there hauled ashore in order to be repaired, on which it fell to pieces, and nothing but a heap of timbers remained of it." Diego Pereira himself was one of the witnesses who were quoted in evidence both of the prediction and of its accomplishment.[1]

Early in February, 1552, Francis arrived at Goa. A large number of fathers and other members of the Society were awaiting him at the College of Santa Fé, for several had been

---

[1] There are several anecdotes about this ship, as is only to be expected. Massei, l. iii. p. 378, tells some of them. The "Santa Croce" once sailed from Malacca to Cochin laden almost to the water's edge, and after sailing about twenty-four miles, began to leak. The people on board fired guns of distress, as she was sailing with a fleet of merchantmen, but no one would consent to relieve her of part of the cargo. The captain turned back to Malacca, and was received with shouts of scorn and hisses, for having doubted of the promise of Francis Xavier. He turned back, then and there, and arrived safe at Cochin.

admitted in his absence by Father Paul of Camerino; others had come to Goa, as Gaspar Baertz, in consequence of letters from himself, or from some other cause, and no less than twelve had arrived from Portugal in the preceding year. Francis on landing proceeded first to the hospitals of the city to visit the sick—his general custom when he returned from a distance—and thence to the monasteries of other religious orders. After this he went on to Santa Fé, where he was received with tears of joy and devotion. After embracing the fathers and brothers collected at the door, he asked if they had any one in the house who was sick. He was told that there was one, whose life was despaired of by the doctors. He went up at once to the sick man's cell, laid his hand upon his head, read a Gospel over him, and gave him his blessing. The sick man, who had heard of his arrival, and had been praying to see him, recovered almost immediately, and lived for many years afterwards.

The majority of those assembled at Santa Fé had never seen the grey-haired man of five-and-forty whom they received with so much reverence.

The period of the stay of Francis Xavier at Goa was not without its cares. He had trouble with Antonio Gomez, rector of the College of Santa Fé, and was obliged first to remove him from the headship of the College, and then to dismiss him from the Order.

Francis occupied himself with letter-writing, and many of the most valuable of the letters which came from his pen were then composed. Not the least interesting is a series to Father Gaspar Baertz, whom he appointed rector of Santa Fé in the room of Gomez, on his duties as a superior, and on his conduct of souls. Some of his advice is most admirable.

"Women," he says, "are generally inconstant in their purposes, and full of chatter when they talk; therefore, I do not wish the fathers to spend much time in the direction even of mothers of families who frequent our churches, however much inclination to be pious they may exhibit. If they do, they lose a vast amount of time, and gain no solid advantage for it.

"Much better give time to the husbands. Men, it is certain, are naturally more able to take in good advice when given, and are more constant in their resolutions to follow it. Should it happen that a wife comes to one of our fathers apart, and says that she has a great desire of serving God, but that an impediment to this lies in the necessity of living with her husband, as being bad and of disorderly habits, and that she has legitimate reasons for separating from him, you must take care not to be moved to approve of this thought of divorce. You should remain firm in advising her to stop with her husband. These tender longings for religion soon grow languid in that inconstant sex, and later on she will condemn her own design and your advice. Supposing them to be constant, still the danger to the husband, and the public scandal which is almost inseparable from such cases, are evils too serious to be overbalanced by the fruit of the devotional advantage of a single soul, which wishes in married life to anticipate the benefits of widowhood. Again, in these cases, carefully avoid blaming the husband before others, even when it is clear that he alone is to blame. See him alone, and gently exhort him to make a general confession, and then take occasion, from his own self-accusation, to scold him, but mildly, and so as to make him understand you are sorry for his own sake for the injury he has done to himself by his fault, rather than that you are moved by the accusations of his wife, who has complained of him.

"Everywhere men require to be treated with gentleness, but nowhere more so than in India. They are as touchy as glass to offence, any violence makes them recoil and break; to gentleness they bend, you can turn them as you will.

Again I repeat this advice; take heed again and again. If a husband and wife take you as umpire, and plead their cause in your presence, never let yourself blame the man before others, however nearly his fault may be brought home to him. The passionate minds of women eagerly take hold of such words, and are incredibly inflated thereby. They are always on the look-out for opportunities of humbling their husbands, and if hints of an inclination to their side are allowed to fall from the men chosen as arbitrators, they triumph openly, and ever after let loose their complaints with greater freedom, their accusations against their husbands, and their excuses of themselves, heaped one on another without end, all poured forth with mad loquacity."

The affair of the Chinese embassy, planned by Francis and Pereira, encountered no opposition at Goa. The Viceroy readily gave the patents constituting Diego Pereira ambassador of Portugal to the Chinese court, and he added letters to the commandant of Malacca, ordering him to favour the expedition in every possible manner. Diego had given Francis letters of credit on his agent in Goa for thirty thousand ducats, and these went to prepare for the embassage on a magnificent scale, by the purchase of rich presents to be made to the Chinese Emperor in the name of the King of Portugal, as well as for the other necessary expenses. The royal treasury also contributed to the outlay, and as we learn from a letter which Francis wrote on the eve of his departure from India, large sums were raised among pious and charitable persons for the general purposes of the voyage, which included also among its objects the liberation of a number of Portuguese captives from the prisons in China. Everything seemed to promise well, and we do not find any note of anticipation or dread of failure either in the letters of Francis himself or in any other record of the time.

It is said that on parting from his friends Francis let them see that he knew that, as S. Paul said to the priests of Ephesus, "they should see his face no more." One of the penitents of Francis, Doña Catalina de Chiaves, began to weep when he told her that this was his last visit, and to comfort her, he added that she should see him again before she died.

On April 25, 1552, Francis Xavier took his final leave of India. He had with him Father Balthasar Gago and four lay brothers, Duarte Silva, Pedro Alcaçeva, Alvaro Ferreira, and Francesco Gonzalez. He had also with him a young Chinese named Antonio, who had been educated at the College of Santa Fé. He was to serve Francis as interpreter, but it turned out, as might have been expected, that the years which he had spent at Goa had made him almost forget his native tongue.

Francis had parted with Diego Pereira at the beginning of the year at Malacca. Diego took his ship, the famous "Santa Croce," to Sunda, and was to return to Malacca in time to meet Francis when he came back from India with the diplomas constituting him envoy to China. Don Alvaro d'Ataide was governor of Malacca. He was a haughty, supercilious man, without religious enthusiasm, or care for anything but his own interests. He was probably also poor, and anxious to make money while in authority at Malacca. We are not told whether he had at first entertained the notion that he himself, and not Diego Pereira, was the proper person to represent the Portuguese Crown in the embassy to China. But he had a secret grudge against Diego Pereira, who, before sailing for Sonda, had refused to lend him a sum of ten thousand ducats. It is only a matter of conjecture whether Francis Xavier was aware of this; but he had armed himself against any possible difficulty on the part of Don Alvaro in two ways—first, by procuring for him some favours from the Viceroy, who conferred on him, at the request of Francis, the "capitanato" of the sea, a naval command, and, secondly, by arming himself with stringent orders from the Viceroy, enjoining on Don Alvaro to further to the utmost the expedition to China, and threatening punishment in case of disobedience.

Diego Pereira returned to Malacca after Francis had been some time on the spot. Francis sent to warn him before he landed, not to assume any pomp or state as ambassador, but to appear in the city as simply and modestly as possible. His arrival forced Don Alvaro to raise his mask, at least partially. The "captaincy of the sea" gave him some authority over the vessels which put into the port, and he availed himself of this—it was the first exercise of his authority—to seize the rudder of Pereira's vessel, and to hang it up defiantly in front of his own palace. His excuse was that he understood that an attack was impending from the Gial, the warlike and hostile tribes in Java, who had furnished a large contingent to the army that had besieged Malacca the year before. This pretext, however, was soon taken from Don Alvaro. A Portuguese ship arrived from the Archipelago with the news that the tribes in question were at war among themselves, and so had no time to think of an attack on Malacca.

It was then that, for the first time since he had left Portugal, Francis Xavier made public the character of Apostolic Nuncio with which he had been invested by the Pope at the request of the king. When he landed in India he had informed the bishop of the briefs which he possessed, but from that time he had kept silence on the subject, and had never acted on his power. He now communicated the briefs to the Vicar of Malacca, Joam Suarez, and begged him to inform Don Alvaro of the danger he was in, inasmuch as all who impeded a Nuncio Apostolic in carrying out his mission were solemnly excommunicated by the Pope.

But Alvaro treated the pontifical briefs as lightly as he had the letters of the Viceroy; he went so far as to accuse Francis Xavier of having forged them. The people of Malacca took the part of the governor, and Francis was insulted in the streets, and unable to set foot outside the College. At last Don Alvaro consented to allow Xavier to proceed to San Chan in the "Santa Croce," but would not allow Diego Pereira to accompany him. There would be no embassy, but the missioner would be allowed to proceed on his way. Alvaro even seized the ships and the merchandize, leaving only a small part to Pereira, and he put some of his own people on board along with the sailors of Pereira. These men were either instructed, or disposed, to pay small regard to Xavier. Pereira knew better than Alvaro the store set by King John on the humble priest, and that this opposition would eventually turn to his own advantage, and the humiliation of the governor. He, therefore, bore all with equanimity, and ordered his people to attend to the wants of Francis, and furnish him with whatever money he might require, in order to effect a landing on the Chinese coast.

S. Francis wrote to Pereira from the vessel:—

"I am confident that this calamity will turn to your advantage; for I doubt not that the king, to whom I have made the request by letter, will worthily reward your admirable zeal for the religion of Jesus Christ. I have ceased to have any dealings with the commandant, who has not hesitated to oppose a voyage which would have done so much for spreading the Christian religion. May God forgive the man! I grieve for his lot, for he will have to suffer a far severer punishment than he imagines."

At length the day came for the "Santa Croce" to sail. Francis once more left the ship, and went up to his favourite shrine of our Lady del Monte. There he remained in prayer until sunset, while a crowd gathered round to see him for the last time. At last he was told that the anchor was weighed, and that sail was being set. He went down the hill to the shore, accompanied by numerous friends weeping and entreating him not to risk himself in so perilous an undertaking as an attempt to enter China. He said he was going whither God called him. Before he reached the strand, the vicar-general, Joam Suarez, came to take leave of him. He was a timid man, wishing to do his duty, and at the same time stand well with Don Alvaro. He asked Francis whether he had taken leave of the "captain?" would it not be better? and might not people think that he had been moved by human feeling if he left without saluting Don Alvaro? Francis answered with firmness and dignity. He and Don Alvaro would meet no more in this life; they would see one another again in the Valley of Jehoshaphat on the day of the terrible judgment, when Jesus Christ, the Son of God, would come to judge the living and the dead, and they would both stand there before Him, and Alvaro would have to give an account of what he had done in preventing him from going to preach to the heathen the Word of Life. They came to the open door of a little church that stood near the shore. Francis knelt down there and prayed aloud. Then he bent himself to the ground, and remained absorbed in silent devotion. After awhile he rose, took off his shoes, and beat them one against another, and against a rock, that he might cast off his feet the very dust of Malacca. The people were aghast. The vicar spoke the last word: "How! Is this your final parting with us?" "As it pleases God," answered Francis, and entered the boat that was to take him to the ship.

After a prosperous voyage the vessel reached San Chan. This little island is described as somewhat barren, covered with brushwood, haunted by tigers, and inhabited by a poor and rude population. As the Portuguese ships were not admitted to Canton, San Chan was a rendezvous for them as well as for the junks of the Chinese traders, who exchanged goods with them. The Portuguese were not allowed to settle even here, but they ran up huts of wood and branches during the few months of their stay in the island. Life at San Chan during this time was wild, jovial, and licentious. Occasions of self-indulgence abounded, money was plentiful, and of restraints there were none. There were gaming and drinking, as well as other kinds of debauchery; and even those who did not go headlong into a course of vice, gave themselves up to enjoyment. The Portuguese, as always, received Francis with great joy. They built for him in a couple of days a little chapel, with a hut attached to it. Here he said mass daily, and administered the sacraments, spending the rest of his time in teaching children, making up quarrels, and other such offices of charity.

Francis reached San Chan in the last week of August, 1552. He had not been long on the island before he was attacked by fever, and was confined to his bed for a fortnight. He, however, recovered, and occupied his mind with forming schemes more or less impracticable for reaching the Chinese coast and preaching there.

He vainly endeavoured to persuade some of the Portuguese merchants to carry him to the Chinese coast, and leave him alone there, to do what he could. No thought of self-defence, no care for his life, crossed his mind. The whole force of his pure, earnest soul was turned towards the salvation of souls in that vast empire that lay in darkness and the shadow of death, and into which as yet no gleam of the light that broke at Bethlehem on the world had yet penetrated. The year before, a vessel commanded by Manuel da Chaves had been driven ashore on the Chinese coast by a storm, and the officers of the emperor had seized on its lading and cast its crew into prison. Indeed, great numbers of venturesome Portuguese lay in the prisons of Canton. Consequently no merchant would run the risk of approaching the dangerous coast.

Francis wrote from San Chan on October 22, 1552, to Francesco Perez, of his Society:—

"May the grace and love of Jesus Christ our Lord always help and favour us! Amen.

"By the grace of God we have reached the port of San Chan, 120 miles from Canton. On disembarking I had a hut constructed for me, in which I offered the Holy Sacrifice every day till I fell ill. I suffered from the fever altogether about a fortnight; however, I am now by God's goodness restored to health. I am not short of work. I hear confessions, appease quarrels, and do other things of that sort. A great number of Chinese merchants from Canton come to this island for the sake of commerce, and the Portuguese have often endeavoured to persuade them to convey me to Canton; but they have all flatly refused, declaring that it would be at great risk to their lives and property if the governor of that town should hear of it, and it was impossible to persuade them to receive us on board their junks.

"However, doubtless by God's arrangement, we have met at last with an honest Canton merchant, who has come to terms with me for 200 gold pieces. He promises to take us in a little vessel, which is to carry no one else but his own sons and a few faithful slaves; so that if the governor of the town ever gets to hear of the affair, he will not be able to find out from the crew who it was who took us to Canton. He has also promised that we shall be in his house for three or four days, with our books and baggage; and then very early one morning he is to take us to the gate of the town and put us on the road leading to the government house. I shall go straight to the governor, telling him that I am come to announce the divine and heavenly law to the emperor of China, and then I shall produce the bishop of Goa's letters addressed to that monarch. The Chinese merchants are always glad to see us, and say they will be glad if the matter is carried out successfully.

"I am aware, as all tell me, of the danger of this enterprise. It is possible that the Chinese merchant after having received the gold may leave us in a desert island, or throw us into the sea to conceal his crime; and again, if we reach Canton, the governor may torture us in all kinds of ways or make us slaves for life. It is a capital crime for a foreigner to enter China without a passport. But there are other dangers besides, greater and more unknown, all of which I cannot enumerate to you, but I will mention some of them.

"First, and foremost, is mistrust of God's goodness and providence. I have come to this country in obedience to God, and from pure love of Him, to declare to the Chinese nation the most holy law of God, and to preach to them His only Son Jesus Christ, the Author of our salvation, and yet—my heart may fail. But since He in His mercy has given me this object, it would indeed be a most terrible danger if I were to doubt His help and protection in the midst of the dangers before me. For neither the devils nor their servants can hurt us, without the permission of Almighty God. If God be our defender, how easily can He dispel all perils! And, besides, we shall follow the precept of the Lord Jesus, 'He that loveth his life shall lose it; and he that hateth his life in this world shall keep it unto life eternal;' words which are in accordance with those other words of Jesus Christ, 'No man, having put his hand to the plough, and looking back, is fit for the kingdom of God.' As, then, we see that these spiritual dangers are more serious and more certain than any perils of the body, we prefer to face those of this life rather than incur everlasting death. Indeed, we are positively determined to enter China, come what may. If God will only prosper our footsteps in the spreading of His faith, then the devils and their army may try their worst, I care not for them. 'If God be for us, who can be against us?'

"I hope that the ships which are shortly leaving for India will bring you letters from me, announcing my entry into Canton. My companions are continually falling ill. The Chinese lad I brought here to act as my interpreter has, I find, forgotten his native tongue; but I have found another well acquainted not only with the language, but with the literature of his country, who has offered to accompany me. May God reward him for it in this life, and in the life to come! I beg you to pray that God will keep him firm in his intention and purpose.

"All the good Chinese who know us take pleasure in our society, and earnestly desire that we may be successful in our attempt to penetrate into China. They have already got an idea that the books which they see us carrying everywhere contain better doctrine than theirs; and though it is possible that this idea may spring only from their love of novelty, they would like to see us enter their country. And yet, in spite of these professions, the Chinese, as I have already told you, refuse altogether to take us there themselves. I am daily expecting the merchant with whom I made the agreement. God grant that he may not fail me! Should that misfortune happen, I know not what I should do, whether return to India, or go to Siam, to join the embassy which the king of Siam is said to be shortly about to send to the emperor of China. I will let you know what we shall do by a ship that sails for Malacca in a few days. May Jesus Christ our Lord grant us His help and guidance, that we may one day come to the possession of the glory of heaven!

"The least of your brothers in Jesus Christ,

"FRANCIS.

"Island of San Chan, October 22, 1552."

S. Francis wrote next to Father Gaspar Baertz, on October 28 :—

"May the grace and love of Jesus Christ our Lord always help and favour us! Amen.

"I do not know whether it was from Malacca or from the Straits of Singapore that I wrote to tell you what had happened to me. God has brought us safe and sound to San Chan, a Chinese island about 120 miles from Canton. Here I am in daily expectation of a Chinese merchant with whom (in consequence of severe edicts forbidding the entrance of a foreigner without a government passport) I have agreed for 200 pardams to be taken to Canton. May God permit this plan to come about! I have heard that the emperor of China has been sending persons into different countries to learn their manners, institutions, and laws. So there is reason to hope (and this the Chinese themselves tell me) that the king will not despise the Christian religion, nor reject it at once. If God grants me life, and deigns to make use of us for His work, I will let you know about it. For the present, I charge you to watch over your soul, for in truth if you do not, I can have no hope of you.

"Remember to read again and again, and observe strictly the rules I left with you, especially those as to self-humiliation, in which I recommended you to exercise yourself every day. Fear above all things lest, in looking round on all that God is pleased to do by means of you and our brothers, you should forget to cultivate your own soul. My great love for you all makes me wish very much that you would consider seriously within yourselves what results God has been hindered from producing through your faults. I would rather see you occupied with this thought than with that of the great works of which you are the instrument. This thought should produce in you shame and humility, by making you sensible of your imperfections and shortcomings;

were it not for these, you might run the danger of falling into presumption, and trust in those good deeds wrought, not by you, but by God, and in the miracles of grace which are the work of God alone. Pray consider how many persons have been led into danger thereby, and how fatal it would be to the whole Society if such a plague should spread through it.

"I also charge you to receive very few postulants into the Society; choose those who are capable of devoting themselves to literary studies, or of attending to the work of the house. I assure you it would be better to buy slaves—yes, slaves—for domestic employments, than to admit into the Society persons unfit for it. If any of those whom I have sent away are at Goa, be sure not to receive them back on any excuse, for they are not suited for our Institute. If one of them should completely reform his life, and give proof of it, by public penance, voluntarily accepted and long persevered in, so as to make full satisfaction, according to the best of your judgment, you may send him to Portugal to the Superior of the Society, with a recommendation from you; he may be made use of there, but not, I am quite satisfied, in India.

"And should any member of the Society, priest or layman, be guilty of serious and scandalous faults, send him away instantly, and do not allow yourself to be persuaded to receive him back, unless his sense of guilt, his repentance, and voluntary penance, have been really satisfactory. Otherwise, on no account receive him; not if the Viceroy and the whole of India were to ask you to do so. I remind you also to send to the Moluccas and Japan none but tried brethren, of great virtue and experience; such are the kind of workmen wanted in these countries.

"Recommend me very much to all the fathers and brothers of our Society, and to all our friends. Greet the Dominican and Franciscan fathers from me, and beg them not to cease to intercede with God for me in prayer, and at the Holy Sacrifice. May God direct us ever, and call us, some day, to His everlasting bliss in heaven!"

The day appointed for the sailing of S. Francis to China in the Chinese junk was November 19th. Before that day arrived, all the Portuguese vessels had left San Chan, except the "Santa Croce." They bore with them the last letters that remain to us from the hand of S. Francis. They are of much sad interest; they exhibit to us how that apostolic heart yearned to the last to spend and be spent for Christ; the great ambition of his soul was to die bearing the Gospel to heathen lands. He had no other wish than this. He was not his own, he was bought with a price; and as the servant of Jesus, he would do his Master's work without a thought of self. He wrote to Father Perez, on November 12:—

"As Gaspar Mendez's ship was weighing anchor, I gave Francesco Sanchez, one of the passengers, a letter for you, which I hope has reached you; and I beg you to take to heart the orders it contains, and which I here repeat, and to give all heed to carry them out. I have been expecting for a week the merchant who is to take me secretly to Canton. I have the fullest confidence in his return, unless some hindrance should occur beyond the power of man to overcome, and I rely on the great value of the reward which I have promised him, and which he himself highly appreciates; for by means of the quantity of pepper which I have agreed to pay him, if he conveys me safe and sound to Canton, he will easily realize a profit of more than 350 gold pieces of our money. I have to thank my dear friend Diego Pereira for the means of buying my passage to China at such a price. He has most generously placed at my disposal this large quantity of valuable merchandize. May God reward him as I cannot, for I shall owe him a debt which I can never repay. I beg you to use your most zealous endeavours to render services to this excellent man, in every part of India where you may be able to assist him; embrace eagerly every means of doing him kindness, without sparing your utmost pains. The most earnest efforts of our united body will never sufficiently repay only this last sacrifice which he has made at so great cost to himself, one so beneficial to the propagation of our holy faith, in order to introduce us into the empire of China, hitherto impenetrably closed against the Gospel. By this means the Society of Jesus will obtain the object of all its constant prayers—the power of spreading the kingdom of Jesus Christ, and bringing into the Church the many nations of that immense empire; and as results are rightly attributed to their origin, it will really owe all these blessings to the generosity of one man, Diego Pereira, who out of his own fortune has provided the funds necessary for my voyage, and for beginning this great work.

"Pray inquire of him whether he has hopes of surmounting the obstacles in the way of his embassy, and if he is coming to Canton next year. I desire this greatly, but I fear I cannot expect it. God grant that my small hopes may be contradicted by a more fortunate issue than I look for! God forgive the man who is the impediment! I greatly fear that before long a terrible vengeance from the God he has offended will overtake him, and it may be that he is even now about to experience its first effects. I am writing to Pereira himself, so that if he obtains a more favourable result than I dare hope for, he may take with him, when he sails for China, some of our Society, whom Father Gaspar will send to him from Goa, if he has notice given him some time beforehand. I have told him this by letter. But if, as I think most likely, Pereira, despairing of the success of his mission, should pass by Malacca, and direct his course towards Sunda, then it will no longer be necessary for the priest who would have gone with him to China to sail from Goa to

Malacca in May. You should give notice of this, as I have told you in good time, to Father Gaspar, the rector of the college at Goa; and I wish you to be clearly informed of Pereira's intentions before your departure for Malacca. I have dismissed Ferreira from the Society, as he was not fitted for it; when, therefore, you arrive at Cochin, and have taken the management of the college, I command you, in virtue of obedience, not to receive him into the house. Do all you can to urge him to enter the Franciscan or Dominican Order; and, if you succeed, ask those fathers to grant him admission. Write also to Father Gaspar Baertz at Goa, saying, that by virtue of my authority, I absolutely forbid his receiving Ferreira into the community or under the college roof; only let him do all he can to help him to get into the Order of S. Francis or of S. Dominic.

"If by God's grace I am able to reach Canton, I will do all in my power that you may hear of my success next year, by letters to India, which I will despatch, if possible, so as to catch the vessel sailing to Coromandel. I shall use for this Pereira's ship on its return to Malacca; I only pray it may reach Malacca in time. If all this can be successfully arranged, you will be able to hear at Cochin during March of my arrival at Canton. With this view, it may be well, when you leave Malacca, to ask Vincent Viegas to be good enough, as soon as he hears that Pereira's vessel has returned from the Chinese coast, to ask for and take charge of any letters from me which it may bring, and to send them to Cochin by way of Coromandel. And that these letters may not be left at Coromandel, especially if, as I think will be the case, there is no immediate opportunity of sending them further by sea, you will do well to beg Diego Pereira himself beforehand to send you my letters to Cochin, together with his own, so as to be forwarded, in case of necessity, overland from Coromandel.

"The interpreter who consented, as I told you, to come with me to China, has been frightened, and has given up the idea. He remains here, after having abandoned me; we are determined to run all risks, relying on God's help. There are three of us—Antonio da Santa Fé (a Chinese educated at our college), Cristoval, and myself. Pray much to God for us, for we are going to expose ourselves to the almost certain danger of dreadful slavery. But our consolation is in the thought with which we are deeply penetrated—that it is infinitely preferable to be a captive in chains for the love of God than to purchase the most delightful liberty by basely and ungratefully deserting the sufferings and the Cross of Jesus Christ. Should it happen that the Chinese merchant, on whom depend our hopes of going to Canton, should change his mind through fear or any other reason, and break his word, I have resolved to sail for the kingdom of Siam, for which voyage I have a favourable opportunity. In fact, I have heard that a ship is being fitted out there for Canton, and if I can get on board, by God's protection I hope, before the end of the year, to land on the shore which is the object of my many prayers. Salute very heartily all our friends for me, and especially Vincent Viegas, and beg them to commend me to our Lord. May He remain with you, and accompany me! May He bring us all to the glory of Paradise! Farewell."

But the object of his ambition was not to be obtained, as he fell ill again with fever on the 20th November, after Mass.

When the fever first attacked him, Francis went on board the "Santa Croce," but the motion of the vessel proved disagreeable, and he was taken ashore at his request, and a Spaniard, Jorge Alvarez, conveyed him into his own hut, and bled him. After this he was very sick, and could eat nothing. Thus he lay racked with fever, and without appetite or power to keep his food down, all one week, lying in a wretched cabin, gazing up at the blue sky through a little window in the side, and murmuring prayers to a crucifix which he held in his hand. On the Monday week after his illness had begun, he became delirious for a time; his wanderings were all about his expedition to China. After this he lost his speech, but on the Wednesday he regained it, and his mind no longer wandered. He begged that the vestments and sacred vessels which he had used for mass, as well as his manuscript of the Christian doctrine in Chinese letters, and the rest, might be taken on board the ship. He spoke a good deal in ejaculations, but chiefly in Latin, so that the Chinese lad who attended him could only remember what was not new to him, such as his favourite exclamations, "O Sanctissima Trinitas," "Jesu Fili David miserere mei," and "Monstra te esse matrem." So the fever went on, and he grew weaker and weaker. He could take nothing for some days before the end came. At last, on the Friday, the 2nd of December, about two in the afternoon, he fixed his eyes lovingly upon his crucifix, his face lighted up with joy, tears poured from his eyes, and he breathed his last, repeating the words of the "Te Deum," "In Thee, O Lord, have I hoped, let me never be confounded!"

The body of Francis Xavier remained unburied till the Sunday after his death. Some of the Portuguese belonging to the ship were touched at the sight of his corpse, but it does not seem that the majority showed any great devotion. The fear of Don Alvaro was strong upon them. The pilot, however, Francesco d'Aghiar, did what was in his power in honour of the saint whose companion he had often been. Jorge Alvarez also had a coffin made, in which the body was placed, clothed in the priestly vestments. Late on the Sunday evening the coffin was lowered into a grave dug on the top of a low spur of hill close to the shore. There was a level space on the summit, and here they planted a wooden cross, at the foot of which was the grave, with two heaps of stones, one at the head and the other at the feet.

One of Don Alvaro's men wrote to him that Master Francis had died, and done no miracle in his death, and that he had been buried at San Chan like every one else; but that the body should be removed to Malacca when the vessel returned. This was done in February, 1553; and thence it was afterwards translated to Goa, where it now reposes.

On looking back on the life of S. Francis Xavier, it is impossible not to be struck with admiration at the inexhaustible patience and perseverance of this truly apostolic character. It stands out before us amidst those of other saints of his time with an individuality of Christian beauty which is most striking He was the great missionary saint of his age. The languid efforts of Christian missionaries at the time were as little successful as the half-hearted efforts of missionaries of the present age. There may have been— there probably was—great piety and great self-denial among those who took the Gospel among the heathen then, as now, but there was not the marvellous apostolic power which brought about success everywhere, which we find in Xavier. He startled Christendom into the conviction that the triumphs of the first preachers of the Gospel were not victories past renewing. The Church had sunk into the belief that Christianity might go on nibbling at the outskirts of heathenism, but could never strike successfully at its heart. Xavier dispelled this delusion. When success is impossible, enthusiasm cannot be very keen. And mission work was prosecuted after routine, and unquickened by any sanguine expectations of success. Xavier reawakened hope. He did more, he made hope triumphant, enthusiastic. It flamed up suddenly and unexpectedly everywhere in a thousand hearts, and men rushed to devote themselves to work in fields white to harvest and ready to admit reapers into them.

The missions in Japan, the glorious church of the martyrs founded there, the heroic efforts of Brébeuf and his gallant band in Canada, the triumphant establishment of a Christian kingdom in Paraguay, the devoted host of martyrs in China, in Cochin China, in Corea, may all trace back their spiritual pedigree to Xavier. It was he who started them on their holy work; it was he who by his successes had stimulated others to emulate his zeal.

Alone on San Chan, when almost all his fellow countrymen had left, with a poor Chinese lad at his side, he died with a work filling his soul, the object of his last prayers, not even begun. That work was begun later: his prayers have produced a great result, and the missions in China deep rooted in blood have proved marvellously successful—they are successful to this very day. It is as though the dying prayers of Xavier had procured for them a special prerogative of endurance, and through blood and prison, mightily in the Celestial Empire grows daily the Word of God, and prevails.

END OF VOL. XIV.

Printed by BALLANTYNE, HANSON & Co.
Edinburgh & London

www.ingramcontent.com/pod-product-compliance
Lightning Source LLC
Chambersburg PA
CBHW020238240426
43672CB00006B/566